Militant Education,
Liberation Struggle,
Consciousness

STUDIA EDUCATIONIS HISTORICA
Studies in the History of Education

Edited by
Marcelo Caruso / Eckhardt Fuchs / Gert Geißler /
Sabine Reh / Eugenia Roldán Vera / Noah W. Sobe

VOL. 4

PETER LANG

Sónia Vaz Borges

Militant Education, Liberation Struggle, Consciousness

The PAIGC education
in Guinea Bissau 1963-1978

PETER LANG

Bibliographic Information published by the Deutsche Nationalbibliothek
The Deutsche Nationalbibliothek lists this publication in the Deutsche Nationalbibliografie; detailed bibliographic data is available in the internet at http://dnb.d-nb.de.

Cover image: PAIGC's Party Pioneers in Moscow in 1973
Source: Teresa Araújo (personal archive)

Printed by CPI books GmbH, Leck

ISSN 2195-5158
ISBN 978-3-631-71942-8 (Print)
E-ISBN 978-3-631-77944-6 (E-PDF)
E-ISBN 978-3-631-77945-3 (EPUB)
E-ISBN 978-3-631-77946-0 (MOBI)
DOI 10.3726/b15150

© Peter Lang GmbH
Internationaler Verlag der Wissenschaften
Berlin 2019
All rights reserved.

Peter Lang – Berlin · Bern · Bruxelles · New York ·
Oxford · Warszawa · Wien

This publication has been peer reviewed.

www.peterlang.com

In memory of Sandra Milena Herrera Restrepo

Acknowledgments

Militant Education, Liberation Struggle, Consciousness: The PAIGC Education in Guinea Bissau 1963-1978, result of my PhD thesis *Militant education, Liberation Struggle, Conscientization and underground educational structures in Guinea Bissau 1963-1978*, is a work that could never have been written without the support and generosity of the great community that surrounds me. My thanks go to the late Rui d' Espiney, the Portuguese intellectual freedom fighter who had the patience to listen and support my first ideas about this project. I also thank my friend Christien Ernst, who during a breakfast meeting when I presented to him my ideas and plans of pursuing a PhD, immediately recommended that I talk with Professor Marcelo Caruso. I thank the Rosa-Luxemburg-Stiftung and their staff who provided me with the invaluable financial and scholarly resources to do this work. I also thank the *Institut für Erziehungswissenschaften Abteilung Historische Bildungforschung* and all its faculty and staff, for all the support and work conditions that it was offered me in order to complete this work.

An invaluable thank you to all PAIGC's militants who dared to share their memories, their knowledge, and opened the doors of their houses, and allowed me a glimpse of their lives and personal belongings. I thank them for the amazing and emotional conversations that we had in their living rooms and gardens, on their balconies, in their offices and at their kitchen tables. Without them a great part of this work would not exist.

My special thanks in this work goes to Professor Marcelo Caruso, for accepting a complete stranger as his PhD student. There are no words to express how thankful I am for the five years of invaluable support and attention, the vibrant intellectual exchanges and remarkable insights during the ongoing process of writing this work.

A special thanks to the amazing support of Ruth Wilson Gilmore, David Harvey, Mary Taylor and Peter Hitchcock members of the Center for Place Culture and Politics (CPCP) – The Graduate Center of the City University of New York. Thanks to my students and my colleagues from the CPCP seminar "Consciousness and revolution" for their great insights on my work. Thanks to Isabel and Tobias for their great helping me with the translation to English of some of the PAIGC documents. Many thanks to Craig, Diana and Emily for helping me with the editing of this work.

Finally, my greatest debt is to my family and friends. To my sisters Sandra, Fernanda, Eduina and Isa. To my crew of beautiful nieces and nephews Erica,

Latiffah, Kayanne, Mayamba, Mizaki, Yuna, Ionas and Aries, for always having pertinent question and observations to do. To my dear friends Tita, Anousck, Christien, Alexia, Paulo, Sónia, Rosana, Carla, Filipa, Juliana, Pietro, Annette, Marianne, Isabelle, Tobias, Diana, Ruthie and Craig for reminding me to always stand up, laugh, cry, struggle and keep my head up wherever I go. Thanks to my colleagues Sandra, Ami, Zang, Lou, Jane, Fanny, Daniel and Johannes for all the support.

To my father José, thank you for teaching me that it's not just what it is in our head that is true or important, and how important it is to remember and listen what it is between the loud voices and silences. Foremost, I would like to thank my mother Bia for always being by my side, and helping me to write and organize my papers and books although she was never able to read them.

Contents

3 Militant education. Ideas and practices during the liberation struggle (1963-1974)

List of Abbreviations

CIPM	Political and Military Instruction Center of Madina do Boé
CLSTP	Movement for the Liberation of São Tomé and Príncipe
DAC	Amílcar Cabral Documents
ISMUN	International Youth & Student Movement for the United Nations
JAAC	African Youth Amílcar Cabral
FARP or F.A.R.P.	People Revolutionary Armed Force.
FRELIMO	Mozambique Liberation Front
INEP	Guinea Bissau National Institute for Studies and Research
MAC	Anti-Colonial Movement
MPLA	People's Movement for the Liberation of Angola
OUA	Organization of African Unity
PAI	African Party for Independence
PAIGC	African Party for the Independence of Guinea and Cape Verde
PIDE-DGS	International Police for the Defense of the State
RENAMO	Mozambican National Resistance
SEP	Branch of the Student s of the Party
UGEAN	General Union of Students from Black Africa under Portuguese Colonial Domination
UN	United Nations
UNITA	National Union for the total Independence of Angola
UNSA	United Nations Students Association
UPA	Union of the Peoples of Angola
WCC	World Council of Churches

The PAIGC. The recovery of the history of 'militant education' and the role of the 'walking archives'

> As you know, this national liberation struggle already has its history, and as all the struggles in the world, it has a beginning, it has a development phase, which is the one that we find ourselves now, but the struggle will never have an end, because it's Man's struggle for the achievement of his ideals of progress, of peace and justice. This struggle will never end as long as these men exist. In the core of the history of our national liberation struggle are men and it is the men that make the history. Some of these men occupy an eminent place, a distinguished place in this gigantic work.[1]
>
> Mário Pinto de Andrade, 1973

Recent studies suggest September of 1959 - and not 1956 as it had previously been thought, as the most plausible date that the African Party for Independence (PAI) was founded in Guinea Bissau by a group of anti-colonialist Guinean and Cape Verdean militants. It was in a meeting that took place in Dakar in October of 1960 that the PAI adopted the final name of "African Party for the Independence of Guinea and Cape Verde," or PAIGC, in order to avoid any confusion with the Malian PAI of Majhemout Diop.[2] In 1963, and after several attempts to negotiate independence with the Portuguese colonial regime, the Party officially started an armed liberation struggle in the Guinean forest in the name of independence for Guinea Bissau and Cape Verde.[3] The armed guerrilla struggle lasted from January

---

1   Mario Pinto de Andrade, *A geração Cabral* (Conakry: Instituto Amizade, 1973), 2.
2   Julião Soares Sousa, *Amílcar Cabral (1924-1973). Vida e morte de um revolucionário africano* (Lisboa: Vega, 2011), 196–205.
3   Part of the Portuguese colonial empire, the territory that corresponds today to Guinea Bissau was under Cape Verdean juridical administration between 1466 and 1879 and it was known as *Os rios grandes da Guiné do Cabo Verde* (The rivers of Guinea and Cape Verde). The historical and cultural connection that developed between both territories – Guinea a and Cape Verde, is part of of the reason why Amílcar Cabral and others comrades created a Party that would fight for the independence of the two territories, with the aim that the unity between them would prevail under the pan-African logic of political unity. Due to the geographic characteristics of the Cape Verde and the unfeasibility and dangers of developing an armed struggle in the archipelago, the liberation struggle took place in Guinea Bissau, but in close partnership with Guinean and Cape Verdean fighters. The Cape Verde independence was recognized by the Portuguese government on July 5th, 1975. Despite their partnership throughout the liberation

23, 1963 until April 25, 1974. In the meantime, challenging Portuguese rule, the PAIGC self-proclaimed the independence of Guinea Bissau on September 24, 1973, although it was only recognized by the Portuguese government on September 10th of the following year.

For the past fifty-four years, much has been written about the PAIGC liberation struggle, with a special emphasis, on the most charismatic figure of the movement: the General Secretary Amílcar Cabral (1924-1973). A review of the literature on the reveals the great difficulty to make a study that separates the liberation struggle from the figure of Amílcar Cabral. Works by Mario Pinto de Andrade,[4] Basil Davidson,[5] Patrick Chabal,[6] Sónia Vaz Borges,[7] and more recently Julião Sousa's biography and Reiland Rabacka's work on the integration of Cabral's thought in the realm of the Africana studies[8] are of particular relevance.

However, the almost exclusive focus on the national and international politics of the military side of the liberation struggle, and the studies on Amílcar Cabral's anti-colonial and decolonial thoughts, and the strategies for liberation, has distracted attention from other strands of the struggle, contributing to the production of silences around other themes. The first silence surrounds the subject of individual experiences and the collective work that the liberation struggle represents. The second silence is related to the specific policies, processes and pragmatisms of the Party ideology in the terrain that were developed during the struggle. Here I am referring to areas such as health practices, the development of justice system, or the commercial exchanges practices within the population. There is also a silence concerning the foreign help that PAIGC received, specifically the ones related with educational ideas, practices and experiences.

---

struggle, the Guinean coup in 1980, put an end to the possibility of political unity between the two countries. For more information on this subject, please see the work of Peter Karibe Mendy, *Colonialismo português em África: A tradição da resistência na Guiné-Bissau (1879-1959)* (Bissau: INEP, 1994).

4   Mário de Andrade, *Amílcar Cabral: Essai de Biographie Politique*, (Paris: François Maspero, 1980).

5   Basil Davidson, *No Fist is Big Enough to Hide the Sky: The liberation of Guinea and Cape Verde: Aspects of an African Revolution* (London: Zed, 1981)

6   Patrick Chabal. Amílcar Cabral. Revolutionary leadership and people's war. (New York: Cambridge University Press, 1983).

7   Borges, Sónia Vaz Borges, Amílcar Cabral: *estratégias políticas e culturais para a independência da Guiné e Cabo Verde* (Lisbon: Universidade de Letras de Lisboa, 2008).

8   Reiland Rabaka, Concepts of Cabralism. Amílcar Cabral and Africana Theory (London: Lexington Books, 2014).

Referring to education, the last process of silence and extracted from PAIGC original documents is the idea of "militant education."

Among the few studies dealing with the PAIGC's educational system are those written by Swedish scholars Birgitta Dahl and Knut Andreasson involved in the events analyzed in their work their work *Guinea-Bissau: rapport om ett land och en befrielserörelse*,[9] 1971, as well as the work of the Swidish scholar Lars Rudebeck *Guinea-Bissau. A study of political mobilization*,[10] 1974. Birgitta Dahl and Knut Andreasson's work is particularly valuable for its inclusion of visual material of PAIGC educational facilities in the liberated areas that the authors obtained when they visited the territory in 1970. To complement this, Lars Rudebeck offers us a first-hand critical analysis of the statistical data provided at the time by the Party. Rudebecks' work is also valuable for the information that provides on the subjects of teacher training, school curricula and the general role of education in the PAIGC's liberation struggle.

The studies that followed these pioneering works, more or less reproduced the same information that these authors had collected and analyzed. These include the works of Paul Bélanger, *Une pratique de contre-ècole: L'expérience éducative du mouvement de libération nationale dans les zones libérées de lá Guinée-Bissau;*[11] Mustafah Dhada, *Warriors at Work: How Guinea was really set free;*[12] and Ocuni Cá, *Perspectiva histórica da Organização do sistema educacional da Guiné Bissau.*[13]

Using these previous studies as references, my aim throughout this work is to explore PAIGC's 'militant education' project, by posing the following questions: What kind of educational structures existed in Guinea Bissau and Cape Verde before the start of the liberation struggle? How did the Party developed its concept of 'militant education' and what were the relations between political education, liberation and 'military'? What kind of curriculum and

9   Birgitta Dahl and Knut Andreasson, *Guinea-Bissau: rapport om ett land och en befrielserörelse.* (Stockholm:Prisma, 1971).

10 Lars Rudebeck, Guinea-Bissau. A study of political mobilization. (Uppsala: The Scandinavian Institute of African Studies, 1974).

11 Paul Bélanger, "Une pratique de Contre-ècole: L' expérience éducative du mouvement de libération nationale dans les zones libérées de lá Guinée-Bissau." Sociologie et Sociétés, 1980: 155–168.

12 Mustafah Dhada, *Warriors at Work: How Guinea was really set free* (Niwot: University Press of Colorado, 1993).

13 Cá, Lourenço Ocuni Cá, *Perspectiva histórica da Organização do sistema educacional da Guiné Bissau* (São Paulo: UNICAMP, 2005).

educational and political projects did the PAIGC put to work during the liberation struggle? How did these initiatives work in an education field marked by the rejection of colonial culture and, simultaneously, the integration into the liberation movement of many of the techniques and practices of the colonizers? How did individuals and groups reshape their identities and practices – in the sense of their comprehensive re-education– in the context of the struggles? And, finally, what were the outcomes of these educational experiences in the aftermath of independence?

Although the PAIGC militant education project is generally historically perceived to have been heavily influenced by Paulo Freire's work on the *Pedagogy of the Oppressed*,[14] it was actually developed *in loco* in Guinea Bissau some years earlier than Freire's work.[15]

Militant education as a liberation struggle idea and practice depicted a process that presupposed a break, rather than a continuity, with the colonial education. Its practices and its concepts of education were strongly difined by an attempt to radically deferentiate from the 'old'. Militant Education oscillated between the ideological aspects of the liberation movements and the stricter conditions dictated by the situation of the liberation struggle. Considerably shaped by utopian elements, militant education depicted a set of representations and practices that linked politics and education in a much stronger and immediate way than the usual description of the political links that education suggests.

The written archives and 'walking archives': the researcher and the oral history recovery

The present book draws on an extended collection of printed archival material, the majority of which is located outside of Guinea Bissau and Cape Verde. Many of the documents related to the liberation struggle are located in Portugal. The materials preserved in the National Archives of Torre do Tombo in Lisbon were largely the result of the activities of the *Polícia Internacional e de Defesa do Estado* - PIDE- DGS (International Police for the Defense of the State) – a central institution of the Portuguese dictatorship. Unsuprisingly the, this collection shows above all the objectives followed by the PIDE and, consequently, it is largely an

---

14 Paulo Freire, *Pedagogy of the oppressed*. (New York: The Seabury Press, 1970).
15 Paulo Freire presence and influence in the Guinea Bissau educational project occured only after independence, when between 1975 and 1978, together with his wife Elza Maia Oliveira, he served as educational advisor for education reform in the territory.

archive built with the intention of defending Portuguese colonial government and thus present a unfavourable picture of the PAIGC and their achievements. Another problem affecting the archival sources conducted for this research is the fragmentary nature of the documentation collected by the Arquivo & Biblioteca Mario Soares Foundation. Finding sequential documents in this valuable material was almost impossible due to interruptions in the series. This unfortunate situation is largely the outcome of the civil war in Guinea-Bissau (1998-1999), during which the building hosting the Amílcar Cabral and PAIGC archives was bombed and looted, resulting in huge losses ofarchival material. However, some useful material can still be found Guinea Bissau and in Cape Verde in Amílcar Cabral Foundation.

However, consideration of the risky tasks of teaching and learning in schools located in the forest as well as the impact of these risks on the spatial mobility and material precariousness of this endeavor, demanded the inclusion of oral testimonies of PAIGC's militants and educationalists. Such approach opened the possibility for addressing aspects of this period for which written documentation may have been lost forever. The inclusion of oral testimonies from the liberation freedom fighters is what distinguishes this present book from the usual descriptions of the PAIGC's militant education program. The book introduces personal experiences into the historical narrative, thereby providing a perspective on the creation and consolidation of 'militant education' beyond the dominant rhetoric of Party documents. The combination of written archival material and oral testimonies presented in this work represents a shift in allows for a shift in historiographical approach. Whereas the political history of the liberation struggle emphasizes the individual figure of Amílcar Cabral, my work treats the liberation struggle and the educational system it produced as a collective endeavor.

Of course, from a historiographical standpoint the reliance on oral history sources poses a set of challenges. For more than forty years, PAIGC-related stories and experiences of 'militant education' were recollected only in small private groups of people who participated in the struggle. During this time, while these people were rebuilding their in Guinea Bissau, Cape Verde or in the diaspora, they traveled and worked, reformulated their ideals and memories about the liberation struggle, they forgot some major details surrounding the events of the struggle. "The struggle was made of walking and marching, a constant walking" was the way many PAIGC militants that I interviewed described the processes of the liberation struggle. This constant walk or march, continues to this very day in time and in space. To symbolize this process and the constant construction an deconstruction of militants' memories, I choose the term walking archive. This concept symbolizes theis group's life processes, their errancy and their itinerancy. The walking archive referes to an collection of memories that is not fixed in one place or house and whose information is not constant or fixed in time, but whose contents are brought to life by the questions and curiosity of those who are interested in accessing them.

The process of interviewing is directly associated with the process of remembering and it relies heavily on how these memories are recalled and the way they are narrated. Describing the process of remembering, Lisa Smith, in her work *Decolonizing Methodologies: Research and Indigenous People*,[16] characterizes it as a painful process "because it involves remembering not just what colonization was about but what being dehumanized meant". Yet she writes, "Both healing and transformation become crucial strategies in any approach which asks a community to remember what they may have decided unconsciously or consciously to forget."[17]

My book on militant education work relies on oral history through people's testimonies to understand the past.[18]These 'rebuilt' memories were revealed to me by my interlocutors in various forms. Cape Verdean and Guinean Creole, Portuguese and English were the languages in which the liberation struggle memories were brought to their present life. It was left to the freedom fighters to choose their language of expression. The places where these memories were shared were also chosen by my interlocutors themselves, and our interviews took place in institutions, work places, living rooms, balconies, gardens and kitchen. Under such circumstances background like the clatter of dishes in the kitchen, cars passing in the street, phones ringing and birds chirping elements were included in the interviewrecordings. Children running outside or playing on the living room floor stopped to listen to their grandparents' past experiences while neigbors passing by decided to stay for a while, hear the story, and perhaps raise a question. All of these aspects, while somewhat at odds with the notion of 'clean' data extracted in almost artificial conditions created an interview atmosphere in which the flow of personal histories could take place in an informal, yet still structured, setting.

Photographs, school manuals, meeting reports, maps and sounds, were always made available from me for consultation before and during the interview

---

16 Linda Tuhiwai Smith, *Decolonizing Methodologies. Research and Indigenous People* (New York: Zed Books Ltd, 1999).

17 Ibid., 146.

18 All interviews present in this work, were conducted, transcribed and translated by the author. The interviews took place in Portugal, Cape Verde, Guinea Bissau, Sweden and Germany.

process, functioned as "sensory memory" triggers.[19] Through the use of these materials, memories returned to my interlocutors and intensified during the course of the intreviewes. They experienced these recollections with great level of details including smells, tastes, sounds, physiological reactions, touch and images - information that unfortunately cannot be translated into words. However, with emotional memories, precise dates and times were not always accurately recalled. The absence of this accurately dates and times was justifird by my interlocutors with the secentece, "Because in a situation of war actions were more important than to write down dates and make notes."[20] However, this lack of specific information has much to do with the memories in later life and the memory lapses. [21]

Interviewing is a process of developing empathy and building trust between the two parties involve, not only during the conversation, but after the interview has taken place. Memories are emotions and although oral historians are concerned with facts and memories, they are often guilty of disregarding the power of emotions in speech.[22] "Feelings, emotions, pain, suffering and happiness all belong to a world historians are not trained to deal with […] Historians are rationally trained to stay away from emotionally stained evidence."[23] The feelings described were an integral part of the interviews and are reflected in this book. However, these emotions affected not just the interviewees in the process of their remembering, but also impacted the interviewer as she posed questions, prompeted memories and listened to her interlocutors responses.

During the interviews (and also during the writing of this work),[24] I was always aware of the various factors that might have affected the interview process and my relationship with my interviewees. Factors such as my age and gender, my social and ethnic background, my profession as a historian, my connectedness

---

19 Alistair Thomson and Robert Perks, *The oral history reader* (New York: Routledge, 2006).

20 Interview with André Corsino Tolentino, August 16, 2013.

21 Joanna Bornat, "Remembering in later life: generating individual and social change," in *The Oxford handbook of oral history*, ed. Donald Richie (Oxford: Oxford University Press, 2011), 202.

22 Paula Hamilton, "The Proust effect: oral history and the senses," in *The Oxford handbook of oral history*, ed. Donald Richie (Oxford: Oxford University Press, 2011), 221.

23 Jacques Depelchin, *Silences in African history. Between the syndromes of discovery and abolition* (Dar es Salaam: Mkuki Publishers, 2005), 151–152.

24 In total, a number of fifty-six people were interviewed for this work. Out of those only twenty-one are an integral part of this work. However, the information and knowledge shared by the other thirty-five were very valuable for the development of this work.

with the theme and my emotional state during the interview influenced the way the questions were posed and how they were answered.

Transferring the recorded word to a written form required a great deal of work, especially when it involved translating interviews from Creole and Portuguese into English. In this work, I tried to retain the speech patterns exactly as they were transmitted to me, only making changes and eliminations (repetitions, interruptions, redundancies)without which the text would have been difficult to read. Nonetheless, I decided to keep some of the temporal forms (e.g. past and present tense) that the interviewees used while telling their stories. However, it is important to keep in mind that the process of transcribing, translating, editing, reorganizing and placing the narratives while writing this book transforms the original interview to some extent, once the full sequence of the conversation is not reported. Creating a text that describes a logical sequence required balancing theinformation from my transcriptions with archival documents. This entailed bridging personal memories and public memories. This was not always possible, but Idid my best by merging the oral testimonies with archival written and visual documents.

Throughout this work, the reader will find long testimonies quoted. The decision to not unpack the words of those I interviewed was made with the intention of keeping as much as possible of their memory and voice intact as well as a gesture of recognition of the centrality of their knowledge in this work. These long quotations was kept also give to the reader a more broad sense of the history of the liberation struggle and those who that took part in it than would a summary of these memories in my analysis would.

This work is about the emergence of collective educational experiences closely associated with the armed guerrilla war in Guinea Bissau during and after the liberation struggle, particularly during the period between 1963 and 1978. It focuses on a specific cultural aspect of the struggle – the militant education front of which – dispite the profuse scholarship about the PAIGC's general history and its achievements – little has been written. The stories told here are the result of highly personal reflections and a legacy of the salient educational experiences of people fighting against colonialism and oppression. Far from being neutral, this history is a collective story that allows us to feel and understand the experiences of the individuals involved and to see how they altered their own lives through their participation in the struggle. In this work, they occupy a central place as subjects and producers of knowledge.[25]

---

25 Donald Ritchie, "Introduction: the evolution of oral history," in *The Oxford handbook of oral history*, ed. Donald Richie (Oxford: Oxford University Press, 2011), 13.

1 The PAIGC's freedom fighter. The process becoming conscious and militant (1940's-1972)

> *"In any way, we wish to start to give, to the indigenous in general a scientific education that their brains cannot yet bear. One or other individual exceptionally intelligent can be admitted in graduation courses, but the crowds mainly need to receive a solid elementary education, and a useful and complementary agricultural and professional training that, valorising the soil and foment the work, would better their economic condition and to powerfully compete for the progress of the colonial economy."*[26]

1 Colonialism, education and the Portuguese colonial policies

In the field of the literature about colonialism and education in African historiography, the chronology of the continent from a Western colonial perspective that is still applied today could be summed up as follows. There was a pre-colonial or traditional period before the arrival of the Europeans followed by a colonial era, particularly after 1800, that lasted until the formal and recognition of independence of African countries by European colonial powers; and finally, a post-colonial period commenced that continues until today. Chronologically this Eurocentric (and somehow pretentiously evolutionary) separation in writing the history of the continent not only largely ignores African agency in resisting European influences, but also tends to silence African initiatives and movements, condemning the continent to merely be reactive to Western agencies.[27]

In the field of education what is usually described as 'colonial education' in substantial fields of scholarship tends to picture Africans as rather passive and uncritical when faced with European expansion. This practice usually results in the acceptance, almost without a critical resistance of European educational models, culture, and values, as shown in the European project to create an *Educated African* or an *Assimilated Indigenous*. However, very little has been

---

26 Lopo Vaz de Sampayo Mello, *Política Indígena* (Porto: Magalhães e Moniz Lda., 1910).

27 Jacques Depelchin, *Silences in African history. Between the syndromes of discovery and abolition* (Dar es Salaam: Mkuki Na Nyota Publishers, 2005).

written about the experiences, effects and even traumatic life experiences under
the colonial educational systems, particularly considering the parallel cultural
environment (family and community) where these practices took place.[28]

Despite some experiences in creating schools in Africa mostly through
initiatives of missionary work or colonial officials, the Berlin Conference (1884-
1885) marked a major interest from colonial powers in an efficacious and substantial occupation of African territories.[29] This implied the design of policies
intended for this purpose, namely the sketching by the metropolitan authorities
of an effective educational system for the colonized territories that promoted
the establishment of economic, social, political and ideological colonial policies.
Walter Rodney in his book *How Europe underdeveloped Africa* described such
policies stating,

> The main purpose of the colonial school system was to train Africans to help the local
> administration at the lowest ranks and to staff the private capitalist firms owned by
> Europeans. In effect, that meant selecting a few Africans to participate in the domina-
> tion and exploitation of the continent as a whole. It was not an educational system that
> grew out of the African environment or one that was designed to promote the most
> rational use of material and social resources. It was not an educational system designed
> to give young people confidence and pride as members of African societies, but one
> which sought to instil a sense of deference towards all that was European and capitalist.[30]

Despite the different educational projects and practices that each European
colonial government applied in the territories that they colonized, the term
'colonial education' is here used as a connected constellation of discourses and
educational practices particularly associated with schooling, developed in the
context of foreign rule by colonial powers with the purpose of disseminating
and inculcating a concurring culture and ideology, both in the colonizer and
the colonized. Despite the differences all were imbibed with racial prejudices
and stereotypes, scientific fallacies about the Black African 'Other,' and the ideology that defended the cultural, economic and political supremacy of the white
western countries.

---

28 Chinua Achebe, *The education of a British-protected child* (New York: Alfred A. Knopf,
    2009). Ngũgĩ wa Thiong'o, *Dreams in a time of war: a childhood memoir* (London: Harvill
    Secker, 2010).

29 Steig Förster, Ronald Robinson, and Mommsen J. Wolfgang. *Bismark, Europe,
    and Africa: The Berlin Africa Conference 1884-1885 and the onset partition,*
    (New York: Oxford University Press, 1988).

30 Walter Rodney, *How Europe underdeveloped Africa* (Dakar: Pambazuka, 2012),
    240–241.

Placed in the hands of the colonial state, the Catholic church, and the missionary Protestant church, the 'colonial education' project across different territories was structured around three groups. The first group is related to the 'colonial education' carried out in the metropolis of the colonial power which intended to prepare a colonial elite and its intermediaries that would ensure the colonial enterprise. The second group, mostly located in the urban centers of the colonized territories, was focused on the development of a specific colonial education for the colonizers and the *assimilated* groups, with the objective of reassuring colonial hegemony and creating a social group of assimilated Africans that would facilitate/moderate the development of colonial policies. The third group focused on the education of the considered 'indigenous' people, particularly those living in the rural areas, with the more specific objective of creating an 'indigenous' working force through mostly practical education.

The schools created for these ends, and especially those that emerged in the colonized territories largely reflected the hegemony and the needs of the colonizers. Very little attention was given to the needs of the indigenous society so that school programs were formulated without the voices and needs of the local population.[31]

Portugal as a colonial agent and although largely influenced by its European counterparts[32] also developed its own 'colonial education' project. Studies about Portuguese education during the colonial period,[33] raise questions about the use of the expression 'Portuguese colonial education' and how such a term is used in the Portuguese educational scholarship without critical reflection. The main

---

31 Gail P. Kelly and Philip G. Altbach, *Education and colonialism* (New York: Longman Inc., 1978), 2.

32 Ana Isabel Madeira , "Portuguese, French and British discourses on colonial education: church-state relations, school expansion and missionary competition in Africa, 1890-1930." Vol. 41, in Paedagogica Historica, 31–60. Routledge Taylor &Francis Group, 2005.

33 João Carlos Paulo, "Vantagens da instrução e do trabalho. 'Escola de massas' e imagens de uma 'educação colonial portuguesa'" *Educação, Sociedade e Culturas* (1996): 99–128; João Carlos Paulo, Da 'educação colonial portuguesa' ao ensino no ultramar, in Ultimo Império e recentramento: 1930-1998, ed. Francisco Betthencourt and Maria F. Alegria (Lisboa: Temas e Debates, 2000), 304–333; João Carlos Paulo, "Èducation Coloniale et «École Portugaise»." In The colonial experience in education, by António' Nóvoa, Marc Depaepe and Erwin V. Johanningemeier, Paedagogica Historica- International journal of History of Education: Paris, 1995: 115-138; and Ana Isabel Madeira, "Popular education and republican ideals: The Portuguese lay missions in colonial Africa." Vol. 47, in Paedagogica Historica, 123–138. Routledge Taylor&Francis Group, 2011.

criticism of this expression developed during the *Estado Novo*[34] regime is that it induced the wrong idea of a single, unitary and uniform educational project applied in all territories colonized by the Portugal.

The idea of homogeneity that this expression transmits not only erases the different discourses, phases and rhythms present in the different political and ideological discourses of the distinct Portuguese regimes. It also doesn't refer to any of the differentiated treatments that the colonial regimes gave to each of the colonized territories due to the economic profits that each of them represented in the Portuguese economy, as well as the racial segregation and cultural prejudices present in the national and diverse legislation (including local policies) applied in those territories, which contributed to the formation of a hierarchical structure not just between the colonized territories but also among its inhabitants.

The institutionalization of State decrees such as the 1926 *Estatuto Político, Social e Criminal dos Indígenas de Angola e Moçambique*[35] later extended to Guinea in 1927,[36] the *Acto Colonial* from 1930,[37] moreover, the approval in 1941 of the *Estatuto do Missionário*,[38] *Código do Trabalho dos Indígenas nas Colónias Portuguesas de África* from 1928[39] and only abolished in 1960, are reminders of the institutionalized hierarchy between the colonized territories and people – the assimilated African and the indigenous African, developed by the successive Portuguese governments.[40]

---

34 *Estado Novo* (New State) was an authoritarian regime in Portugal between (1933-1974). The face of the regime was the Prime Minister António de Oliveira Salazar, substituted in 1968 by Marcelo Caetano that governed the country until 1974.

35 "Political, Social and Criminal Statute of the Indigenous of Angola and Mozambique" (The Indigenous Statute) Decree 12.533 from 23rd October 1926. The Indigenous Statute was already provided by the Law 277, 15th August 15, 1914. During the authoritarian regime, the Statute was revised two times. First in 1929 by the Decree 16.473 of 6th February 1929 and a second time by the Decree 39.666 of 20th May 1954 in the sequence of the constitutional reform in 1951. The Statute was extinct in the law by the Decree 43.893 from 6th September 1961.

36 Decree 13.968 30th May 1927.

37 "Colonial Act" approved by the Decree 18.570 from 8th July 1930.

38 "Missionary Statute", Decree 31.2017 from 5th April 1941.

39 "Labor Code for the Indigenous of the Portuguese Colonies in Africa" approved by the Decree 16.199 from 6th December 1928.

40 Mário Moutinho, *O indígena no pensamento colonial português*, (Lisboa: Edições Universitárias Lusófonas, 2000).

1.1 Colonial educational structures in Guinea-Bissau and Cape Verde

Colonial education structures in the contemporary territory of Guinea Bissau was mostly relegated to the hands of the Catholic church and civilians. Only in May of 1958, the territory officially inaugurated its first high school, the *Liceu Honório Barreto*, followed months later by the creation of the *Escola Industrial e Comercial de Bissau*, the first State vocational training center in the territory. The educational system in the territory was regulated by the Indigenous and the Missionary Statutes that implemented a discriminatory and dual educational structure.

One structure for the Africans named *educação rudimentar*[41] mostly for those located in the rural areas whose aim was to "gradually lead the wild indigenous to a civilized life" to "mentor in them a consciousness of being Portuguese" and to "prepare [the indigenous] for the struggle of life, making [the indigenous] more useful to the society and himself."[42] The other educational structure called *educação regular*,[43] located mainly in urban centers was designated for Europeans and the 'assimilated' Africans. Here the educational program followed the same structure applied by schools in Portugal.

However, the freedom that Catholic church and local priests had on how they administered and regulated their school population, created situations where families and pupils in order to attend school, were forced to convert to Catholicism,[44] and such demands had several consequences such as forced conversion, skepticism of parents concerning their children attending school, and family/community separation, as Felinto Vaz Martins recalls:

> The most cruel childhood memory I have is that I was expelled from school for religious reasons. In my time, all schools of the municipality, Bissau, Bafatá, Bolama, Gabu, were municipal schools and all the rest of Guinea was entrusted to Catholic mission. Moreover, there was the obligation to go to the church on weekends. I did not profess that religion, nor did my father. It was cruel because I had many friends. My dad said,

---

41 Translation: rudimentary education.
42 Decree 238 of May 17 of 1930.
43 Translation: regular education.
44 It is important to note the diversity of religious beliefs existent in Guinea-Bissau – Animist, Muslims or Islamicized. The catholic were minority group located mostly in the urban centers. For more information on this subject please consult table Annex 1 for "Ethnic groups and sub-groups from Guinea Bissau," and Annex 2 "Ethnographic map of Guinea Bissau," for the distribution of the population in the territory, in the annexes section.

'the only solution is to send you to Bolama. You were born by chance in Bolama, now is
not by chance but forcibly you have to leave Empada, your colleagues, your friends to go
to study in Bolama'. It is a memory. It hurt me a lot. First, my father started teaching me
some things at home. How could a man who did not have the fourth grade? But he was a
scholar. He taught me. He helped me a lot. And when he saw that he had already reached
the limit of what he knew, he had to accept the idea of me going to Bolama to continue
my studies. This is the most difficult memory for me to accept that time.[45]

Felinto Vaz Martins testimony reveals the ambiguous rules of how Catholic
church regulated their rudimentary schools and the emotional and material
impacts on family life. Most of all, it reveals the contradictions within the educational system especially between the policies applied in the rural areas and those
implemented in the urban centers. Having to send children to live in the urban
areas to escape the arbitrary regulation but also the limited future which rudimentary education offered was by design, it was a solution that not every parent
could afford. Having done his primary studies in Bolama, and due to the non-
existent high school in that urban center, Filinto Vaz Martins was again forced to
move, this time to Bissau:

From Bolama I came to Bissau. There was still no high school in Bissau. However, there
was an enormous pressure from Portuguese public employees to create a high school.
They called it *Colégio Liceu de Bissau*. The teachers were recruited from the Portuguese
top staff and workers in service mission here in Guinea. They were military, staff from
higher health services, the wives who accompanied their husbands, who by chance had a
very good education. They were recruited and with them, the high school was founded.
It was located in the *Casa da Cultura*. The administrators gave part of [the building] for
classrooms. I finished [school] as the first of my class that year. It is good to be poor. It
stimulates. I managed to be the first of the group. However, there was a Portuguese and
a mixed Portuguese - Cape Verdean [pupil] whose parents had a high reputation. The
colonial [government] would only give two annual scholarships to go to Portugal to
continue the studies, and though I was as the first in my class, they had the opportunity
and were chosen for the award. There was something like Ah! [sadness] And so I left.
There was no other way![46]

Contrary to the situation in Guinea-Bissau, the colonial investment in education
in Cape Verde had a different trajectory. The first high school, *Liceu Nacional*,
was established in 1860 in the Santiago Island, followed by the creation in 1866
of a seminary, *Seminário-Liceu* in São Nicolau Island, and later the foundation of

---

45 Interview with Filinto Vaz Martins, June 5, 2014.
46 Ibid.

the *Liceu Infante Dom Henrique* (later named *Liceu Gil Eanes*) in Mindelo, São Vicente island.

The three Islands – Santiago, São Nicolau and São Vicente, were the colonial educational hubs in the archipelago which were complemented by primary schools dispersed in the other seven islands of the archipelago.

The existence of a more organized educational structure, where the discriminatory separation between regular and rudimentary school did not exist, and with a similar educational program like the one in practice in Portugal.[47] The life of the Cape Verdean pupil was not much easier than the pupil in Guinea Bissau. André Corsino Tolentino, born in Cape Verde in Santo Antão island in 1946, son of small landowners recalls his educational trajectory Cape Verde:

> [Life in Cape Verde in late 1950's] was a harsh life. Education was seen as a very serious matter that one should not play with. [...] It was an austere education that the moral of the time required. Also, it required labour. Required study and demanded that one should be consistent with certain objectives. [...]. I have done the fourth grade of primary school in Santo Antão island,] [...] There was a distance between home and the school of probably three kilometres, but nothing serious. There I did the fourth grade. In that time we would do the fourth grade. Those, the very few of the agricultural islands whose parents dared [or could] send [their children] to continue the studies in São Vicente or Praia, in my case was to São Vicente Island, we had to do an admission examination for the secondary education. Normally this would take a year to do. I have done it in Coucu
li, parish of Santo Cruxifixo, Ribeira Grande municipality. I have done this process travelling a distance of maybe ten kilometres daily, round trip. The teacher, by chance a renowned teacher, Pedro Josénio Delgado, was my relative and was one of the few primary school teachers who had completed high school.
>
> He had the famous seventh grade of high school. During my youth [to have] the seventh grade of high school was something very respected. [...] I did the preparation for high school with him, and later that year, it should have been 1959, I went to do the exam in São Vicente, for admission in the *Liceu Gil Eanes*. I was successfully admitted. However, had arrived in my village, so to speak o *meu lugar*,[48] a young woman who had completed

---

47 The school organization was the same that was in practice in the metropolis. According to the Decree n° 13.619 from May 17th of 1927, school were divided into three groups: early childhood; elementary, primary education (from 7 to 11 years old), complementary primary school (from 11 to 13 years old). The secondary school, was divided into three groups: the first middle school (corresponded two or three years of training), and the second middle school (three years of training), and lastly the high school that was also known as the seventh grade (corresponding to two years training), was the highest education level that one could study in the colonized territories.

48 A Portuguese kind expression to refer to the village where one grown up. A literal translation is would be "my place."

the seventh grade and she was hoping to continue her studies abroad. [...] I returned to Santo Antão to take advantage of this circumstance and prepare myself to do the first and second year of high school as an external student. I returned to Santo Antão, and two years later I returned to São Vicente to stay and to do the exams for the second year of high school and continue until the seventh grade.

This was my school trajectory. It was, let's say, in three phases. The first in my village; the second phase already in the parish with Professor Josénio Delgado and preparation for the admission; and the third step still in Santo Antão, again in my village to seize that particular circumstance and to prepare me for the second grade of high school. [When] I finished the second year of high school, there was no other option. One could continue or give up. I continued to make the seventh grade in 1966.[49]

Both trajectories from Felinto Vaz Martins in Guinea Bissau and André Corsino Tolentino in Cape Verde reinforce the argument of the nonexistence a homogeneous and unitary Portuguese colonial educational structure all over the then considered Portuguese territory. The investment in the creation of educational facilities is crucial for the understanding of the educational gaps and opportunities that each colonized territory could offer. Compared to Cape Verde, the late investment on the creation of educational facilities in the territory of Guinea Bissau is an example of the hierarchies between territories, but also a result of the Portuguese racial and cultural prejudices concerning each territory.

1.2 Everyday realities: legislation, school and the daily life

Another aim of Portuguese colonization was to transform Africans into 'true Portuguese' through work and education. However, such plans crashed daily with the discriminatory produced legislation and practice, and the life outside the school gates. Anselmo Cabral, like Felinto Vaz Martins, had done his primary studies in Bolama, and in 1959 moved Bissau to continue the secondary school in the recently founded high school *Liceu Honório Barreto*. Coming from a family considered to be *assimilada* by the Portuguese colonial regime, Anselmo recalls how the Portuguese discriminatory legislation was experienced in the territory and how the school environment dealt such situation:

In high school, there were Portuguese, Cape Verdean and assimilated Guinean [pupils]. That was it. Those who did not have the identity card for the assimilated, they could not matriculate. [...] There was inadequate treatment. Yes! [We] saw how the Portuguese mistreated the people. There was forced labour on the roads and there were fights with

---

49   Interview with André Corsino Tolentino, August 16, 2013.

the *Cipaios*,[50] the administration guards. If you came from a *tabanca*[51] [village] without a permission license, because you need to have a permission license[52] to come to Bissau, and if you were caught without it, you would be punished and beaten. That angered the people. Besides that, there was a lot of abuse. The people could not argue, and sometimes in their workplace, there was always trouble [work injustices], and if you argued they [the Portuguese] would kick you out of work. And if you tried to argue they would sue you. The injustice was blatant on a daily basis. Daily you could see the difference [like] the people's purchasing power. The people that lived in the outskirts neighbourhood lived with many difficulties. They could not attend school, or have access to the health services. There was this injustice. [...] The entire population was considered indigenous. There was whole process that the indigenous should go through to be considered assimilated. They had to know how to eat at the table. The [Portuguese] administration would come [to their house] to observe how their home was, if you had normal things, like a table, a house with latrines, with bathroom, beds, etc. There was this process [that the Portuguese administration] imposed and only when people went through all process, then automatically the Portuguese administration would give the identity card. The process was long. And you had to know how to speak Portuguese, and you need to have a school education. Because [of the Portuguese Indigenous legislation] only a tiny group had access to school. There was always an elite that they [the Portuguese administration] prepared and needed, only for a matter of work. [...] The school was very serious. Because it was not a school for Guineans, it was a school for the Portuguese. [...] The Guineans would go there, with hard work [...] Then in the school, the class subjects

---

50 The Guinean colonial administrative structure was divided in six groups, 1) the Governor; 2) the administrators; 3) station chiefs, 4) traditional chiefs (*régulos*); 5) village chiefs (*chefes de tabanca*) and 6) the Sipaios (*Cipaios*) a paramilitary force whose task was to make Indigenous population obey the Portuguese laws.

51 Translation: Guinean creole word that means village.

52 The *Caderneta o Indígena* (The Indigenous Passbook) was an identity card or passport only for the African people considered by Portuguese colonial law as being Indigenous (uncivilized). Through this document, the Portuguese could control the "transit, setting and moving" of all male Indigenous more than 16 years old. This document should contain information about health, employment, and taxes. The Indigenous population was also a) forbidden "transit on colony roads and in the European towns" if not correctly dressed and between the period of 9 pm and 5 am; b) they could not live in the European town unless their "parents or tutors" had a legal profession; c) the legislation established a maximum period of 10 days for the Indigenous to find work in the city (otherwise he would run the danger of being considered a vagrant, be arrested and designed to compelled work for a period of no less 18 months). The infringement of the law was punished with a fine or days of correctional labour. The incapacity of the majority to pay these fines gave the administrators a source of free labour. All these restrictions, especially to the capital city of Bissau, promoted the existence of labour reserves in neighbourhoods euphemistically called "Indigenous neighbourhoods."

were the same that were taught in Portugal. We just studied with books that came from Portugal. The Portuguese idiom was required, and you could not even speak Creole outside [in the playground] only Portuguese. It was an assimilation system. [...] They [Portuguese administration] did not want too much contact between us, who studied in high school, with the people of the surroundings [indigenous]. We could not go there. Only here in the city, like going to the cinema, or when there were things like the activities of the *Mocidade Portuguesa*.[53] It was mandatory. Everyone should participate in the *Mocidade Portuguesa*, to be good Portuguese. I took part in the *Mocidade Portuguesa*, I did not have another choice. I was a good Portuguese until a certain time, but then I stopped being, and I walked away.[54]

In Guinea Bissau, the daily life of a regular African student was captured in the contradictory world of everyday life that their African peers were subjugated under the colonial regime and a discriminatory educational structure that only a few had access to, whose goal was to coach them on how to become a good 'assimilated' Portuguese. Although the Indigenous legislation was not applied in Cape Verde, the reality in the territory was not much different. These contradictions in the Cape Verdean territory were recalled by André Corsino Tolentino:

I must say that there was a gap. An extraordinary gap between what was the education system, or what it was conceived as such through the tangible materials such as the school manual. I remember for example my mother with a big book teaching me the first letters and nothing [in the book] had to do with what I observed in my daily life. Neither the human figures, nor the animals, nor the content. For example, it was a white, a little boy or a little girl, Portuguese from Portugal of Europe. Or it was a train. Or they would talk about a bus on a certain road, or it was an animal I had never seen. I remember this discomfort, this thing that led us to think that education was something from a world very different from ours. Then the teachers, the anecdotes, the popular sayings that had nothing to do with our reality. I remember having this thing, this feeling that I didn't know how to explain but which seemed extremely strange. I also remember that because of this implicit comparison between what were the education signs of the Portuguese empire and our real life, I remember finding myself in a situation of watching myself

---

53 The *Mocidade Portuguesa* meaning The Portuguese Youth, created on May 14th 1936 by the Decree n° 26.611, stated in art.40 its main objective, "cover all youth, schooled or not, and is designed to stimulate the comprehensive development of their physical capacity, the formation of character and devotion to the fatherland, the sentiment of order, in the taste for discipline and military service". Its extension to the colonized territories through the Decree 29.453 17 February 1939, extinguished, substituted and appropriated the already grounded patrimony of a previous organization in Cape Verde – The *Falcões Portugueses de Cabo Verde* or Skols de Cabo Verde (founded in Mindelo in 1934).

54 Interview with Anselmo Cabral, June 25, 2014.

in the mirror in the hope that I could be considered more pale or white or more so-so. Because in the school we were learning that there was a kind of primitive Kaffirs, and a kind of citizens, who were not even the first citizens because they [the Portuguese] were the citizens. Then I remember to quarrel this with my peers, and it always came [in our discussions] this surreptitious thing of a racist language that we ourselves used and even if we are very attentive we can still detect in Cape Verde, or between Cape Verdeans, even living abroad. Anyway, I remember this huge contrast between the signs of education, of civilization, and what was our real life, which was something to overcome. I believe there was an implicit desire for us to overcome this situation. But then on the other side there was a very strong conviction and found that in my family, in the neighbourhood, *no meu lugar*, that education was the only way at least in that context, the only thing that could take us out from that contradiction, of that situation, of that sort of social paralysis. This is to say, that through education it was possible to climb, it was possible to rise, and possible to change the status. It is possible to change life. The teachers sometimes made a kind of miracle. Because I when I studied my fourth school grade, we were all classes of first, second; third and fourth grade in the same classroom. The teacher had to deal with all that, and the most interesting is that they could get [positive] results. [Concerning the social life in the islands] In São Vicente it was a little bit more different. Because São Vicente was characterized by some advanced urbanization thanks to the influence of probably many things, namely a kind of distance from the Governor and the people that surrounded him, and that had a significant influence in the society. For example, in Praia [Santiago island] in the Square Alexandre Albuquerque, there was one level for the people who used shoes, and that normally were part of the administration. The Governor himself would go for a walk in the Square, and very few merchants would have access to that nucleus. Then [in the same square] in a lower step were the barefoot people. This was something that we in São Vicente didn't know, probably because of the distance with the Governor, and maybe because of the presence of the English, the Italians and others with a more open mind than the Portuguese colonial administration.[55]

The hierarchies, discrimination, and conflicts experienced in the daily life, and the contradictions featured in the school manuals, were also transferred to the school corridors involving teachers, pupils and the administration's arbitrary rules and values. Continuing his recollections of his school years is Cape Verde André Corsino Tolentino spoke about two of these episodes that marked this period as a student in high school *Liceu Gil Eanes*:

The first episode was in my fourth grade of high school. For reasons that had to do with a certain revolt, but not yet rationalized or politically framed, but my classmates and I, we thought that the exaggerations of *Mocidade Portuguesa* had no suitability in the context of our school. However, some teachers and specifically the president of *Liceu*

---

55 Interview with André Corsino Tolentino, August 16, 2013.

Gil Eanes, the Professor Anterro Simões, who at the time acted more as an agent of the order than as director of an organization dedicated to education, insisted on having everybody enrolled in the activities of *Mocidade Portuguesa* with the symbol of Salazar and those things. We decided -we were a group- not to care much with that. Quite the contrary, in a way we acted with a certain disdain, towards *Mocidade Portuguesa*, the symbol of Salazar and so forth, though our reasons were not very clear. The truth is that I was administratively forced to leave school in the third period of the fourth year of high school. I have done the first period and I pass. I made the second period pass. But when I presented myself after the vacation holidays in agricultural islands - to do the third period of the fourth year, I was not admitted. The president of the *Liceu Gil Eanes* came to my classroom - a little bit to impose respect to the other classmates said: "Mr. Tolentino cannot continue in this school because he did not respect a number of rules and, had [a certain number of] faults in *Mocidade Portuguesa* activities."

There was a very important episode that followed. At the time the head of Cape Verde's education services - a kind of minister of education of Cape Verde province, was called was Anterro Barros, a native of São Vicente. He had been rector of *Liceu Gil Eanes*, but there were those discriminations between Portuguese and Cape Verdeans, and the relation between Anterro Simoes and Anterro Barros seemed not to be very good, because, Anterro Barros ran from mouth to mouth that he was a patriot and had met Amílcar Cabral in New York.

Paraphrasing what people say about the inhabitants of Santo Antão – that "we born with a foolscap sheet of paper under the arm", which means that we like requirements or have an obsession for paper. I wrote to the director of education in Cape Verde, Anterro Barros, and I expressed what was going on, adding that I expected the approval of my document in order to be allowed to continue school. I remained in Santo Antão all the third period. The truth is that before the beginning of next year the director's resolution arrived saying that my case had been studied, that it was verified that the grades I had from the first and second period and if I had had the normal conditions it could be deduced that I would transit to for the fifth grade. This about the procedure. Then concerning the question of merit, he understood that the faults that I received on the grounds of *Mocidade Portuguesa*, were not enough to keep me from continuing my studies in the next year. Conclusion, I signed up for the fifth grade without completing the fourth.[56]

Contrary to Corsino Tolentino's experience with the *Mocidade Portuguesa* organization and the conflicts with the school administration, in Guinea Bissau the use of the funds of the *Mocidade Portuguesa* was responsible for the scholarship that Filinto Vaz Martins received and that allowed him to continue his studies in Lisbon, as he described:

---

56 Ibid.

In the year of 1959, the political police - PIDE[57]- was installed here [Guinea Bissau]. The headquarters were where today is the office of FUNDEI.[58] It was a little house and with a yard inside where people were beaten. [During colonial period] to leave the colony you need to have permission from the political police, the PIDE. For me there was no problem because I could not afford to leave the colony, and my parents had no money to give me to leave and to continue my studies [in Lisbon]. I present myself in a public tenure for a working place as a customs register. I got the position and I started to work, doing calculation. At that time there were no calculating machines, there were no computers, there was nothing. [I had to do] sums, huge rows of sums that one person had to do. By chance, sometimes there are things that is not possible to understand, how it happened that a Portuguese complained about my situation: - 'How does this boy who was the first in his class, first he does not receive a scholarship, and second is here all day doing calculations?'

And he went [to the Customs Director Office] with a group of employees to meet with the Customs Director, the Governor who was a kind of a president here, and the heads of finance departments. [...]. He put the problem, which seems that generated a lot of talk, and an element of PIDE that attended the meeting suggested that I was granted a scholarship of *Mocidade Portuguesa*. Though I had nothing to do with *Mocidade Portuguesa*, they gave me a scholarship. I worked [as a customs register] only one month, and I was benefited with a scholarship from *Mocidade Portuguesa*. I was in Portugal two years in *Instituto Superior Técnico* in the course higher engineering in Lisbon.[59]

Both testimonies from André Corsino Tolentino and Filinto Vaz Martins are a reflection of the inconsistency and disparities of the Portuguese colonial structure and how much of the decisions were more dependent on the willingness of individuals and employees in each territory than on the actual colonial regulation. Their experiences along their educational path in the Guinea Bissau and Cape Verde are important in understanding the student life and lived emotional and physical contradictions under a colonial regime with the ambiguous ideal of promoting assimilation through education.

The prohibition of African languages in the schools, the representation in the school manuals of the colonizers as superiors and as heroes and the Africans as inferiors and shameful, the teaching of Portuguese history, geography and Portuguese idiom, are the themes transversal to all Portuguese colonial educational structures - in the metropole and overseas. The outcome of such policies

---

57   PIDE-DGS - Polícia Internacional e de defesa do Estado (International Police for the Defense of the State). The organization was created in 1945 for Portugal by the Salazar Regime, and extended to Africa in 1954.

58   Fundação Guineense para o Desenvolvimento Empresarial Industrial, today located in Rua General Omar Torrijos nº 49.

59   Interview with Filinto Vaz Martins June 5, 2014.

and practices was that "as soon as African children enter elementary school, they develop an inferiority complex. They learn to fear the white man and to feel ashamed of being Africans."[60]

1.3 The arrival to Portugal: the consciousness and militancy spaces

"The black man in the Portuguese colonies in Africa, like the other Black man in the other foreign colonies, generally does not possess the economic resources compatible with his human dignity. The structure of the colonial regime reserves him, explicit or tacitly, positions that in the capitalist social structure corresponds to a socio-economic level consider inferior [and] when the black man achieves the limited field of 'opportunities that are offered to him', he finds explicit or tacit limitations imposed by racism"[61]

Amílcar Cabral, 1978

Amílcar Cabral in the article *The role of the African student* written in 1953 for the special edition of *Présence Africaine* approached several issues concerning the situation of the Black African student and the academic life within the framework of Portuguese colonialism. The article gives a general overview of the different Portuguese educational policies and focused on the situation of the African student and their lack of resources - the fact that only a small number of students could actually pursue their higher studies abroad, this being dependent on their family's economic situation to finance their education, or the dependence on the few scholarships that the colonial government provided, but also that that largely limited the student courses choice. Even after the course conclusion the African student still had to face the difficulties of working in Africa or Portugal due to the existent colonial racist structure.

To welcome students from overseas, to defend their interest, to strengthen the solidarity and friendship between the overseas students and the ones from the metropole, and above all to propagate the Portuguese ideology of the 'great' empire from '*Minho a Timor*',[62] the Portuguese government founded the 'associative and cultural' platform *Casa dos Estudantes do Império* in 1944 in Lisbon.[63] In the same year the institution opened a delegation in Coimbra, followed in 1960

---

60 Amílcar Cabral, *Unidade e Luta. A arma da teoria* (Lisboa: Seara Nova, 1978), 64.

61 Ibid., 30.

62 The expression from "Minho to Timor", was used during the colonial period to describe the greatness and the extension of the Portuguese empire, being Minho the northest province point of Portugal, and East Timor also know as Piortuguse Timor, a southeast Asian nation and Portugues colony until November 28th, 1978.

63 Translation: House of the Students of the Empire.

by a delegation in Porto. The *Casa dos Estudantes do Império* became the meeting point of every African student in the Metropole.[64] From the several activities the students organized with relative autonomy, it was the publication of the student magazine *Mensagem* (1948-1965) that most impacts on the student consciousness about colonialism and their situation as oppressed and colonized subjects. The magazine that counted on the participation and writing from students from the different colonized territories approached themes such as history, social life, economy, linguistics, prose, poetry and drawings, with a special focus on the territories colonized by Portugal.

Complementary to this initiative were the publication of magazines with similar characteristics in *Casa dos Estudantes do Império* in Coimbra with the magazine *Meridiano* (1947) followed by the magazine *Momento* (1950), not to mention the organization of periodic balls of conviviality and fund raising, sports leagues, and the holding of conferences and debates that contributed to the dissemination of African cultures, the reaffirmation of the African subject as self, and in between the lines, condemnation of the Portuguese colonialism and the need to organize for its end.

Such activities had not gone unnoticed by the Portuguese political police –PIDE-DGS, that in 1952 started to follow the *Casa dos Estudantes do Império* activities and their members, as Maria da Luz Boal recalls:

> In the *Casa dos Estudantes do Império*, we felt that something was not going well. Already in that time, we felt there that Portugal was with political problems as well. So there was a certain control, a certain follow-up of our steps. I remember once I was contracted to make an inventory of people's home furnishings. And that was terrible. You would to people's house, knock the door, and say that you want to know how many dishes they had, how many cups they had [...] I mean, that was something to test me. I went a couple of times and then I gave up. I said I did not want continue. I began to think that it would be perhaps the PIDE manoeuvre to catch me. To see if I actually had the ability to investigate, find out about people's lives. So I stopped.[65]

In 1965/1666 the *Casa dos Estudantes do Império* was replaced by the *Procuradoria dos Estudantes Utramarinos*,[66] an institution that at the same time that it offered scholarships, was used to control and frame their political activities. André Corsino Tolentino, who arrived in Lisbon in 1966 to further his higher studies

---

64 António Faria, *Linha Estreita da Liberdade. A Casa dos Estudantes do Império*, (Lisboa: Edições Colibri, 1997).

65 Interview with Maria da Luz Boal, September 2, 2013.

66 Translation: Procuratorate of the Students of the Empire.

in the course of public administration at *Instituto Superior de Ciências Sociais e Política Ultramarina*, recalls his experience with the Portuguese political police:

> In Portugal, because I had a scholarship I went to *Lar Ultramarino* near Santo Amaro. The *Procuradoria dos Estudantes Ultramarinos* had inherited the *Casa dos Estudantes do Império*. The *Procuradoria* paid the scholarships and tried to control the students. It was very infiltrated by the PIDE. I was in Lisbon for about a year and a half, in the years 1966 and 1968 [...] I must say that we were already on the list. [...] I remember one joke. In the year 1966, when I finished high school to go to Lisbon, we had to present parental permission, certainly to facilitate control over the departures from Cape Verde. I managed to embark with a false authorization. They let me travel, and I thought eventually that PIDE-DGS apparatus in Cape Verde was quite ineffective. It is ridiculous but true. Only a few days after I left to Lisbon they started to announce my name on the radio requesting for my appearance [in their office]. I got to know this from a friend's letter who asked me:
>
> - Ah! so the guys do not know that you left São Vincente to the Metropole?
>
> This is to say that sometimes we thought that the political police were very powerful, but they had incredible weaknesses. I travel to Portugal in 1966, right on time to start the school year. There, I was somehow surprised by the structure that my Cape Verdean peers from previous years, had created for me, in the PAIGC. They were already recognized as Party activists, and they included me. [...] The political police started to visit me with increasing frequency, searching my bookshelves [looking for] what I was reading. They would confiscate books even if they were sold in the city bookstores. [...] Another detail that probably worth telling is that there was a contradiction between what the PIDE intentions were and what actually happened. For example, there were many booksellers - Portuguese booksellers, and of course, they were known to sell some books that they knew were not properly appreciated by the PIDE and the *Salazaristas*,[67] or were simply prohibited [in the country]. However, they sold them under the counter because there was this semi-clandestine market. At another point, the PIDE came and made a raid on the students' and teachers' bookshelves. They took everything [I had] because of that aberrant category of prohibited works. They pilfered from my shelves at *Lar Ultramarino* books like *Vidas Secas* from Graciliano Ramos, *Catacumbas da Liberdade* from Jorge Amado or works of Portuguese authors sold in the market but that at the same time were prohibited. We also had books of Marxists, existentialists and Social Democrats. They [the political police] had this kind of contradictions.[68]

However, parallel to the existence of these two institutions highly infiltrated by the political police, other clandestine political groups contributed to the political consciousness and training of the African students. Among them were the Portuguese left political movements, as the *Partido Comunista*[69] or the *Movimento*

---

67 Expression used to define the supporters of the Salazar regime.
68 Interview with André Corsino Tolentino, August 21, 2013.
69 Translation: Comunist Party.

Juvenil de Unidade Democrática,[70] clandestine groups that some African students had political relations with, a fact that contributed to the political police putting the institution under surveillance.

1.4 Underground self-re-education centers in Lisbon

The life of the African student in Portugal-Lisbon of the 1940s, 50s and 60's was centered on three poles - the *Casa dos Estudantes do Império*, the *Centro de Estudos Africanos*[71] a clandestine study group created by students in 1951, and the *Clube Marítimo Africano*[72] founded in 1954, whose aim was to function as a sports and cultural recreational center that supported the African community in Lisbon.

Mario Pinto de Andrade, one of the founders of the *Centro de Estudos Africanos* recalled in an interview the origins, activities, and impact of the study group on the political consciousness formation of the African students:

> [The Center] has its story, with its adventures. As we exchanged impressions, we were to form a collective consciousness, from a group that thought the same things. I no longer know in what circumstances we meet a man of the old generation, Arthur Castro, a journalist from Sao Tomé, João de Castro's brother. This João de Castro's was a man who had militated, was one of the leaders of the associations of the 1920's and was a member of the directorates of these associations, and the Junta, and *Liga Africana*[73] [...] and then took positions in favour of Portugal in League of Nations [...] We had relations with his brother, Artur Castro, because he was the leader - perhaps the only one - of a *Casa de África* [House of Africa], [...] The *Casa de África* had no members, no one, no movement, but there was a building, an administration, and we wanted to take possession over this administration [...] We wanted, to lay hold of the *Casa de África* and to then carry out a cultural action was a façade. It should culminate naturally in politics. We wanted to do a study centre. And that's why Tenreiro and myself [...]came together and built a work plan that was called Study Centre of the Portuguese African House: that was the name of the first work plan [...]But this attempted coup, of taking the small Bastille which was the *Casa de África* did not take place [...] we had to find a way to do

---

70 Translation: Juvenile Movement of Democratic Unity.

71 Translation: Center of African Studies.

72 Translation: African Maritime Club.

73 The *Junta* (Coolective) and the *Liga Africana* (African League), corresponds to proto-nationalist organizations created by Africans living in Lisbon and in the colonized territories in the beginning of the twentieth century. For more information on this subject, please consult the work of Mário Pinto de Andrade, *Origens do nacionalismo africano. Continuidade e ruptura nos movimentos unitários emergentes da luta contra a dominação portuguesa: 1911-1961* (Lisboa: Dom Quixote, 1998).

make the Center of African Students exist in some place, and we chose the family that was - for us – was in better situation at the time, that was the Espírito Santos' family, because they had a [...] big room. [...] In fact, the goal was to study Africa: [...] we had to get to know, know ourselves to ourselves. For the Portuguese, we were assimilated. [...] From Africa we had the experience, the material experience, social experience, but we had not reflected on our own culture, we had not had in our respective countries the possibility of thinking about our own culture: it was not bound in our language – it's an evidence - many of us didn't even speak the language or languages of the country [...] it was necessary to become aware of it: it was a self-consciousness of African culture and the different cultures in the continental framework, and the black world and beyond the black world.[...] A work plan of this type was operational - as we say today. It took us to our culture; it made us think about our problems and then it would open polit-ical perspectives. It was not a pure reflection over African situations of the past, but it plunged us directly in the real, the real in movement. Various topics flowed directly into the social reality in our lives and the need to act.[74]

Alongside the Center activities, another and a more selective group emerged that concentrated their energies on detecting conscious people that would be able to join the development of the liberation struggle in the colonized territo-ries. The *Centro de Estudos Africanos* remained in operation until 1954, a period when most of its members left Portugal and started to work clandestinely on the organization of the liberation struggle in the colonized territories. Nonetheless, the existence of a network of clandestine study groups continued to develop in Lisbon, with the task of continuing to study Africa, Portuguese colonialism and other international movements and literature, but also to detect the conscious and trustworthy people who would adhere to the already ongoing process of the liberation struggle.

Upon his arrival to Lisbon, André Corsino Tolentino was integrated into one clandestine study group or *célula* in Lisbon. Reading and debating were cen-tral to the group activities and central in the process of becoming conscious about colonialism and strategies of resistance and of visualizing a future for their homelands. Corsino's recalls some of the literature of the PAIGC cell in Lisbon and the group's modus operandi:

[The group] had followed the tradition that Amílcar Cabral left in Lisbon - the study groups. We were challenged. The thing was serious! [...] The students and young people in general, devoted to the study of key issues for the history, economy, and culture of Cape Verde. We studied history from the perspective of Sena Barcelos, but also from other scholars, and we tried to interpret certain information, with the help of Antonio

---

74   Michel Laban, *Mário Pinto de Andrade. Uma entrevista a Michel Laban,* (Lisboa: Edições Sá da Costa, 1997), 66–75. (author translation)

Carreira for example. Universal themes such as social justice, political organization and national liberation interested us very much. We studied agriculture in Cape Verde based on the studies of Gandveaux Barbosa, Orlando Ribeiro, Ilídio do Amaral, Amílcar Cabral, etc. The scientific perspective and the world knowledge stimulated our intellect and our attitudes. The overt or camouflaged political position was important. We used experts to strengthen our training because we had the ambition to be useful [...]. The ones who studied Agronomy dedicated themselves to agriculture and livestock studies. They would compare sources and led the colleagues in the debates. The ones who studied administration did the same, and jurists and economists too. [...] These courses were a kind of university *avant la lettre*, a parallel university that we did. These study and observation groups were part of training in politics and policies. Those who have had formal ties with the PAIGC were somehow responsible for initiating others and to report to the Party. Let's say that that was the path followed in the study groups, an innovative tradition.[75]

The PAIGC study group that André Corsino Tolentino attended was not the only one in the city. Agnelo Regala, a Guinean recalls his student years in Lisbon during the 1960's and the government policies of separating the African students. His testimony reveals the existence of other clandestine study groups in Lisbon, their diversity and the group interaction with other students and artistic movements from other countries:

The colonial regime separated the African students for three universities. The *Instituto Superior de Economia*, the *Instituto Superior de Ciências do Trabalho e da Empresa*, and the *Instituto Superior de Ciências Sociais e Políticas*. The African students who were in those universities were separated. I remember a friend who was Angolan, who was sent to in *Instituto Superior de Economia*, the other was sent to *Instituto Superior de Ciências Socias e Políticas*, and I was sent to *Instituto Superior de Ciências do Trabalho e da Empresa*. [...] From there I integrated into the Party [PAIGC] clandestine cell. We were doing great debates, in an apartment in Rua da Estefânia. We were essentially people from Guinea, from Angola there was one member, and there was people from Cape Verde. [We had] debates on ideological issues, on the issue of the liberation struggle. It was a question of consciousness, the consciousness of the people. [There were also] interactions, because there were many Cape Verdeans [living] in France and that came to Portugal in vacations. The social gatherings were much wider. They had another vision, the vision of freedom was other. While there [in France] they already lived in a democracy, in Portugal there was still the dictatorship. They brought a certain fresh air of hope to the group.[76]

---

75 Interview with André Corsino Tolentino, August 21, 2013.
76 Interview with Agnelo Augusto Regala, June 5, 2014.

The constant control of the political police, the government list of forbidden literature, and the Portuguese dictatorial regime were significant obstacles for student's intellectual emancipation. It was within that social and political conjuncture that the contact network with the outside was an added value for the consciousness process of the African student in Lisbon. The *Clube Marítimo Africano* and the contact with the African sailors facilitated the circulation of international literature that otherwise would be difficult to access, contributing to the dangerous practice of book smuggling in the city. Mario Pinto de Andrade recalled the important role of sailors in this process:

> We ordered many books through the sailors. The sailors were not only young proletarians that we had to literate [...] Some were literate, were men who already had a political consciousness [...] the books were brought from Brazil, the United States [...] We knew the New Negro movement; we followed, we read everything Langston Hughes wrote, we made our consciousness courses, always with the Native Son from Richard Wright, reading it in the original. And in Brazil, for sure [...] we read poets of the West Indies, West Indies - Nicolás Guillén. We recited the poems of Nicolás Guillén, it was mandatory, part of our heritage, part of the baggage of progressive and informed African intellectual in Lisbon at the time.[77]

1.5 The world outside the Portuguese colonial dictatorship and the escapes towards the struggle

The climate of fear and intimidation that African students and all the dissident voices against Portuguese dictatorship and colonialist regime lived through in Portugal under the political police persecution contributed to a series of clandestine escapes using various strategies and schemes. The use of clandestine smuggling trails in the Portuguese north and western borders with Spain, the payment of bribes to the corrupt Portuguese police to escape military service or to obtain permission to travel were some of the methods that several African students used to escape from Portugal.

By the end of 1950's and 1960's, the African liberation movements in the colonized territories were already in significant development by the first generation of students that attended the *Casa dos Estudantes do Império*. For this generation, Mario Pinto de Andrade coined the term, *Geração Cabral*.[78] The second generation was then to join on the liberation path. The democratic world outside, the

---

77 Laban, *Mário Pinto de Andrade. Uma entrevista a Michel Laban*, 77.
78 Translation: Cabral's Generation. Referring to the generation of African students in Portugal during the 1940's that initiated the liberation struggle. Other members of this group were Agostinho Neto, Amílcar Cabral.

independence of African countries like Ghana in 1957, Guinea in 1958, Senegal in 1960, and Algeria in 1962, just to mention a few, and the civil rights movement in the United States of America, deeply influenced the students to join the liberation and independence struggle.

It was in the summer, June 16th and July 2nd of 1961,[79] in Portugal that the largest African student clandestine escape took place, with the help of *Cimade - Comité inter-mouvements auprès des évacués*,[80] an international ecumenical service agency of the French Protestant Federation founded at the beguining of the World war II, in contact with the World Council of Churches. The escape was organized in two groups, being the first group composed of nineteen students, and the second group forty-one others. In total, they were sixty students, most of them college students, some of them under the political police radar. Filinto Vaz Martins recalled his experience in the first group that escaped:

> The harassment by the political police was very strong. We had the *Casa dos Estudantes do Império* where people began to talk about politics. Conakry was already free, the whole area of Africa began to move and then the Angolans had already started the first movements with the *União dos Povos de Angola*.[81] All that action created a huge distrust [of Portuguese authorities] in the students that were coming from the colonies. This was exacerbated by the fact that I was living in a boarding school run by a group of Americans that received Angolan students. I got there by coincidence. I met an Angolan friend. We lived there together, and they gave us the same room with a bunk bed. At certain point the political police began to call us for interrogations. Why? We did not know. Also, because our actions were not yet very clear [obvious]. We were sometimes called in the morning and stayed until the end of the day for interrogations. [The political police wanted] to know what we do, what our thoughts were. They would do questions like, 'We saw you on the other day in a youth meeting what was the conversation about? Who was there from your group?'
> They would make the connections to see if we were saying the same thing.
> Then we [realize that there was no] solution, 'Or we leave Portugal, or somehow we will finish in jail.'
> With the support of the same people from this American society that we could not know who was behind for necessary reasons of confidentiality [we escape]. We only knew that there were people interested in helping us to get out of that situation. Everything was kept in silence.

---

79 The book from Charles R. Harper and William J. Nottinghan, *Escape from Portugal - The church in action. The secret flight of 60 African students to France* (St. Louis -Missouri: Lucas Park, 2015), documents with detail the reasons, the preparation and the flight of this student flight from Portugal.

80 Translation: Inter-Movement Committee for Evacuees

81 Translation: Union of the Peoples of Angola – UPA.

One day they around seven o'clock they told us, 'Prepare a bag, only with some small things, it not worth to take many things.' And were taken from Lisbon to Porto. In the middle of the night two cars arrived. We [drove until we were] two kilometres from the Spanish border and we crossed. There were smugglers. They gave us a laissez-passer from the Congo of Patrice Lumumba. The documents had pictures that were not ours. They kept us in a place, until a strange hour. [When] we left, we found a group of Spanish *carabinieri* [border police] and they told us to stop. We were a group of nineteen [people]. They stopped us and asked for our identification. We showed them our passports. They did not even look at us and knew that we were not the person [in the passport]. They told us, 'But this does not have a Spanish allowance entrance stamp? How did you get this?'

After many conversations, one of those people who supported us talked with them, and of course, in these conversations, there was some bribery money and the *carabinieri* said, 'Go quickly, never pass, here again, we did not see anything.'

We reach the border of Spain with France, and we made a request for France to let us pass. Unfortunately, it was a weekend. They [the American] started working on the French side, and at the end they to let us pass to go to sleep. There was one French hotel [that was] one kilometre from the border. The policeman stayed by [the hotel] door.

The next day was Monday, around nine o'clock in the morning, things worked in France, and they let us pass. We went to CIMADE [boarding house], but after some time the French government was clear: that we could not stay, and they gave us a deadline to leave. Fortunately, the Swiss civil society made pressure, and they convinced the Swiss Confederation to allow us to enter the country. They did not give us anything else because they had good relations with Portugal. However, that same organization managed to put us in different universities or schools where we could continue our studies. Fortunately, I communicated immediately to Cabral, when this situation was stable. Cabral told me to travel to Conakry. I went to Conakry, and we talk, and he told me, 'No. The chances that you have to continue your work in Switzerland, to acquire more knowledge, it very worthwhile. You will be much more useful to the independent Guinea [if you remain there to study], than if you come here and work. The only place we could get for you here is to teach at the Pilot School.'

Then they send me back. I worked [in Switzerland] in various companies, and with the death of Cabral, I said, 'No. I really have to go back.' I returned via Algeria. Me, my wife and three children. We came to Conakry, and from Conakry, they sent us all to *Escola de Teranga* in Ziguinchor where we became teachers.[82]

The escape, also known as *O Salto*[83] were also taken individually. André Corsino Tolentino recalls the impact that his visit to Paris in 1968, had on him, and how the political situation in Portugal lead him to join the liberation struggle:

---

82 Interview with Filinto Vaz Martins, June 5, 2014.
83 Translation: The Jump.

There was also the possibility in some circles to bribe someone, particularly the military. For example, I was forbidden to leave Portugal until I had done obligatory military service. However, this was being postponed because of my studies. However, if I paid a good tip to a sergeant who dealt with the paperwork, I could obtain the signature of an entitled person [to leave the country], and many young people were leaving, fleeing the troops in this way. Others went to visit European cities and did not return for as long as the colonial war lasted. Colonial war for some and the national liberation for others. I had the opportunity to visit Paris in 1968, and you cannot imagine! An unforgettable feeling. [A felling] that contrasted with that lead gray that Portugal was at the time, where the police wear that ugly uniform. When I arrived in the *Champs-'lysees* in mid-May 1968, I saw the bookstores, the intellectual animation, newspapers, and magazines. My feet barely stand on the ground. I almost levitated. I saw so many things, so many books and drawings. So many works of literature on liberation movements. Both works from communist authors of all tendencies, existentialist and Social Democrats. At a certain point, I could not keep my feet on the ground. I was somehow in a sort of levitation. [...] It was in Paris that I exploded and [the city] made me see how backward we were in Cape Verde and Portugal. The possibilities beyond the borders of the Portuguese empire were so many that no one could remain indifferent. So yes, from emotional, intellectual and the cosmopolitan knowledge point of view I can say that May 68 was the culmination of a slow and long process. [...] In my time, according to the style of the 1960s, O Salto was in vogue. There was a film that was a metaphor about the jump to freedom, from the land of the Salazar dictatorship beyond the Pyrenees, because in Spain there was [Francisco] Franco.

Another way to achieve the same result was through bribes [as already mentioned]. People could purchase an authorization of the Armed Forces to get the passport. In 1968, I chose this way. [...] The best thing that could happen to a militant of the national liberation struggle was to be called by the PAIGC. That was what happened to me in 1970. Without hesitation, I interrupted my studies, and I fulfilled the [Party] order [...] Paris and May 68 confirmed a decision already taken, through the study groups [...] plus that I was tagged in PIDE and I was tagged in the PAIGC, for opposite reasons. However, I mentioned the episode of Paris to say that in the personal formation there are indelible moments for their emotional force or decisive character in the intellectual life. [...] I was doing a course in economy at the University of Louvain, the order [from the Party] arrived [together with the] plane ticket. I immediately went to Conakry, via Berlin German Democratic Republic - GDR. Commitments were to be fulfilled [...]

I did not travel alone. [...] Some of us received tickets, but it was not really necessary for us to wait to receive the tickets and the order come, to go to the struggle with too much time in advance, because we were already fully available.

Certain discussions were meaningless. Things like 'I have exams' or 'I will interrupt the studies,' 'there is a rent to be paid' or my girlfriend or my boyfriend. No, we did not have these types of discussions, because everything revolved around a bigger issue that was national liberation. The ethics of responsibility commanded that everything else was subordinate to the struggle. [...] I remember like today, to be called, as we said with pride, by Amílcar Cabral, it was the ultimate aspiration. This was not discussed. Report to the comrades, yes. 'Comrade,' this word that today is so trivialized, [in that time] had that load of trust and belonging to the same cause and future.

- Look, I am going on the day so and so. Don't tell anyone.

And it was that. We received the ticket in the city of Leuven, Belgium, where we had a particular situation. We received guidelines for working with the group of students in Belgium and the workers who were in the Netherlands and France, especially in Rotterdam and Moselle, [...]. We made a kind of come and go [between the cities/countries]. The studies were secondary, *i.e* the liberation struggle was the number one priority, and only after that came the other commitments or occupations. We knew the importance that Amílcar Cabral gave to education in the fight, and we agreed with him. Our tickets came from the German Democratic Republic, whose government provided under that collaboration they had with the PAIGC. We waited in Berlin for three days, I think. From Berlin, we travel via a company that no longer exists, the Interflug, toward Conakry, where we were received and distributed to our tasks.[84]

The situation in the colonized territories was not different. According to Albano Correia, rector of *Liceu Adriano Moreira* in Cape Verde between 1965 and 1967, recalled the disappearance of students and other people from the island without leaving trace, certainly to join the struggle:

> Every month someone would disappear from the islands, inclusively students in the last years of high school. Without leaving a trace. Only sometime later we would receive the news that they had passed to the "enemy side" the military in the ranks that opposed to Portugal and our colonialism [...] Many of them belonged to families that we all know and with whom we dealt on a daily basis: a mother who sold us some products; a brother, a graduate brother of *Mocidade Portuguesa*; the girlfriend employee in the high school. The Cabrais, the Graças, the Barbosas were some of these [family] names. [...] So, those nearby relations were seen, mostly as a "minefield," always ready to explode. [...] On the other hand, this intimacy [contact] with the "enemy" [or people of his kin] was something that seduced me, by the new experience that this meant to me [...] in sight to understand what was the colonialism and the anti-colonialism.[85]

In Guinea Bissau, people knowing from recently independent countries struggle (Republic of Guinea and Republic of Senegal) shared the consciousness process and adherence to the struggle right across the wall from the high school *Liceu Honório Barreto*. Anselmo Cabral, a high school student recalls how his consciousness process arose and how he was mobilized by the PAIGC militant Rafael Barbosa to adhere the liberation struggle:

---

84 Interview with André Corsino Tolentino, August 21, 2013.

85 In, Maria Adriana Sousa Carvalho, *O Liceu em Cabo Verde. Um Imperativo de Cidadania* (1917-1975) (Praia: Edições Uni-CV, 2011), 316.

My mobilization process was as follows. Rafael Barbosa who was a civil construction worker worked in the house construction next to the school. He saw us [in the school playground] playing football, and from time to time we would have some trouble with the Portuguese, and fights here and there. After school, he called us and explained to us, - Look the world will change. There are countries already where the Africans are masters of their country. There is a wind that is running towards independence. You should study. Tomorrow you will be the future of this country. Listen to this radio, listen to this and that...

And that was how it started. And he would continue,

And the boys started to be interested in [knowing] more. The boys started to listen to Radio Moscow, that spoke about the liberation struggle in Africa. Or to Radio Senegal. It was the moment that France gave independence to its former colonies. The boys followed that, but secretly because it was forbidden [and] it was very difficult to tune those radios. Because there was always movement at the border from the Senegalese, it was through them that we had access to a radio, which occasionally tuned in those broadcasts. Another thing was that there was a Center created by the Portuguese, where in the afternoon the boys went there to learn about the "social good manners" as they say, [like] to learn to play ping pong, learn to play billiards, chess, etc. And there they had magazines from Senegal and other magazines that came from France. They did not realize that we saw the independence of Senegal, the independence of other colonies. We would steal the magazines, and with the little French we learned we could understand much of what we read, and we would distribute for our classmates. [It was like this] that the turmoil started.

And we went to the *Homem Grande*[86] [Rafael Barbosa] and said, 'In fact Mr. you are right. We saw in the newspaper, the independence, etc.' As he saw that the boys started to be interested he said,

- Guinea can also achieve the same level as other countries for the conquest of independence. And we [the boys] would answer:

-But how can we? We do not have doctors, we have nothing!

And he would reply:

-No, you will graduate, etc.

And he managed to convince the us to go to secret meetings. When we had a class break, the boys spent the time talking to each other at the same time they played football.

We would adapt [our speech] and slowly we were mobilizing other fellows who were not in school, [raising questions like] 'Do you know what's going on?'; 'Look, Senegal is independent. Guinea Conakry is independent. We will also be independent'.

They would answer, 'Oh! No, here we will never be, we do not have cadres, we have nothing.'

We would answer back, 'No! It will come in time. The people will be trained'

---

86 The term *Homem Grande* (Great Man), is a term used to refer to a person of a certain age, but also someone respected in the community with great wisdom and knowledge.

Then the young boys began to be interested and he [Rafael Barbosa] was able to mobilize a lot of young guys in the high school.
Then when the fight began, and I got to know, I went.
I was a good Portuguese until a certain point, but then I was not anymore, and I left.[87]

1.6 The development of anti-colonial consciousness and political organizations. The role of education in the struggle for liberation

Colonialism as a practice of domination, involves the subjugation and oppression of one people by another through the creation of a colonial structure, which implies the domination of geographical space; the creation of policies of domestication and reformation of native bodies, minds and emotions; the repression of traditional and cultural manifestations; the appropriation and the integration of local economic histories into the colonizer's culture,[88] and the creation of two interrelated and antagonistic groups, the colonizer/oppressor and the colonized/oppressed.

Clinical studies define consciousness as a subjective state of awareness of the self, the environment and of a momentary experience interpreted in the context of personal memory and present state. This state is determined by the level and content of the awareness.[89] In the work *Contribution to the critique of political economy* Karl Marx defended the impact that external factors have in the production of consciousness "The mode of production in material life determines the general character of the social, political and spiritual processes of life. It is not the consciousness of men that determines their being, but on the contrary, their social being that determines their consciousness."[90]

This chapter is built on the testimonies of PAIGC militants and their life experience under the Portuguese colonial regime and unveils some of the external factors that contributed to the rise and development of consciousness, namely by colonial policies, and how this emergent social, political, economic, anti-colonial and de-colonial consciousness of the colonial subject, materialized in the emergence of liberation movements/struggle.

87 Interview with Anselmo Cabral, June 25, 2014.
88 V.Y. Mudimbe, *The invention of Africa* (London: Indiana University Press, 1988).
89 E. Roy John, "A theory of consciousness," *Sage Journals. Current Directions in Psychological Science*, December 3, 2003, http://journals.sagepub.com/doi/abs/10.1046/j.09637214.2003.01271.x?journalCode=cdpa (accessed June 26, 2017).
90 Karl Marx, *A contribution to the critique of political economy* (Calcutta: Abinash Chandra Saha, 1904), 11–12.

In this process of becoming conscious, the testimonials allow us to understand how the social space of the colonial school and schooling played a crucial role in the process. Their testimonies presented the several facets of colonial school, such as an arbitrary space of policies, as a place of exclusion and conflicts, and the dissonance between schooling and the pupil's realities and daily life in colonized territory. However, this same space and the progression within it, highly contributed to the consciousness emerging in the pupils of their oppressed "social being" inside the colonial system.

In the case of some of PAIGC militants, especially those who went to study abroad, it was through the contact with the reality lived in the metropole and the contact with dissident clandestine anti-fascist organizations, but above all the contact and exchange with their peers from other colonized territories and the understanding of their common situation that this consciousness started to develop and took a materialized shape:

> Lisbon was the place where my horizon expanded. It was in Lisbon that I met and reunited with some of my fellow of Lyceum of São Vincente, and I met other students from Angola, Mozambique, Cape Verde. I attended, as most students did the *Casa dos Estudantes do Império*. It was our political university and was from there that we engaged in what would be our national liberation struggle. Certainly, there were others who in this matter were more informed and more involved in this fight for national liberation as my Angolan friends at the time. So, it's there that in fact we participated in the debate and took on a mission. It is necessary to note that we are the fruit of our time. My time was that. It was half of the 1950s, beginning of 1960s. That was our time. The time of the struggle against colonial domination. The great aspiration of all African people and other peoples was liberation. We all engaged in it - to answer the call of our time. I think that it was our time, and in that time it was necessary to participate and finally integrate into this movement of change, the African liberation.[91]

Casa dos Estudantes do Império, Centro de Estudos Africanos, Clube Marítimo Africano, the many clandestine study groups that were created in the Metropole and their bonds with the ongoing liberation struggle, as well as with the international network of support that developed around the liberation struggle spread through different countries, are some of the signs of how a 'social being' consciousness was being developed, and how the emergence of a decolonial and anti-colonial self was being revealed within the colonial system.

The materialization of this process of consciousness took one of its forms with the foundation of anti-colonial organizations. *Movimento Anti-Colonial – MAC*[92]

---

91 Interview with Commander Pedro de Verona Rodrigues Pires, September 11, 2013.
92 Translation: Anti-Colonial Movement.

in 1959, whose clandestine network was spread in four European cities (Lisbon, Paris, Frankfurt, and Berlin) was one of these organizations. MAC's goal was to "raise, develop and coordinate the unity of Africans in the fight against Portuguese colonialism. [to seek] the immediate conquest of the national independence of African countries under Portuguese colonial domination and total liquidation of Portuguese colonialism in Africa [to] Denounce and condemn the brutal repression that African patriots are subject [...] and alert to all patriotic organizations and all Africans from the Portuguese colonies for whom, in a united and invincible front, to start already with the preparation, the structuring and development of bases and means that will allow our people to respond with violence to all the violence of Portuguese colonialism."[93]

As an organization the Movimento Anti-Colonial had contributed to the development of the liberation movements across the colonized territories, namely the People's Movement for the Liberation of Angola -MPLA (1956), the African Party for the Independence of Guinea and Cape Verde -PAIGC (1959), the *Mozambique Liberation Front*-FRELIMO (1962), and the *Movement for the Liberation of São Tomé and Príncipe* -CLSTP (1961). To describe these political movements as simply struggling for independence, decolonization and the right of self-determination defended by international law[94] not only limits the way we perceive these movements but also diminishes their purposes in the scope of the liberation struggle - to imagine and struggle for the world beyond the colonial structure and their practices of oppression, exploitation, racism, and capitalism.

The term liberation struggle (or liberation movements) is used in this work as a general term to refer to a social and political phenomenon that I define as an individual-collective process-response of people who, becoming conscious of the racialization, dehumanization, oppression and exploitation through which they are subjugated under colonial-oppressive government inside and outside their 'country', organize themselves to dismantle or destroy the institutions and practices to which they are subjugated, employing towards this end any means at their disposal, including (violent acts, such as an armed guerrilla struggle) and

---

93 Lúcio Lara, *Documentos e comentários para a história do MPLA* (Porto: Edições Afrontamento, 1995).

94 Christopher O. Quaye, *Liberation Struggle in international law* (Philadelphia: University Press, 1991). Robert Macquordale, *Self-determination in international law* (Dartmouth: Aldershot Publishing Company, 2000).

nonviolent acts (such as strikes, educational projects and programs, or cultural and civil resistance, or any combination thereof).[95]

Julius Nyerere (1922-1999), professor and president of Tanzania (1960-1985) stated that "a liberated nation, in Africa or elsewhere, is not just a nation which has overcome alien occupation. That is an essential first part of liberation, but only the first. Liberation means more than that. A truly liberated nation is a self-reliant nation, one which has freed itself from economic and cultural dependence on other nations, and is therefore able to develop itself in free and equal cooperation with other members of the world community."[96]

Throughout this chapter, we saw the role that school and schooling played in the consciousness process of the liberation struggle militants and in how a clandestine network of self-re-education contributed to the creation of anti-colonial and decolonial organizations. Like how the term and practices of 'colonial education' was unfolded throughout this chapter to help explain the necessity and the emergence of a social and political consciousness of the African, and how they themselves took advantage of the 'colonial education' contradictions to re-educate themselves. In the following chapter I will disclose the centrality of education as radical practice in the process of the revolutionary Guinean liberation struggle.

---

95 Aimê Césaire, *Discourse on Colonialism* (London: Monthly Review Press, 1972); Siba n'Zatioula Grovogui, *Sovereigns, Quasi Sovereigns, and Africans: Race and Self-Determination in International Law*, (Minneapolis: University of Minnesota, 1996), Martiza Montero, and Christopher C. Sonn. *Psychology of Liberation. Theory and applications*, (Venezuela: Springer, 2009);Maciej J. Bartkowski, *Recovering nonviolent history. Civil resistance in liberation struggles*, (London: Lynne Reinner Publishers, 2013); Quaye, Christopher O. Quaye, *Liberation Struggles in International Law*, (Philadelphia: Temple University Press, 1991); Albert Memmi, *The colonizer and the colonized*, (UK: Earthscan Publications Ltd, 2003) and Frantz Fanon, *Os condenados da Terra*, (Lisboa: Editora Ulisseia, 1961).

96 Elieshi Lema et al., *Nyerere on Education* (Dar es Salaam: The Mwalimu Nyerere Foundation, 2004), 124.

2 Building and organizing educational structures in Guinea Bissau (1960-1972)

> *Guiné has 85 478 indigenous agricultural holdings. This is the number of indigenous families which make their living from agricultural activity. [...] The true cultivated area is 410 801 hectares, which is 12-21 percent of the surface are of Guiné (3 363 700 hectares), minus the part under water. Crops cover an area of 428 177 hectares, with a multiple cropped area of 71 376 hectares.[97]*
>
> Amílcar Cabral, 1979

> *The guerrilla manuals once told us that without mountains you cannot make guerrilla war. But in my country, there are no mountains, only the people.[98]*
> *As for the mountains, we decided that our people had to take their place [...]. So, our people are our mountains.[99]*
>
> Amílcar Cabral, 1972

1 The PAIGC educational project within its minor and major program

The moment of the development of a liberation struggle corresponds to a significant phase in a country and on its people. Such struggle is a remarkable and articulated response to any form of colonialism, racism, oppression, and exploitation. This reaction can take many shapes, and it is dependent on the internal and external circumstances of the country and its people during the struggle period. To sum up some of Amílcar Cabral's thoughts about the liberation struggle, he recalled that to fulfill the objectives of the national liberation movement and to put in practice the program and the strategies designed for liberation, one had to be ready to face significant obstacles. First, to overthrow the colonial institution of oppression and exploitation, second to fight against the several toxic residues

---

97 Amílcar Cabral, *Unity and Struggle. Speeches and writing* (New York: Monthly Review Press, 1979), 4–5.

98 *Return to the source: selected speeches of Amílcar Cabral* (New York: Monthly Review, 1973), 77.

99 *Our people are our mountains. Amílcar Cabral on Guinean revolution* (London: Committee for Freedom in Mozambique, Angola & Guinea, 1972).

left by this same structure in the body and minds of the people, and third to fight against the high percentage of illiteracy and ignorance so that people could reclaim and regain their voice as active members in world history.

Although political independence was a clear goal in the struggle for liberation, it should not be seen as the ultimate aim, but only as an important phase of a long process, "we are not struggling merely so that we may have a flag, an anthem and ministers."[100] The broader and bigger goal was social and human liberation through the destruction of the colonial institution and ideology and the construction of a 'new' decolonized society. Such process implied the knowledge of how the domination system of colonial institutions functioned and the different forms it could take, and it implied the vision of the kind of society that one wanted to build, how it would be built and with whom it would be built.

The Party PAIGC's was defined by Cabral's as being "the base instrument, the mother instrument. [...] the principle means which creates other means linked to it. It is the root and the trunk which produces other brunches for the development of our struggle."[101] and "the effective instrument for the construction of freedom, peace, progress and happiness for [the] people of Guinea and Cape Verde".[102] As a Party, in the sense of an organization of people fighting for independence against foreign rule and who laid down the common plans for the struggle and the future national reconstruction, would make use of "all the gains and discoveries of value by human culture for the progress of the peoples of Guinea and Cape Verde" and to "restore the peace and dignity [and progressively eliminate the] man's exploitation of man, of all forms of subservience of the human person for the profit of individual groups or classes."[103]

The Party Major Program was elaborated around nine segments. For instance, the first section demanded the "national, total and unconditional independence for the people of 'Portuguese' Guinea and Cape Verde [and] the end of all colonialist or imperialistic relationships [...] revision or revocation of all agreements, treaties, alliances made by the Portuguese colonialist."[104] The second and third section defended the national "economic, political, social and cultural unity"[105] and the union between Guinea and Cape Verde for the "construction of a strong

---

100 Cabral, *Amílcar Cabral. Unity and struggle*, 86.
101 Ibid., 85.
102 Ibid., 250.
103 PAIGC, Programa Maior do Partido, 1959.
104 Ibid.
105 Ibid.

and progressive fatherland based on opportunely consulted popular will."[106] The seventh section complemented these last two by defending the African unity.

The fifth section focused on the kind of regime to be implanted in the country after independence, namely a "democratic, anti-colonialist, and anti- imperialist regime [where all citizens would be equal] before the law, with no distinction as to nationality or ethnic group, sex, origin, cultural level, profession, wealth, religious, beliefs, or philosophical convictions".[107] This was topped up with the sixth section focused on "economic independence, a structured economy, and the development of production", the seventh section on "justice and progress" at the social and educational level, the eighth section on "national defense" and finally ninth section on "international policy to be developed in the interest of the nation of Africa of peace and of the progress of humanity."[108]

1.1 The educational project within the PAIGC's program

General educational systems and goals may often vary from society to society, but they have in common the matters of "producing good people who are faithful citizens with the ability to contribute to the nation's development."[109] However, these goals are greatly influenced by historical events, the socioeconomic needs of a particular society in any specific time. These circumstances dictate the specific desired educational outcomes.[110]

PAIGC's First Party Congress – the Cassacá Congress, took place between 13-17th February 1964 in the liberated areas of the Guinean forest.[111] The

---

106 Ibid.

107 Ibid.

108 For more information on each of the sections, please consult the Annex 3 "PAIGC's Minor and Major Program" in the annexes section.

109 Ali A. Abdi and Ailie Cleghorn, *Issue in African history* (New York: Palgrave Macmillan, 2005), 12.

110 Ibid., 12.

111 The called 'liberated areas' or 'liberated zones' "meant a large area duringthe struggle proportional to the size of the country, to the north, east and south of Guinea Bissau. It had the following characteristics: to mobilize and to serve as a model for future states; to be defended by its citizens; to provide the main services of agriculture, education and health given that its rural population was illiterate and extremely poor. In the liberation movement and in the liberated ares, the political function was essential. (Corsino Tolentino)." They were also areas of the Guinean territory where the Portuguese colonial troops could not circulate freely. It refers to areas of the territory where the population was organized under PAIGC's direction. See Annex 2.1 in the annexes section.

outcomes of the congress were the political and military reorganization of the Party, namely reforms in the reinforcement of the popular power, the regulation of the economic, administrative, judicial, educational[112] and social assistance activities in the liberated areas and the creation of the *Forças Armadas Revolucionárias do Povo* - FARP[113] that included the guerrilla, the popular army, and the popular militia.

Within the resolutions that came out from this meeting was the defense for improvement of knowledge through the creation of schools, the investment in the education of pupils and adults, and the self-investment in one's own education for the betterment of the Party cadres. In the directives written by Amílcar Cabral for the Congress he states:

> To carry on the victorious development of our struggle, we must: set up schools and develop teaching in the liberated areas. [...] Improve the work in the existing schools, avoid high number which might prejudice the advantage to all. Found schools but bear in mind the real potential at our disposal, to prevent later to close some schools through lack of resources. [...] Constantly strengthen the political training of teachers [...] Set up courses to teach adults to read and write, whether they are combatants or elements of the population. [...] Little by little create simple libraries in the liberated areas, lend others the books we possess, help others to learn to read a book, the newspaper and to understand what is read.[114]

Under the struggle watchwords, "all those who know should teach those who don't know,"[115] the PAIGC developed two simultaneous educational projects, one for adults and another for pupils. To achieve the later, it was important to advance adult education, not only in the teaching of writing and reading but above all in the mobilization and consciousness about the reasons for and the goals of the future struggle.

1.2 The mobilization campaign as an integral part of PAIGC's educational project

The Party directives from the Cassacá Congress invited the PAIGC militants to, "give the widest possible distribution of the Party newspaper, hold sessions for collective reading (in a group) and lead those who are reading into a discussion

---

112 For full, information on the Cassacá Congress directives concerning education, please see Annex 18 at the annexes section.

113 Translation: Revolutionary Army Forces of the People.

114 Amílcar Cabral, *Amílcar Cabral. Unity and struggle*, 242–244.

115 Cabral, *Amílcar Cabral. Unity and struggle*, 242.

and into expressing views on what they have read."[116] The PAIGC's need to create a national consciousness about Portuguese colonialism and the need to struggle for national independence and reconstruction under the common cloud of a pluralistic but singular Guinean identity was the significant obstacle that the Party had to face at the beginning of the struggle. Through the work of the *Comissário Político*,[117] the Party mobilization and consciousness campaigns were a significant activity. The conversations with the population and the investment in education would contribute to PAIGC's aim to "combat without violence harmful practices, the negative aspects of the beliefs and tradition of [Guinean] people. [and] all particularisms (separatist feeling) prejudicial to the unity of people, [and] all demonstrations of tribalism, or racial or religious discrimination."[118]

Open sessions in forest with the population was part of the Party mobilization and consciousness campaign as the Photo 1 exemplifies through the development of collective discussions. In the Photo 1, Carmem Pereira (at the center), PAIGC *comissária política* from the inter-regional south Committee dialogues with a group of peasants men and women in the Guinean forest. Her right-hand holds a piece of folded paper, of what might well be PAIGC's propaganda information. The conversation unfolds within the circle, and the layout of people in the place contribute for the erasure of a hierarchical, top-down conversation. The mobilization speech concentrated its rhetoric in practical aspects of the daily life under the Portuguese colonial rule. In 1969, during an interview recorded at the Khartoum Conference in January 1969, Amílcar Cabral revealed some of the content of the conversations and the goals that they aimed to achieve:

> Telling the people that "the land belongs to those who work on it" was not enough to mobilize them, because we have more than enough land, there is all we need. We had to find appropriate formulae for mobilizing our peasants, instead of using terms that our people could not yet understand. We could never mobilize our people simply on the basis of the struggle against colonialism- that has no effect. To speak of the fight against imperialism is not convincing enough. Instead, we use a direct language that all can understand: "Why are you going to fight? What are you? What is your father? What has happened to your father up to now? What is the situation? Did you pay taxes? Did your father pay taxes? What have you seen from those taxes? How much do you get for your ground nuts? Have you thought about how much you will earn with your ground nuts? How much sweat has it cost your family? Which of you has been imprisoned? You are going to work on the road-building: who gives you the tools? You are bringing the tools.

---

116 Ibid., 244.
117 Translation: political commissar.
118 Ibid. 242–243.

Photo 1. PAIGC's political mobilization and consciecialization. Source: *Arquivo & Biblioteca o Mário Soares Foundation. DAC –Amílcar CabralDocuments*

The fact that there is a woman who delivers the message to a group mostly composed men (behind Carmen Pereira at the center there is another female in the group) constitutes a great achievement of the struggle that defended and promoted gender inequality and rights in the territory.

> Who provides your meals? You provide your meals. But who walks on the road? Who has a car? And your daughter who was raped – are you happy about that?"[119]

This form of political teaching endorsed by the Party intended to raise the people's conscience about what was happening to them on their land and the meaning and impact of colonialism at a most personal and daily level of their lives. Such open-air sessions were crucial to PAIGC. They raised and solidify popular consciousness, they also contributed to the establishment of an administrative political, judicial, economic and social structure in the

---

119 Amílcar Cabral, *Revolution in Guinea: Selected texts by Amílcar Cabral* (New York: Monthly Press Review), 159.

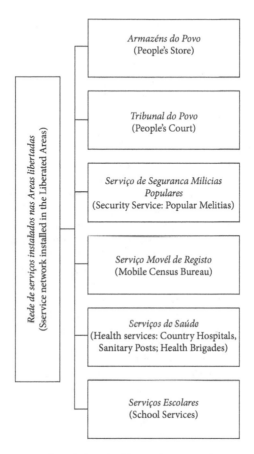

Fig. 1. Civil organization of PAIGC in the liberated areas in Guinea Bissau. Source: own elaboration based on the document - *Apontamentos das Aulas de Política do Centro de Aperfeiçoamento de Professores* 1966. Translation: Notes on Political Lessons of the Centre for Improving and Retraining of Teachers.

territory, namely the liberated areas (see Fig. 1). The creation of these social structures was crucial in the consciousness development of the people as Amílcar Cabral's noted:

> The people struggle and accept the sacrifices demanded by the struggle, but in order to gain material advantages, to be able to live in peace, to see their lives progress and to ensure their children's future. National liberation, the struggle against colonialism, working for peace and progress – independence – all these are empty words without meaning for the people unless they are translated into a real improvement in standards

of living. It is useless to liberate an area if the people of that area are left without the necessities of life.[120]

Anselmo Cabral, who became after his escape to the struggle, a political commissar and *responsavél*[121] for education in the north region recalled the Party mobilization initiatives and its outcomes with the development of the administrative and social structure:

> In the liberated areas, PAIGC was able to organize very early. In the time of mobilization, we were going to propagate the PAIGC's guidelines to prepare the people for the referendum after the struggle. In all *tabancas*, the PAIGC would always leave an imprint. That imprint was to political organize the population. There was the *responsável* and the second *responsável*. Then we would go to another *tabanca* and again do the same thing. After the mobilization, the tabanca was organized, and again there was a *responsável* and a second responsável. This was made in every *tabanca*. Later, when the zone was completely freed with the struggle advances, there was already in those *tabancas* some organization which allowed us to continue the [PAIGC] work. We organized what the Party called the Party committee [...] There was one responsible for education in the *tabanca* committee. The *responsável* for education had the obligation of not letting any children stay at home during the school period. He would do the school inspection. The children were forbidden to go to the pasture, rice cultivation, etc. To this *responsável*, three or four people would join, the *responsável* for culture, the *responsável* for health and neatness of the *tabanca*, and another for logistics issue. This was at the level of the liberated zones, which was called *tabanca* committees. Based on these committees, PAIGC organized a group of three or four committees that would form a section. Each group had an assembly, each section had an assembly, and so on until you reach the zone level. Then it was the region level, and all regions also had an assembly, and they were represented by sections and groups. In the group's meeting, one could already implement what was called democratic centralism, criticism, and self-criticism. At the meeting, everyone would do their criticism and self-criticism of what was done. You criticize, I accept the criticism that you made, constructive criticism, and I agree that I was wrong, and I will correct it, and from now on I will do better.[122]

Within the Guinean territory, the total of liberated areas was divided into two inter-regions - the north and the south inter-region, that functioned through people's administration as is shown on Fig. 2 It was inside this structure that PAIGC's educational project took place, first as it was already referenced with the practice of political teaching about the Party ideology, the integration of

---

120 Cabral, *Amílcar Cabral. Unity and struggle*, 241.

121 The word '*responsavél*' refer to the person in charge of something, or responsible for the organization and coordination of activities, or of an institution.

122 Interview with Anselmo Cabral, June 25, 2014.

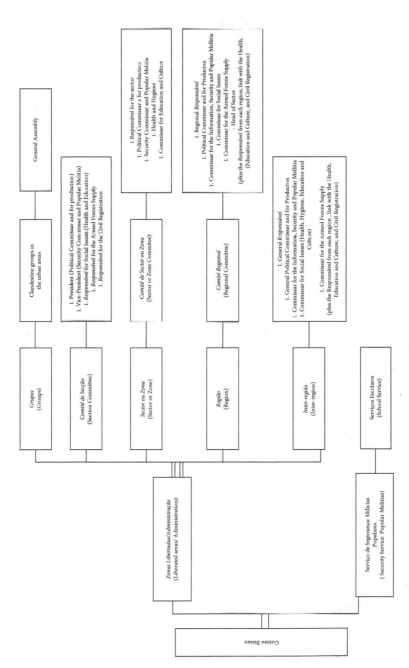

Fig. 2. Political organization in PAIGC's liberated areas in Guinea Bissau defined in the Cassacá Congress (1964). Source: own elaboration based on the document - *Apontamentos das Aulas de Política do Centro de Aperfeiçoamento de Professores* 1966

democratic values in coexistence with traditional forms of organization, and the development of a collective and unified administrative structure governed by the people through the process of a learning practice. With such practice the PAIGC aim was to provide the Guinean people with the experience of "a new life [so they could] see the difference between the colonial era and the liberation struggle, and [with such structure] how would the country be when it became independent.?"[123]

1.3 Conscencialize[124] parents towards the benefits of education for their children

The Cassacá Congress resolution of creating schools and develop education throughout the country in the liberated areas, had as goals the destruction of "everything that [was] an obstacle to the progress" of the people of Guinea Bissau, and to create "concrete and equal possibilities [for] man or woman, to advance as a human being [so they can] give all their capacity, develop their physical and their spirit to be a man or a woman at the height of their actual capacity"[125]

Nevertheless, the practice of such resolution faced obstacles. One of the directives from the 1964 Congress was to "persuade parents of the absolute necessity for their sons and daughters to attend school."[126] Mobilize parents to allow their children to attend school, and to conscencialize them for the importance of the school created by the Party. This practice was another aspect of the PAIGC political education. Parents resistance to send their children to school can be analyzed in three groups. First, concerning the school schedule, agricultural labor, and the domestic tasks. Second resistance aspect is related to religious beliefs. The third aspect was the gender domestic and cultural obligations with a focus on the female group.

Although the PAIGC's popular mobilization started at the beginning of the 1960's and schools began to be implemented in 1964, in 1971 the Party continued

---

123 Interview with Ana Maria Cabral, September 9, 2013
124 The term 'conscencialize' is used in this work as a synonymous of the process of raising awareness about something. However, the choice to use this term is the political connotation that it carries, in the sense raising of awareness in a political form and the politicization of the individual, that is followed by the phase of consciousness meaning the state of being aware.
125 Amílcar Cabral, Análise de alguns tipos de Resistência (Bolama: Imprensa Nacional, 1979) 11–12.
126 Cabral, Amílcar Cabral. Unity and struggle, 242. For full, information on the Cassacá Congress directives concerning education, please see Annex 18 at the annexes section.

to face parents resistance to send their children to schools. In 1971 during a Party committee meeting, the issue was still being discussed, and the opposition still existed:

> Another aspect that has an interest is the parents' attitude towards school. In all countries of the world, comrades, especially in countries where the peasants are the majority, there is a great resistance against the schools. We should not be discouraged because in our country there are folks of the population who do not want schools. We must have pity, but not be discouraged. In Portugal, for example, especially in the northern part of Portugal, when schools were open in the villages, the population arose and burned the schools. But it happened in other countries. The peasants burnt schools because with school children have to leave home, which affects them [parents] at work because the children are the arms that keep the house, the pigs, the sheep, herding the cattle, etc. They sweep the house, help in the fields, fetch water. And suddenly we take the children from them to take them to school. This is a normal thing, and we do not have to be discouraged about it. We have to be able to understand that the best possible manner, and create an acceptable solution, without much serious conflict between schools (i.e., the Party) and the population. And we said from the beginning in the party slogans as follows: we are going to make schools and put children in school, but establish a kind of schedule and work that allows children to help their parents. It was or was not said? It was said specifically so that parents did not think that we are taking their children away.[127]

The pupils' frequency in attending schools was conditioned through a work of negotiation, adaptation, and organization of the person responsible for its operation and his understanding of the local and cultural realities. To solve the situation the Party organized the school periods according to the daily life and the agricultural activities of the community, as well as with the year's seasons. PAIGC's 1965 school regulation -*Regulamento de Escolas do Partido*[128] school matriculations could start in October, but the lessons could only start in November after the rainy season. School took place therefore only between November 1st and June 30th. The school period was divided into two semesters separated by more than one month vacation between December 15th and January 31th. However, due to the territorial diversity as in people's culture and agricultural activities, the struggle development and the necessity to feed the people during the struggle, to avoid the implementation standard schedule that could create more conflicts

---

127 PAIGC, *Reunião do Conselho Superior da Luta. Sobre alguns problemas práticos da nossa luta. Intervenção do camarada Amílcar Cabral*, 1971, 24.

128 Translation: Regulation of the Schools Party. See Annex 4 "Regulation of the schools of the Party" in the annexes section.

with the population in each region, a new resolution was taken, giving more freedom the region *responsavéis*, about how to organize the school routines:

> [...] it is necessary to produce to feed our people and our fighters. Work in the field is therefore essential. Especially during the rainy season, the students work hard in the farms. The classes in each school, although presenting characteristics that are common to the other locals, vary with local conditions. Generally, it can be said that; a) schools work for all days of the week. Some schools also work on Sundays; b) the daily number of hours of classes ranges from 4 to 10 hours. In some cases, only work in the morning (from 7 am to 11 am or noon), in others work in the morning and afternoon. It depends on the specific conditions of each school [...] c) frequency of classes is organized by groups, so that it can conveniently carry out the work or cultivation of the crop fields.[129]

A look at the agricultural calendar of Guinea Bissau allows an understanding of its compatibility with PAIGC's school schedules. In the case of largest subsistence farming activity in the territory - *Arroz de Bolanha*,[130] the sowing happens during the months of July and August corresponding in this way to the school's vacation break, and its harvest corresponds to the vacation during the months of December and January.[131] Other important agricultural cultures such as peanuts or cashews, their planting, and harvest happen during the months of June and November, which it is again the school vacation period.

Religion beliefs was another ground of the parents' resistance. Such resistance had to do with the diversity of educational structures existent in the territories according to the religious practices. In the Guinean territory, there were the Portuguese Catholic and colonial schools,[132] there was the Koranic school directed toward the Islamicized groups,[133] and finally the Animist group and their educational practices.

Portuguese studies dated from 1954 reveal in the territory a total of four hundred and thirty-five Islamic schools for children and fifty Islamic cultural centers

---

129 PAIGC, A nossa luta pela educação de massas e pela formação de quadros, 1965, (Conakry: PAIGC, 1965), 4–5.

130 Cultivation of rice in paddy fields: Lowland (*Bolanha*) rice (*arroz*).

131 Olavo Borges de Oliveira and Philip J. Havik and Ulrich Schiefer, *Armazenamento traditional na Guiné Bissau* (Münster: Institut für Soziologie Universitat Münster), 1993.

132 The Portuguese colonial school was already characterized in Chapter one through the experience of African students in the territory of Guinea Bissau and Cape Verde. Therefore, I shall focus here in the Koranic and Animist education.

133 See Annex 1 "Ethnic groups and subgroups from Guinea Bissau," and for their distribution along the Guinean territory, see Annex 2 "Ethnographic map of Guinea Bissau," in the annexes section.

for adults that functioned as specialized centers whose aim was to improve the acquired learnings in the school. The teaching in these schools included the Arabic alphabet, which was an important tool for the cultural preservation of the Guinean knowledge as the author of the studies described, "though little suitable to the negro-African languages, [the Arabic alphabet] became a form of preservation and cultivation of literature and the native thoughts. Applied to their mother tongues, especially Fulani and Mandingo, it allowed literary work to be scripted and to circulate – poetry, short stories and proverbs, historical traditions [*Tárticas*], and even philosophical themes."[134]

The imbalance between the Portuguese-Christian and the Arab –Muslim teaching was evident if we take into consideration the existence the total of two hundred and five Portuguese primary schools in the territory in 1961, forty-two of them private administration.[135] However, the Muslim community in the territory found ways of profiting from the two educational systems namely, by using both as the same studies described, "the fact is that the Mandingo and Fulani of Gabu and Bafatá sent their children to Bissau, particularly the chiefs and leaders, in order to follow or pursue their Koranic studies on guidance of *Caramôs*. Children stayed at homes of these masters, with accommodation pension paid by their parents, and simultaneously learned to read and write in Arab characters at night, and during the day attended Portuguese schools. They conciliated in this way the urge to get a European culture and to conserve the Muslim tradition."[136]

Giving this situation in the territory, the development of PAIGC's school in the same territory represented a concurrent system that could unbalance this unwritten conciliation between the Koranic and colonial schools and consequently create a conflict within the community. Therefore, negotiation was a key strategy that the Party adopted. Testimonies of the Party *comissários político*, responsible for the mobilization and the creation of the schools, although devaluing the importance of the Koranic school in the territory, that at the same time prove the teaching technique described in Portuguese studies about the Koranic school, reveals some of the adopted strategies and the dialog of the Party *comissários político* with the community leaders for the allowance of PAIGC school implementation in their villages:

---

134 António Carreira, "Aspectos históricos do islamismo na Guiné Bissau. Achagas para o seu estudo," *Boletim Cultural da Guiné Portuguesa*, 84 No (1966): 446–447

135 Rafael Ávila de Azevedo, Relação sobre a educação em África (Lisboa: Estudos Ciências Sociais e Políticas), 1963.

136 António Carreira, *Aspectos históricos do islamismo na Guiné Bissau*, 447. (author translation).

The issue of Koranic school, the real meaning of Islam, did not exist. Most of those people that were Islamicized were animists [before the conversion]. There were places where, for example, the grandfather was Muslim, and the grandmother was not Muslim. She would make all the animism ceremonies, but her grandson could say 'Allahu Akbar.' However, they all lived together which means that there was not a deep Islamization, it was something very superficial. [Their schools] well, it was not really a school, because they would have had the writing paper, but [the people who taught] had no knowledge of Islamic literature. They went to Senegal to learn some things and then returned [to teach]. But there was more a religious thing, it was more learn, repeat, speak and repeat the Koran themes. So, the Koranic school did not have a big impact. The children would learn the Koran at night. They usually learn this at night, or evening, because during the day they went to work in the farms. Then when they return to the village, and because the teaching was not highly developed, the 'big' man spoke, and they repeated [what he said]. Usually, those who are Mandingo spoke in Mandingo, those who are Fulani would cite that in Fulani. Each recited in their mother tongue. [With the creation of PAIGC's school in the territory] The problem was this: when we would open a school in a *tabanca*, first of all, we would go there with the political *responsavél* of that area and we would have a meeting with the *Homem Grande*[137] or the *Grande Marabou*[138] of that *tabanca*, and we would make a good friendship with him. And then I would say 'The liberation struggle is for these kids, for your kids, not for us. They are the ones who will take care of our country in the future. Do you want to remain in this situation [referring to colonialism]? If they study and became men, you will see. We do not dismiss the Koran. It is your religion. It is a personal choice. We accept. You can continue practicing it, but please let the kids go to school.'

And there was some who understood this very well. In the evening they would do the Koranic lecture, in the morning, they would go to the grassland, and in the afternoon they would go to our schools, that they called *Escola dos Brancos*. In the beginning, in fact, there were difficulties, because Morés was a Muslim area, but with the struggle all that fell apart, so to say, the Muslim scepticism [in relation with the Party]. PAIGC's ideology was able to get through, and things became easier. The Party gained respect and value, and there was a formidable acceptance. [...] Amílcar would use this strategy, but he never spoke or took part for any religious group, because of the needs of the struggle. He needed both the Muslims and the Animists. He put everyone on the same level to push the fight. There was also a ceremony of adherence to Party politics. With the Islamicized, we would do it with the kola nuts, and with the Animist, we would use palm wine. These elements because they were important for each group symbolized their complicity and the commitment to the Party.[139]

---

137 The denomination *Homem Grande* (*Big Men*) *is* a term use to refer to the village chief or the oldest person in a group. The term is used as a symbol of respect.

138 Muslim religious leader and teacher.

139 Interview with Anselmo Cabral, June 25, 2014.

Established gender roles, especially for the female group, was the third factor of resistance. Such resistance was transversal to all groups in the territory, despite their religious beliefs. In general the presence of girls in school was not well received in the community, because of the domestic tasks that girls needed to perform, such as cleaning, cooking, fetching water, caring for the children and elders, but above all, was the question of marriage and the danger that their school attendance would delay the ceremony or make it impossible to happen. The problem was approached in the 1971 meeting:

> Of course, it is also very natural there is resistance to women attending school. In Azerbaijan, the Soviet Union, today, in Tajikistan, etc., parents resisted the fact of children going to school, especially in the Muslim families regarding girls. There is a deep mind-set concerning that. For us, and Muslims in particular, the idea of preventing girls from going to school is the idea that they cannot perform all those functions that they perform without the girls' education that represent more wealth, more cows, etc. when they marry. We have to understand this first, so then we can require and work so that girls can go to school. But only understanding this very well, and understanding that it is not just us who have this problem. We cannot be discouraged with that work and must look for the best way to solve this problem. What it needs to be done is to think. The *responsáveis* have to think about the problems, study our issues and not proceed as if we were administrators. We are fundamentally politicians, comrades.[140]

To avoid major conflicts, the Party adopted some strategies. One of them was to convince parents with the material advantages and status condition in the social milieu that these could bring to the family:

> But there were also problems with the girls in the Islamicized areas. They did not want the girls to attend school. And with the boys, they would say that 'they need to work in the fields and with the cattle.' They would mount a great resistance. They didn't want to let the girls go to school. It was their law. We could keep the boys, but with the girls, it was a problem. But Amílcar would always say to them that the school was for boys and girls. But one time, they sent a group of girls to the Soviet Union, to be trained as nurses, most of them Animist. When they returned, and the other group saw them, a lot of other girls started to go to school.[141]

Another strategy was to create a specific time schedule for girls so that only they could attend classes (see Photo 2). The photo lets us understand that the majority of students in the classroom are female pupils. Having in mind the problems

---

140 PAIGC, *Reunião do Conselho Superior da Luta*, 5.
141 Interview with Anselmo Cabral, June 25, 2014.

Photo 2. PAIGC's group of girls in the classroom. Source: The Nordic Africa Institute - Knut Andreassen

School attendance and participation in the liberation struggle as nurses or *responsáveis* was used for girls as a way to avoid marriage. PAIGC's sometimes used school to keep some girls from marriage and protect them from angry families by sending them to schools located far away from home. Such practice was narrated to Lars Rudebeck during his visit to the liberated areas in 1972, "It is unusual, very unusual, Luís says, at least among the Muslim groups, that girls gets beyond (*reaches?*) second grade, at least in the village schools. Therefore, they have to go to the *internato (boarding school)*, which is why second grade will be kept for the girls in the *Internato Norte*. Marriage age comes early, at 14-15. The only way to 'save' the girls, Luis says, is to get them away from villages." Note: This excerpt is part of Rudebeck's personal hand-written notebook of observations, during his visit to the northern part of PAIGC's liberated area in 1972. The text was translated from Swedish to English by the author and kindly provided for this work.

faced by the PAIGC in trying to practice the principle of gender equality in the school system, the photo reveals one important aspect of the negotiation with the community and school adaptation. Girls class attendance happened only after their domestic tasks were concluded.[142]

---

142 For more information about the women's experiences during PAIGC's liberation struggle, Stephanie Urdgang, *Fighting two colonialisms. Women in Guinea Bissau* (London: Monthly Review Press, 1979), it's a pioneer work in what refers the two

1.4 Pupils trajectories to school

The children's trajectories to school during the liberation struggle are crucial to understand some of the parents' resistance to send their children to school. Apart from the fears already approached – religion, domestic and farm tasks, gender, the risk of being trapped in an open-armed conflict between the two antagonist forces – PAIGC's guerrilla and Portuguese military was a very present risk. Students personal memories of those days elucidate some of the parents fears and resistance as well as their own trajectory, difficulties, and losses in order to attend PAIGC schools. Testimonies also reveal PAIGC's initial authoritarian behaviors over families choices when selecting the first children that who would attend their schools, an attitude recognized by Amílcar Cabral in 1970 as necessary to set an example, but that could not continue, especially when bringing small children and orphans to the Party boarding schools.

Recalling her student years in PAIGC schools in the liberated areas, Mamai Badinca, remembers her path to school and how she was selected by one Party member to enroll in the school, despite her family's fears:

> One day, during the night, the Portuguese, the *tugas*[143] came [to my village] and surrounded our *tabanca*. They enter my house and arrested my father and my brother. They were searching for guns. They said that the people from our *tabanca* had guns and were collaborating with the terrorists[144] [PAIGC militants]. They arrested my father, my brother and my uncle and tied their hands behind their backs. They stayed all night tied in the truck while they [the Portuguese] were searching the entire *tabanca* for guns. They didn't find any guns. They killed one woman of my family in front of my father. They arrested my father, my uncle and the other members of the community. For weeks we didn't know where they were. We all cried. Three months later my father returned and said that we really had to do something. They took a group of young adults to the barracks, and they give them guns.
> I always wanted to learn how to read. One of the youngsters who studied in the barracks, told me about schools in the barracks, about the teachers and that they had already started to give classes. I ran away from my family [to go to school], and I stayed there. The barracks name was Faier. It was between the Farim river and Senegal, and it was located in the forest.

---

colonial struggles that women had to face. One the struggle against colonialism, and second the struggle against oppressive elements of their traditions.

143 The term *tugas*' is pejorative slang word used by the liberation movements to in Guinea and Cape Verde when referring to the white Portuguese colonialists.

144 . The term 'terrorist' was the way the Portuguese press and colonial governments referred to the Africans involved in the liberation struggle. In the Portuguese press of the time the liberation movements were described as 'terrorist organizations'.

A year has gone, when the Portuguese got to know about our barracks location. One day I went to fetch water. The Portuguese found our barracks, and they started a combat. I heard gunshots, and I went to hide. Then I heard noises, turmoil and I left the place where I was hidden. Right after I left, I meet the *tugas*, and shots were fired. I was hit in my right leg. All my colleagues ran in different directions, and I found a place to hide. When the combat finished, I went alone to the barracks to find someone who could help me. When I could not walk anymore, I stopped to rest in a place. When the guerrillas came to search for survivors, they found me. One military took me to the barracks, and together with another seriously injured military, they wanted to take us to Ziguinchor. At the border, they left me at my father's house, and only the next day they took me with the car to the border. PAIGC had Lar Sami where they would do first aid, and patients in a more serious condition they would take to Ziguinchor hospital. I was treated there. However, my uncle did not allow me to return to Guinea because of the war, and my family took me from Lar Sami. [...] It was Luís Cabral, who already had seen me when I was still in the Lar Sami, who gave the order to take me to the *Escola Piloto* in Conakry.[145]

Besides the family resistance and the Party authoritarianism that Mamai Badinca's testimony reveals two aspects that are important to highlight, namely the early contact with Portuguese colonial troops, first in her village followed by the barracks attack where the school was located. Both experiences reveal the presence of the constant danger that pupils faced on their difficult way to school alone or in the company of other adults. Similar experiences to the ones that Mamai Badinca recalled are also found in other students testimonies. Braima Sambu Auó, a Muslim boy, and grandson of a Marabou whose mother wanted him to follow his grandfather steps, recalled a quite similar and dangerous experience:

I remember that we were walking on the road that goes to Guinea Conakry, that today we call Caminho de Cacine. It was the end of the day. I remember very well. We were a group of men, women, and children, and at the front, there was a [PAIGC] guerrilla group. When, during the walk and it was already night, we saw houses on fire, and cars lights. The guerrilla gave the alarm. It was a Portuguese patrol, and everybody went to the bush. My uncle Dauda was carrying me on his shoulders. When everybody run to the bush, he tried to take me out, but I refused, and I grabbed him even tighter. Everybody ran. Just on the next day, we continued our walk. I don't remember how I got to the gas truck. In the truck, there was a colleague, Toumani. We were the only children in that truck.[146]

In other cases, children were also victims of PAIGC attacks and armed clashes between the Party guerrilla and the population sectors that supported the

---

145 Interview with Mamai Badinca, June 24, 2014.
146 Interview with Braima Sambu Auó, June 24, 2014.

Portuguese troops. Califa Seidi, one of PAIGC first students in *Escola Piloto* in Conakry, recalled how during a PAIGC attack on his village separated him from his family and the war circumstances forced him to go against the religious practices of his community:

> When I was seven years old, my mother took me to a *tabanca* named Tchakali. In Tchakali was my uncle, my mother's older brother. My mother gave me to him so he could take care. In Tchakali, there was Portuguese military, that would attack the barrack where Domingos Ramos was, Gancarnaste near Tchakali. Upset with that situation, Domingos Ramos decided to attack the tabanca where I lived. He made it during the night. That night they burned houses, and the Fulani militias who were favored by the Portuguese ran away. We were caught that night. We were four kids, seven, eight, nine years old. I was around seven or eight years old. They took us to Domingos Ramos barracks. Unfortunately, one girl who was the sister of another colleague that was with me, Cherno Sissé, passed away due to a shot that caught her. We were three in the barracks, me, Cherno Sissé and Tomango Candé. As a form of protest for all that happened, we refused to eat. We decided to do a hunger strike. Especially because the food that was served was pork meat. For us who left a Muslim *tabanca*, it was unthinkable to eat pork meat. Domingos Ramos, upset with our behavior, threatened us and said that if we did not eat, he would kill us. We were scared, and so we had to eat. It was the first time that we ate pork meat. There was nothing else to eat, just pork or monkey meat. As there were other kids there [in the barrack], they opened a school. From there at the end of 1964, they took us to Conakry. [...] We stayed in *Lar do Bomfim*, before the creation of *Escola Piloto*. They were preparing the *Escola Piloto*. From *Lar do Bonfim*, we went to *Escola Piloto* after it was completed. In fact, we participated in finishing the work. It was like that.[147]

The early contact with death is a relevant aspect from the testimonies of Mamai Badinca and Califa Seidi. Pupils' experiences with war and death on their school trajectories and the physical and emotional traumas that they carried, had a great influenced on how the PAIGC developed their school curriculum and manuals, the pedagogy that should be adopted toward the student and their experiences in what concerns the teachers and their teaching practices. These last aspects will be shown in chapter three.

1.5 Building and organizing school structures in the liberated areas of the Guinean territory

Between 1963 and 1972, PAIGC developed three groups of educational facilities. Most of these facilities were located in the liberated areas of Guinea Bissau, with

---

147 Interview with Califa Seidi, June 24, 2014.

the exception of two boarding schools located in the neighboring countries of the Republic of Senegal and the Republic of Guinea. The schools were coordinated by *Instituto Amizade*,[148] a "non-political organization with educational and humanitarian purposes" created by the Party in 1965 with permanent representative offices in Dakar and Conakry.

According to the Institute statutes dated from 1969, its purpose was to "informing, protecting and educating children effected/victimized by the colonial war; educating selected young people in schools in the liberated areas of Guinea-Bissau; training the future leadership of Guinea Bissau and Cape Verde; studying and developing methods for literacy and school education with the aim to help the people of Guinea Bissau and Cape Verde to liberate themselves from their ignorance."[149]

The Institute statutes described the organization as a non-political working with close collaboration with the Educational Department of the liberated areas of Guinea Bissau, according to interviews, the Institute itself functioned as a "sort of outline of a Ministry of Education" within the Party structure.[150] The directives of how schools should work, the curriculum and the development of school manuals, how many schools should be opened or closed, the management scholarships or any other social help offered by foreign countries, to select, organize travel for students who would continue their studies abroad. All these activities were coordinated by the *Instituto Amizade*. The *Instituto Amizade* was also responsible for the organization and coordination of adult seminars for the training of cadres, namely the training of school teachers.

During the liberation struggle, *Instituto Amizade* coordinated three sets of educational facilities. They were, the *Escolas de Tabanca*[151] (village schools) located near to villages in the liberated areas, the *Internatos* (boarding schools) and the *Semi-Internatos* (semi-boarding schools) located in the liberated areas and in the neighboring countries, and finally, the *Jardim de Infância* (kindergarten) also located in the Guinea Conakry (see Fig. 3 and Fig. 4).

---

148 Translation: Friendship Institute.
149 PAIGC, *Instituto Amizade* – Estatutos, 1969. See Annex 5 in the annex section.
150 Interview with Ana Maria Cabral, September 5, 2013.
151 *Escolas de mato* (bush schools) and *escolas em bases de guerrilha* (barrack schools), were replaced by the *escolas de tabanca* (village schools). The reasons behind this substitution were the danger that their location could cause to the school population. One danger was the sudden attacks to schools as Mamai Badinca testimony already mentionedth, but also the conflict that arose in the barracks schools within the military and their conduct toward the female presence in the barracks.

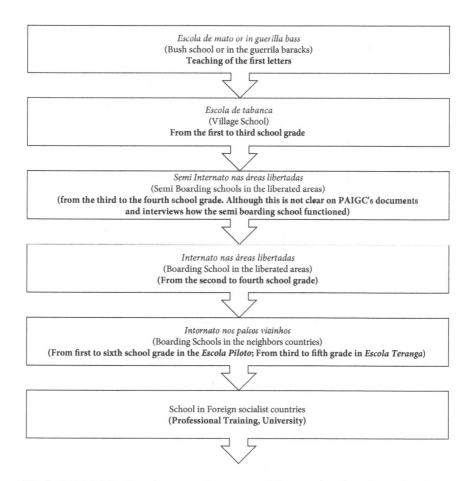

Fig. 3. PAIGC School grade system. *Source: own elaboration based on the conducted interviews, and PAIGC's diverse documents, and the youth magazine* Blufo. Orgão dos Pioneiros do Partido

1.5.1 *The* Tabanca *schools*

After the Cassacá Congress and the PAIGC directive highlighting the need to create schools throughout the territory, the Party sent second groups of militants on a mission to fulfill this principle throughout the territory. In 1964, a group of militants reached the Quitafene region, located in the south of Guinea Bissau. This same group, in a letter to PAIGC headquarters reported their experience in establishing a village school in the territory:

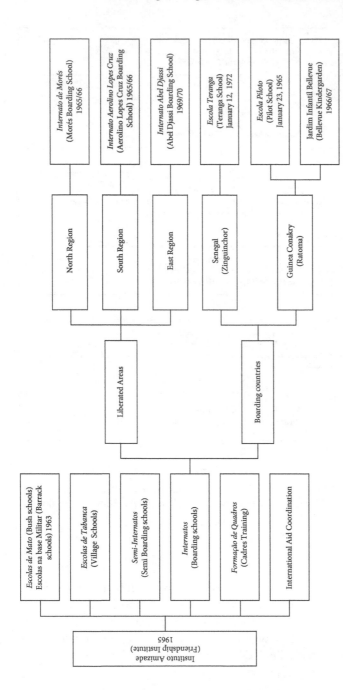

Fig. 4. PAIGC's schools under *Instituto Amizade* coordination. Source: own elaboration based on the conducted interviews and PAIGC's diverse documents and magazines

As is known, we were sent by the Party Leadership to the interior of our country on a six-month mission for the alphabetization of our people, but given very serious difficulties it was impossible to entirely fulfil it the order, contrary to our will. We reached Quitafene on 26 February 1964 after a two-day trip with a stop in Boké. Since that time we could not do any kind of positive work, except some meetings with the population. These were our first contact for the execution of our mission. Enemy bombing from planes caused the withdrawal of populations and destruction of houses, etc., lasting until May 1st date on which date built the first school tent. By mid-June were already operating four schools, namely: Cassacá school, whose classes started on May 1st, 1964. This had 41 students of both sexes directed by Professor Julius Semedo. Having overcome the initial difficulties, we gained courage and with it, more experience and knowledge in the performance of our task. On June 1st, we opened a school in Comissorà with a total of 23 students having as teachers the comrades Anastácio Furtado and Ignatius Semedo Jr.. Ten days later the comrades Adelino Nunes Correia and Pio Gomes Correia had already started classes at Caçumba school that held 50 students of both sexes. Later, with the constantly growing number of students, we found necessary to create another -School Calaque - where they had 20 students assisted by Comrade António Monteiro Freire. We always try to carry out our work in close collaboration with the Party *responsável* and always submit the opinion of Party leaders regarding the choice of the sites for the construction of school tents, since they are more than anyone connoisseurs of the terrain. We also sought to secure the tents in safe places to avoid any surprise from our enemy. When there are, for example, two or more villages near to each other, we make the school between them, according to the circumstances, to save a long walk for our pupils. It sometimes happens that there are students who cannot attend the two periods of classes, just because they live quite far from their schools and the time is not enough for them to go home to eat and then return to school. For these students we made a kind of semi-boarding school, and the students bring their food, which we give to the local Party leaders to prepare. In the afternoon, after the last period of classes, they return (they leave sooner than other students) to their homes. Altogether we counted 134 students of both sexes ages between seven and seventeen frequenting two periods of classes: morning from 8 to 12 hours and in the afternoon from 14 to 17 hours. We take every working day for lessons, except Sundays and holidays. At night, any person receives school tutoring - men or women - often elderly people whose duties do not allow them to attend the daytime classes. [...] Regarding sports activities, from time to time, we conduct football challenges, and lately, we started with volleyball coaching. Together with this report, we send some notebooks of our students, registration books, accounts and an example of the reading book we use.[152]

---

152 Julio Semedo, "Carta relatório sobre as escolas nas regiões libertadas do sul da Guiné", August 31, 1964. (author translation)

The above report raises several issues that PAIGC militants had to face to successfully establish a school in the liberated areas. The report lets us understand the school creation as a collective process between teachers, the Party *responsavél* and the population. The document show that such a process required a constant negotiation and adjustment of place, school periods and school population and their routines. The construction of schools near the *tabanca* was to facilitate the pupils' journey to school, some other factors needed to be taken into account when opening a school, namely the security measures and the protection from the air bombings; the population's capacity to provide food and other school needs.

Although located near the villages, schools should be constructed in a place relatively safe due to the war situation, but at the same time not far from a water source and relatively accessible by a bush path which motorized vehicles could access. The school structure was not permanent due to the war circumstances that forced them to have a sort of an itinerant life and structure. Therefore, the building materials should be easy to transport in order to rebuild in another region. The main material used to build the school were the natural material such as leaves, tree trunks, and branches collected from the forest.[153] One example of this school construction can be seen Photo 3, which provides us a clear view of the classrooms of village schools or boarding schools.

The photo reveals two groups of tables separated by a corridor. The terrain is flat and clean. The table and the seats were constructed with flattened planks and the school structure – pilar and roof , with tree trunks and branches . The trees and the surrounding vegetation protected the school from reconnaissance aircraft and well as from the sun. The roof construction in the form of small squares is prepared to hold palm tree leaves for protection from the rain. The construction reveals a school completely integrated into the forest environment and by the simplicity of the material its possible to understand that such structure were easy to dismantle and to transport in the case the school needed to be transferred to another location.

The forest environment provided a natural protection for school reconnaissance from the aircraft. At the same time, it was necessary to protect schools on the ground from possible attacks. In this way, teachers were supposed to be armed and be trained to evacuate the school in safety to bomb shelters (see Photo 4). Such military training did not put aside the presence of another military during classes to watch over the school defense (see Photo 5).

---

153 Interview with André Corsino Tolentino, August 21, 2013.

Photo 3. PAIGC's classroom detail in the liberated area in Guinea Bissau. Source: The Nordic African Institut - Knut Andreassen

Not all PAIGC schools in the liberated areas had the same characteristics. In regions of the country with no forest to provide the necessary material and protection, schools were sometimes built in wetlands and mangrove fields. Marcelino Mutna, who studied for four years in a mangrove school describe the condition:

> We studied in the mud. When the water came up to here [referring a little bit above the ankle], we would stay there, until we finish the lesson. Then we would go down and walk all through the water to go home. We lived and studied in the mangrove fields for four years (1966-1969), it was our refugee against the bombings.[154]

When Marcelino's refers "to go down," he is referring to how the school was constructed. The school seats and tables were built with higher legs, to avoid the feet being in the water; another small structure was constructed so that students could rest their feet during the classes during the high tide (see Photo 6).

---

154 Interview with Marcelino Mutna, June 5, 2014.

Photo 4. School bomb shelter in a liberated area. Source: Amílcar Cabral Foundation – Praia-Cape Verde

1.5.2 *The boarding schools in the liberated areas of the Guinean territory*

The creation of boarding schools aimed to respond to the families' situation, in particular children whose parents were at the war front or who were war orphans. The rules and diligence in the creation and location of a boarding school were similar to the ones for *escolas de tabanca*. According to the internal Party regulations, students who attended the boarding school would receive "the necessary preparation that later will allow them to attend other schools" (photo 9).

In the liberated areas of Guinea Bissau, PAIGC established three boarding schools with dorms (photo 8). The first boarding schools that opened in the territory was located in the north region of the country, in area called Morés between the years of 1965-1966. Years later, for safety reasons the school was transferred to the Sara region (see Photo 16). Lassana Seidi, one of the first students of the boarding school, recalls the school creation and its conditions:

> The teacher, Anselmo Cabral, was one of the *responsável* for education created the first school in Morés military base. The first professor was Paulo Cabral de Almada, the

Photo 5. PAIGC's school in the liberated area guarded by a soldier during the class period. Source: Mário SoaresFoundation . DAC- Amílcar Cabral Documents

younger brother of Fidelis Cabral de Almada. Simultaneously, [the Party] ordered that the surrounding villages to create schools. For example, there was a village near to the second military base, in the direction towards Mansoa, and there they created a school, with professor Adão Touré. When they created schools in the military base and the surrounding villages, those schools were the first PAIGC schools in the North. […] The first boarding school launched in the North was named *Internato de Norte* in Morés. We could not say the location due to the war situation, so the only reference was *Internato Norte*. The students who had finished the first class in the semi-boarding school with a good grade were selected and sent to the *Internato Norte*.

In that time, there were no tables. We were in the forest. You would search for trees, cut the branches, and some palm trees, and we would make tables out of them, on the open spaces in the forest. The blackboard would be hung in a tree, and in this way, the teacher would give the classes. In the beginning, there was no school material. When we were learning the A-B-C-D, a normal pencil was cut in two, sometimes even three, according to the numbers of students. During that time, we would search for paper, or even […] pasteboard. On these pasteboards, the teacher would write the alphabet, and you would repeat and copy.[155]

---

155 Interview with Lassana Seidi, June 3, 2014.

Photo 6. School Plan located in the liberated area of Quitafene. Source: Draw by Marcelino Mutna and Rui Néné N'Jata in Bissau 2014

Legend: 1) Plateau; 2) Terrace; 3) Mangrove trees

Around the same period, the teacher Adelino Sousa Delgado created in the south region of Guinea Bissau the second Party boarding school. The name under which the boarding school came to be known – *Internato Aerolino Lopes Cruz* (see Photo 7), was a tribute to a teacher who, according to testimonies lost his life during an air raid when taking his pupils to a bomb shelter. Following the same life rhythm and organization of *Internato* in Morés, the *Internato Aerolino Lopes Cruz* stands out for the constant change of location due to the constant Portuguese air raids of which it was victim (see Photo 16). From its creation in 1965/66 to 1974 the school changed places ten times. Professor José Sambe recalled some of these movements through the Guinean territory:

> The first school was located in Caiquene village. The founder and director of the boarding was Adelino Sousa Delgado. The second village was Flandene, where the 30th April bombing occurred. The third place was Nhambrem. That was a Fulani region. The fourth location was Colibui. The fifth Madina, the sixth Candjafra [located in the

Republic of Guinea at the boarder with Guinea Bissau]. Then we left Candjafra and we returned to a region named Cadiyala. The eighth was Empada and then ninth, Cufar. The tenth location, and this after the independence was Bolama, where the students of the two big boarding schools – the Aerolino Lopes Cruz and Escola Piloto were gathered. I was teacher in Flandene, Nhambrem, Colibui and Candjafra.[156]

The *Escola-Colégio Militar Abel Djassi*,[157] located in the east region in Madina do Boé was the third and last boarding school created by PAIGC (see Photo 16). The school directors Segunda Lopes and Mario Cabral founded the school in the year of 1969-1970. Segunda Lopes, recalls her task as school director:

> The school had 275 students, all of them were under my responsibility. But we had other teachers. […] I was responsible to get the school materials in Conakry and to bring all the material to Lugajole, the place where the State of Guinea Bissau was proclaimed. The boarding school was located there too. The material was kept in the warehouse. In addition to teaching and coordinating the boarding school, I also cooked for all those kids and washed their clothes too. […] At that time we built tents to teach, but we were always alert to the airplane noise. If you heard the sound of one, you take all the kids to hide under the rocks. We stayed there lying until the airplane disappeared. It was a weariness, a very great weariness. But […] nothing bad happened to those kids while under my responsibility until we left East Boé and went to install the boarding school in Saco Vaz near Cacheu. There we stayed two years. After Independence, we moved to the barracks in Pelundo.[158]

The regular maintenance of these boarding schools was always difficult for PAIGC. Security questions, number of students, teacher and teaching capacities and conditions, lack of school supplies, but above all the inability to provide enough nourishment to students in these facilities were some of the problems that the Party and the boarding schools directors and regional *responsavéis* had to deal on a daily basis. A meeting held in 1971 marked the closure of the East boarding school. In that meeting, there was an appeal to the *responsavéis* of each region to be realistic and responsible when considering to open a new school:

> We are willing to give the maximum so that the boarding schools can do their work. But we have to be realistic. The boarding school is made there where it is possible to do it, where it's possible to have food for the boarding school. If that is not possible, comrades, it is better not to create a boarding school. We cannot create a big boarding school and then put hands to the head because we have no food to give to the children. The Party can give clothes, all the work material, even some products like milk, but the Party cannot

---

156 Interview with José Sambe, June 19, 2014.
157 The name *Abel Djassi* was the pseudonym name adopted by Amílcar Cabral in 1960.
158 Interview with Segunda Lopes, May 26, 2014.

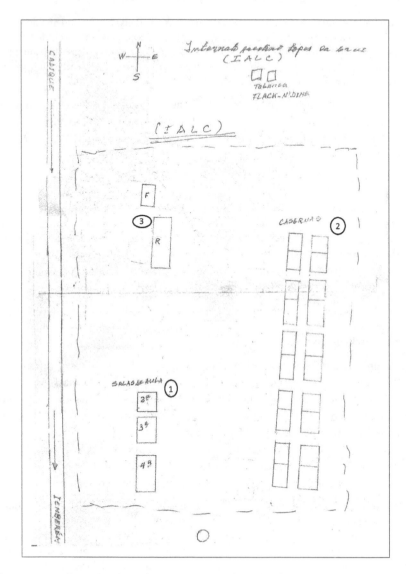

Photo 7. Boarding school Aerolino Lopes Cruz plan when located in Flandene village.
Source: Draw by José Sambe in Bissau 2014

Legend: 1) classrooms from the 2nd to the 4th class; 2) dormitory; 3) bomb shelter

Photo 8. School dormitory in the liberated area in Guinea Bissau. Source: Lars Rudebeck personal archive – Uppsala

guarantee rice for boarding schools, there is no way to do it. And where there is no rice for boarding school, then we closed them, even if we stay ignorant ten years longer […] Another issue that was raised was the closure of the eastern front boarding school. I knew that it was going to be closed […] I was against the closure of the boarding school in the East but didn't refuse because of the situation at that moment the only thing we could do was to close it, there was no other solution. Even if we reopen it later, but at that time we needed to close it because there was so much confusion, so much disorientation and on top of it the school had no support of the population as it should have.[159]

1.5.3 The boarding schools in the neighbour countries of Republic of Guinea and Republic of Senegal

Escola Piloto[160] and the kindergarten *Jardim de Infância Bellevue* located in the Republic of Guinea, and the *Escola Teranga*[161] situated in the Republic of Senegal,

---

159 PAIGC, *Reunião do Conselho Superior da Luta, 1971,* 5–6.
160 Translation: Experimental School.
161 Translation: Friendship School.

Photo 9. PAIGC's group of boy's students in the liberated areas. Source: The Nordic Africa Institute - Knut Andreassen

A group of students (probably between 13 and 17 years old) pose for the photograph with their school material, possibly in their everyday school track. During some interviews conducted with PAIGC students, this photo was described as *a altura do vale tudo* (it was the period that everything was worth), referring to the student's clothes and bare feet. The first student on the left carries small a bag with his school material. The same type of bag we can see in Photo 3 on page 77. The bag symbolizes the importance and care that one should have with the school material especially the school manual. This was a precious object during the struggle, and sometimes one book under the responsibility of one student was shared by between other ten. Another aspect to highlight in this picture is the diversity hats that they are wearing and their symbolic meaning at the time. The black hat, much associated with the liberation movements and personalities (the Black Panther Party or Che Guevara), and the *Sumbia* (that the three first students from the left are using). The *Sumbia*, made of wool, very much use by the Balanta ethnic group, during the struggle was very much associate with the personality of Amílcar Cabral. The hat became a symbol of PAIGC's liberation struggle. Source: Interview with Faustino Pok, May 16, 2014.

were PAIGC's extraterritorial boarding schools. A result of Cassacá Congress, the idea of creating a boarding school that would set an example for all PAIGC schools, and a space where experimental pedagogies and programs would be developed, and where the future of the Guinean education would be designed, emerged the *Escola Piloto* inaugurated on January 23rd of 1965.

Founded with some of the youngsters present at the Cassacá Congress as well as with some others who for various reasons were evacuated from the liberated areas, the first space where the school functioned was in *Lar do Bonfim*, a space that functioned as a hospital, but also as a Party training center, where militants would learn how to read and write and receive political training. Despite the enthusiasm that emerged from the congress described by Luís Cabral as the "great reward [to give to the youth] instruction in order to form cadres to better serve our Party and our people [...] young people who would become founders of our *Escola Piloto* [...] boarding school specially designed for them,"[162] other testimonies revealed other reason behind the school creation:

> One day, in the Lar [PAIGC militants], saw the comrade Domingos Brito, teaching the kids, entertaining them. Because they were playing and running around all day. He was a good person who had proven to be patient. In this way we tried to a find a way to create a school, that would be an experimental school. The school would receive the children who already had finished the first studies in the countryside so that they could continue their studies and then they could travel abroad to do their technical and professional courses.[163]

Ana Maria Cabral's testimony together with Luís Cabral's memories recalling the first school life in *Lar do Bonfim*, referring to "the girls who came with us (between 12 to 15 years old), taking one or two of them, that had never attended school. The first letters that were taught to them in our boarding school, and there were a few who learned to put together syllables and form words or sentences and read even without understanding"[164] lets us understand that the PAIGC although it had an idea of creating the school for all ages in the beginning, focused more concentrated on youth with age range between 12 to 17 years old.

The plan for an educational facility for younger ages was still in process, and such was a result of Domingos Ramos' initiative and the support that PAIGC received from the Sekou Touré government who donated the space where the *Escola Piloto* facility was developed with the help of militants and foreign contributions, where future pupils played a significant role in the school construction and cleaning, as some of them recalled, "I remember PAIGC got the place for *Escola Piloto*. Before all students were transferred to the school, we would go there and do volunteer work on Saturdays and Sundays. I was very young, but I remember very well the time that we went there to clean and organize the space. One day the school opened, and we were sent [to live] there"[165] (photo 11).

---

162 Luis Cabral, *Crónica da libertação*, 187.
163 Interview with Ana Maria Cabral, September 5, 2013.
164 Luis Cabral, *Crónica da libertação*, 188.
165 Interview with Braima Sambu Auó, June 24, 2014.

Located in Ratoma neighborhood, the school was initially a set of "shacks and a courtyard that latter the Party slowly extended and built more shacks inside that space."[166] With improvements made, by the year of 1973, the school area had five classrooms, a kitchen and two canteens, a pharmacy and health center, three dorms (one for girls, one for boys and one for female teachers), one storehouse, a sports camp, a house garden and a pigsty (see Photo 10).

The PAIGC kindergarten *Jardim de Infância Bellevue* was located not far from Escola Piloto. According to testimonies, its location was halfway from the Party headquarters in Miniére and *Escola Piloto* in Ratoma. Inaugurated on November 1 of 1970, the kindergarten (see Photos 12 and 13) emerged from two big Party militant needs. One was the need to transform the *Escola Piloto* into a more functional space where students could concentrate solely on their studies without having to take care of the smaller toddlers. The presence of toddlers and younger students was disruptive in *Escola Piloto*. The second reason had to do with the teachers and other PAIGC militants who worked at the Party headquarters. There was a great need to have space where the children could be during the day so that parents could be free for the Party work:

> The small children also lived with the teenagers, and that was not good. And our kids were growing, and they also went to school, so it was all in the same space, the school and the kindergarten. We had to train comrades who would take care of the young children, and it was necessary to find another space. It was for this reason that the kindergarten was created, to separate the young children from the teenagers because when they were together, the teens took care of the small children. The kindergarten appears first in a place not so far from the school, but later we found a better place, with a wall around it, that was near to Miniére. There, they had a big space to play, and we build other houses and a kitchen. And that place was the kindergarten. If my memory is not wrong the last director of the kindergarten was Maria das Dores Silveira.[167]

In a regime of *Internato* and *Semi-Internato* (according to the family needs), the kindergarten was directed by Teodora Inácia Gomes, a PAIGC militant who had studied Pedagogy and Psychology in Gorki Institute in U.S.S.R. (now in Kiev-Ukraine). The inauguration of the kindergarten was reported on the twenty-first series of the PAIGC youth magazine, of November 1970. The article dedicated to its opening described the space:

> [A] big school yard and a playing field. The classrooms are in the yard, far from the canteen. Each grade has their classroom away from each other. The classroom is roundish,

---

166 Interview with Maria da Luz Boal September 2, 2013.
167 Interview with Ana Maria Cabral, September 5, 2013.

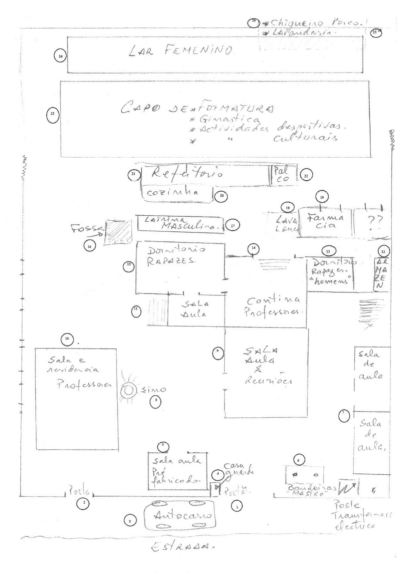

Photo 10. Boarding school *Escola Piloto* in Ratoma-Conakry, Republic of Guinea.
Source: Draw by Teresa Araújo, Maria da Luz Boal and Luísa Batista in Praia – Cape
Verde 2013

Legend: 1) main entrance gate; 2) second entrance gate; 3) Bus stop; 4) guardhouse; 5) classroom;
6) flagpole; 7) classroom; 8) bell; 9) Classroom and meeting room; 10) room and teachers residence;
11) classroom; 12) storehouse; 13) boys dormitory; 14) teachers canteen; 15) boys dormitory;
16) sewage; 17) boys toilet; 18) dishwasher; 19) pharmacy; 20) kitchen; 21) students canteen; 22) stage;
23) sport camp (for gymnastic, cultural activities and prom); 24) girls house; 25) laundry; 26) pigsty.

Photo 11. PAIGC group of students from *Escola Piloto*. Source Arquivo & Biblioteca Mário Soares Foundation . DAC- Amílcar Cabral Documents

Two important details are important to emphasize in this photo, first the students' outfit. The student's outfit can be understanding as a symbol of transition to another school if we compare it with photo 2 on page 68 and photo 9 on page 84. But it was also a symbol of equality between the student's erasure any social, cultural and economic background. The second important characteristic is the fact that in this picture we have mixed gender group, which can be understood as a symbol of equality between girls and boys.

and they are made as the houses of "djemerem" of our country [...]. Another thing that pleased us much was the room decoration. All the rooms have puppets drawn glue to the wall, and the wall shelves also have toys. We have a big canteen with several windows from where we got much light. In this canteen, there are two columns from to ground to the ceiling and have several toys. The teachers have their rooms in one block or house on the right side of our [room] and each night one teacher sleeps in this service room, that is next to the butterfly room (nursery room).[168]

The *Escola de Teranga*,[169] was the last boarding school created by the PAIGC. Inaugurated on January 12th, 1972 (see Photo 14), the school was located

---

168 Djamila Cabral, "O novo jardim dos pequeninos," Blufo, November 1970, 2.

169 The name *"Teranga"* is also written by some persons as *"Terranga."* But both refer to the same school. In Wolof idiom, the language of native Wolof people who are

Photo 12. PAIGC's Kindergarten bungalow inside view. Source: Amílcar Cabral Foundation Praia-Cape Verde

Contrary to the classroom photos that were shown before, the kindergarten classroom has another disposition as well as the building. The classroom is circular, as is the tables disposition. This allows the teacher to see the students in an equal manner, and the signs of hierarchy in the classroom are almost imperceptible, once the teacher table is part of the big circle. Something to highlight in the building construction is that it is very much similar to the circular house constructions used in the country's interior.

in Zinguinchor in the Republic of Senegal. Very little is known about the circumstances and the construction of this boarding school. The PAIGC's archives and militant testimonies did not have any information on how the Senegalese government allowed the construction of the school on its territory, or how much was spent on its construction. The scant information that it was possible to obtain, was that some of the resources to build the school (see Photo 15) came with the support of the Red Cross and the United Nations High Commissioner at the time, who was Algerian and a "friend" of PAIGC liberation struggle.[170]

---

distributed along the territory of Senegal, Gambia and Mauritania, the word Teranga means 'Friendship.'

170 Interview with Maria da Luz Boal, September 2, 2013.

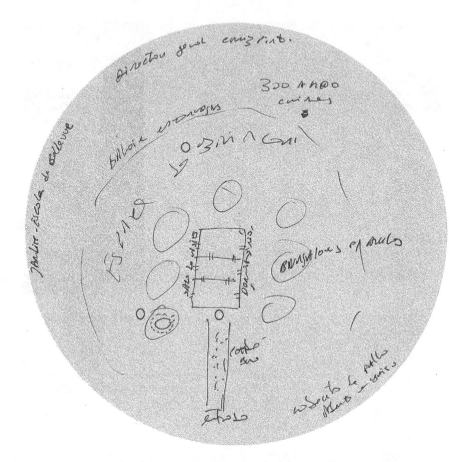

Photo 13. PAIGC's kindergarten. Plan of *Jardim de Infância Bellevue* in Guinea Conakry. Source: Draw with the help of Teodora Inácia Gomes in Bissau-Guinea Bissau 2014

Legend: 1) main entrance; 2) children's dormitory and visit room; 3) bungalows for children's activities; 4) playground.

The initial school population was formed by students and teachers from liberated areas, in particular from the north boarding school of Morés, and the semiboarding school in Campada. The reason behind its construction was to alleviate the high flow of students to *Escola Piloto*, which by the time had achieved its limit. In this, the construction of *Escola Teranga* was not only to alleviate the number of students in *Escola Piloto* but also to help to maintain the teaching quality of PAIGC schools to better prepare students to study abroad.

Photo 14. Inauguration day of *Escola Teranga* in Senegal-Ziguinchor. Source *Arquivo & Biblioteca Mário Soares Foundation DAC- Amílcar Cabral Documents*

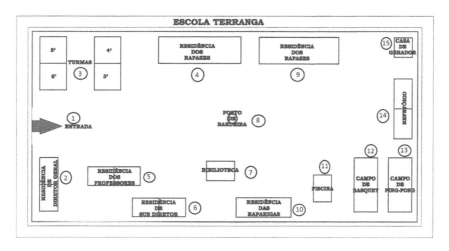

Photo 15. Boarding school *Escola Teranga* plan in Zinguinchor – Republic of Senegal. Source: Draw by Marcelino Mutna and Rui N'Jata in Bissau 2014

Legend: 1) main entrance; 2) school director residence; 3) classrooms from the 3rd to 6th grade; 4) boys dormitory; 5) teachers residence; 6) sub-director residence; 7) library; 8) flagpole; 9) boys dormitory; 10) girls dormitory; 11) swimming pool; 12) basketball field; 13) ping-pong field; 14) canteen; 15) electricity/generator house

Marcelino Mutna, a student from the south area in Quitafene, recalls his trajectory to *Escola Teranga*, and the learning and living conditions:

> I went to school in 1965, in the *tabanca* Tafore, in Quitafene. My first tabanca was near the Cacine river, and we could not stay there because we were constantly being bombed by the enemy boats, that would come from the barracks in Cameconde. My first professor was Guilherme Pereira, then Marciano Lima, and later Leonel Dioma. Those three professors gave us classes until 1969. In 1968, I finished the fourth grade, but there was no professor for the fifth grade, so we continued to do a class that they called 4A and 4B until they opened the boarding school in Campon, which was in another tabanca. There we had a teacher Mr. Cupadjuda, who gave us classes, and with him, I've done the fourth grade to the fifth grade. Carmem Pereira, who was the political commissar took me and other colleagues to *Escola Piloto*. We informed them that we had done the exam for the fifth grade, but during that time there was not really a certificate to prove it. So we had to repeat the exam. We succeed in the exam, and they told us that we would be part of the fifth class in Escola de Teranga. In Teranga again we studied the fourth grade. José Toure was the school director. Later came the professor Felinto Vaz Martins, who guided us all the time. He would teach math, physics, chemistry, and French. His wife taught us Portuguese. Iva Cabral taught history. Carlos Barros taught us drawing and geometry, Hipólito Djata taught sciences and the engineer Sadjo Baió taught geography. We studied the fifth and the sixth grade. With what the professor Felinto taught us, sometimes me and Néné Njata and other colleagues would compete with the Inhabô high school in Ziguinchor. They were in more advanced classes, but we were more advanced than them because in the school we had excellent material to do experiments with oxygen and hydrogen and other chemistry exercises.[171]

1.5.4 Locate PAIGC's school in the Portuguese colonial map

From all PAIGC educational facilities presented throughout these pages, only some of them can be located on the map. However, even this location is still a complicated process for different reasons. One of the major difficulties has to do with finding on the map the location names that archive documents and oral testimonies provided. This difficulty is intrinsically connected with how maps are made, and who had made them and their purpose. In the PAIGC case we are dealing with two different maps. On one hand we have the Portuguese colonial map, in this case, we use the chart *Carta da Provincia da Guiné*[172] (Photo 16) dated from 1961. On the other hand, there is the cognitive map of the local population with completely different location names, roads, regions, only understandable by those who share this similar cognitive map and interpretation of

---

171 Interview with Marcelino Mutna, June 5, 2014.
172 Translation: Chart of the Guinea Province

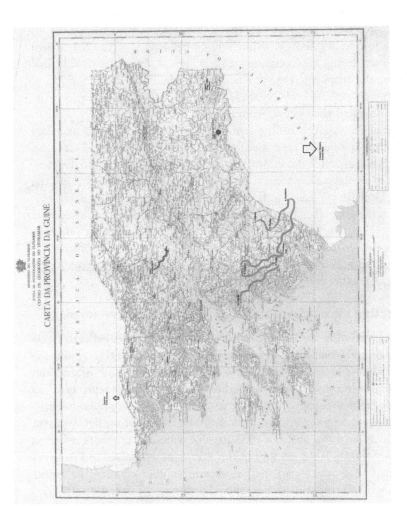

Photo 16. PAIGC's main boarding school location and itinerary 1963-1974. Source: http://www.ensp.unl.pt/luis.graca/guine_guerracolonial10_mapageral.html

Legend: Red: itinerary Boarding school Morés to Sara; Yellow: itinerary of *Escola-Colégio Militar Abel Djassi* from Lugajole to Saco Vaz and finally Pelundo; Green: itinerary from Boarding school Aerolino Lopes Cruz; Blue: CIPM in Quembra (see chapter three). Down arrow, direction of *Escola Piloto in the Republic of Guinea*; Up arrow direction of *Escola Teranga in the Republic of Senegal*

the territory. Another major difficulty in tracing the school locations has to do with the constant change of place of some of the schools, due to the war environment.

Based on oral testimonies and some PAIGC archive documents, the map (Photo 16) is an attempt to combine these both of these charts – the written colonial and the native cognitive. [173] The locations presented here gives an approximate location of PAIGC boarding schools between 1965 to 1974, as well as their itinerary during the liberation struggle. The absence of a straight line when showing the schools change of place, and instead, the use of wavy lines symbolizes the schools' and probably students' itinerary through the paths in the bushes of the liberated areas of the Guinean territory.

With a focus on PAIGC boarding schools in the liberated areas – *Internato de Morés*; *Internato Aerolino Lopes Cruz* and the *Internato Colégio Militar Abel Djassi*, there is one aspect that is important to highlight I'm referring to the great travel distance that the students and school had to cross in order to establish the school in a new location. Such can be seen with *Internato Aerolino Lopes Cruz*, represented by the green line, that at some point was established in the Republic of Guinean territory. The long way that students had to travel when the *Internato Colégio Militar Abel Djassi* here represented with the yellow line, in order to be placed in other schools on the other side of the territory. Students were distributed almost to the other side of the territory.

1.6 Interpreting the numbers of PAIGC's educational development

PAIGC's characterization and location of the educational facilities between 1963-1974, cannot be completed without an analysis of its evolution throughout the years and an attempt to decipher the sparse and disperse statistical information that can be found in original archive documents that had been reproduced in the few bibliographies that approached the issue of PAIGC educational system.

In 1973, a statistics report from *Instituto da Amizade*, about the development of PAIGC educational system from 1963 to 1964, the total numbers referring to school, teachers, students, number of the Party trained cadres and students training abroad or about to start their studies in another country, the report claimed in numbers a "rapid growth of school life during the liberation struggle" through the following numbers:

---

173 Morag Bell, *Geography and Imperialism, 1820-1940*, (New York: Manchester University Press, 1995).

[I]n 1964-65 there was 4000 students divided among 50 schools, in 1965-66: 13,361 students in 127 schools and 191 teachers, in 1966-67: 14 386 students in 159 schools, 220 teachers. [...] Today, the party has 164 primary schools in their liberated areas, where education is taught by 258 teachers, serving a total of 14,531 students, of whom about a third are girls. [...] Today, in less than ten years, the PAIGC formed 36 university cadres, we have 46 cadres of higher technical training; 241 cadres of professional and specialized education; 174 trade union and policy cadres; 410 cadres of sanitary assistance. In addition to these already formed, we have at this moment, receiving middle and higher training abroad, 422 students, to whom this year will join by about 100 students.[174]

Previously, in a hand written report dated from 1972, these same numbers once again appeared.[175] Domingos Brito, director of the Party boarding school *Escola Piloto* between the years of 1965-1969, was the person responsible to collect and organize these numbers. Since their first appearance, these numbers have been reproduced in the few studies that approached the theme of PAIGC's education during the liberation struggle, as well in studies about the history of education in Guinea Bissau. Such was the work of Lars Rudebeck *Guinea Bissau. A study of political mobilization* from 1974; Birgitta Dahl and Knut Andreasson, *Guinea-Bissau: rapport om ett land och en befrielserörelse* from 1971; Inocencio Cá - *Perspectiva histórica da organização do sistema educacional na Guiné Bissau* from 2005; and Mustapha Dhada – *Warriors at work. How Guinea was really set free* from 1993.

However, the analysis of PAIGC educational system development between 1963 and 1974, it is not an easy task. The major problem that this statistical data poses to the researcher trying to analyze them correctly is that due to the Guinean civil war from 1998, today there is no other document sources from where and how the numbers[176] were extracted to achieve this final form.[177] The second

---

174 PAIGC, O analfabetismo na nossa terra. Suas causas e consequências, 1973 4–5.

175 For the original notes see Annex 6 "Domingos Brito original document of PAIGC's school" in the annex section (not translated).

176 During the liberation struggle PAIGC school teachers had to present to the Party education responsible an annual report of students enrolled in the schools. Domingos Brito handwritten documents (see Annex 6) is the most likely source from where the final data was based. However, due to the loss of several archive documents during the transference of PAIGC headquarters from Republic of Guinea to Bissau and the country civil war in 1998, and the destruction of PAIGC archives, there is today no concrete example of this student enrollment lists.

177 See Annex 7 "School enrollment registration document" and Annex 8 "PAIGC school attendance card", that exemplifies a possible way of how teachers registered

problem that arises from these statistics is to know to whom they were directed, what was the purpose behind them? Were they just for the internal organization? Or was they made to foreign institutions to reveal PAIGC's struggle for education in in this way obtain more support from foreign countries and institutions, including from the United Nations? Was this information a way to question and to contradict the Portuguese discourse and colonial ideology about their presence in the territory?

These are some of the questions that this statistics number raise. Nonetheless, a closer look at diversity of PAIGC documents containing quantitative information about their educational system development, when closely analysed, allows usto see and understand some discrepancies, the difficulties that arose from the war condition that was lived at the time. Above all, they allow us to see how limited these numbers were if we take into consideration a broader picture of the struggle and the practice of education in other fields where the struggle was developed, for example the fields of health and military.

Lars Rudebeck, in his book, *Guinea Bissau. A study of political mobilization*, reproduced Domingos Brito's original information in his book from 1974 (see Tab. 1) and problematized the difficulties in the analysis of Brito's numbers posing the problem on the unknown number of people living in the liberated areas to "estimate [...] parameters as "percentage enrolled of the population in school-age" or other similar measures,"[178] recognizing that although the numbers presented were an important achievement, they do demonstrate, however, that in spite of significant efforts to develop a sustainable educational structure under conditions of extreme difficulty. PAIGC by 1970-1972 was "still far from having achieved the goal of universal education for the children of liberated Guinea-Bissau."[179]

Analyzing the statistics from the time and drawing upon the same table published in Rudebeck's book (Tab. 1), it is possible to see that the number of schools in the territory between 1964-1972, there was an increase of schools until 1968, followed with a relative stablility in the following years. Compared with the number of students between the same period there was a relative decrease in the numbers of students after 1968 followed by a stable period and then again another great increase in the year of 1971/1972, surpassing the numbers of the

---

their student enrollment and class attendance. It is possible that it was from these documents that most of the PAIGC statistic information was extracted.

178 Lars Rudebeck, *Guinea Bissau. A study of political mobilization* (Uppsala: The Scandinavian Institute of African Studies, 1974), 209.

179 Ibid., 209.

Tab. 1. Number of students, teachers and village schools in the liberated areas of Guinea Bissau 1965-1972

	1964-65	1965-66	1966-67	1967-68	1968-69	1969-70	1970-1971	1971-1972
Students	4000	13 361	14 386	9 384	8 130	8 559	8 574	14.531
Male		9 821	10 865	6 737	5 907	6 232	6 419	10898
Female		3 540	3 521	2 647	2 223	2 327	243	248
Teachers		191	220	284	243	248	251	258
Schools	50	127	159	158	134	149	157	164
% Female students		26	24	28	27	27	25	25
Students/ School		105	90	59	61	57	55	89
Students/ Teacher		70	61	33	33	35	34	56

Source: Lars Rudebeck "Guinea Bissau. A study of political mobilization". Interview with Faustino Pok, May 16, 2014, 206

first years of school establishment. The official report justified the decrease of students in the years 1967-1968 as follows "sending candidates for an average technical training abroad, and the massive integration of adult students of our schools in the various Party activity areas: military, navy, telecommunications, political organization, security, militia, health, education, production, etc. This decrease is due in a way, to the closure of twenty-five schools, which almost become unproductive due to the war constraints."[180] The reading of other PAIGC documents drives us to the conclusion that the years 1968-1969, was a hard period for PAIGC at the military level.

The analysis of the growing number of teachers between 1965 to 1968 followed again by a small decrease and a stable period over the following years allows us to present two important points. First, is the great increase in the number of teachers for the years of 1964-1965 then more than doubling to more than double in the years 1965 to 1966. One plausible explanation for this fact has to do with the emergence of the teacher category which was made official in 1966, the year that corresponds with the creation of the PAIGC first teacher training – *Centro de Formação e Reciclagem de Professores*.[181] Before that date,

---

180 Domingos Brito's hand writing report. See Annex 6 in the annexes section (not translate).

181 Translation: Centre for Improving and Retraining of Teachers. More information about this course will be giving on chapter three.

Tab. 2. PAIGC's student's distribution by school year.

School level	Kindergarten	1st class	2nd class	3rd class	4th class	5th class	6th class
Number of students	38 students	11 201 students	1 890 students	967 students	409 students	26 students	n.d.

Source: PAIGC – *Reconstrução Nacional* 1973

the teacher category was somehow blended in with the figure of the *Comissário Político*, but also embedded in the Party watchword "all those who know should teach those who don't know" which made everyone who could read and write a teacher candidate. If we take into account that the category of the *Comissário Político* continued to exist throughout the struggle doing the work of mobilization and alphabetization, these statistics fail to represent not only them, but all the civilian population who was able to learn to read and write during that period.

A deeper look at the distribution of students according to school grade (Tab. 2), it is easy to perceive that the majority of students were concentrated in the first and second grade. The explanation for this has to do with the fact that the majority of PAIGC were people from the liberated areas that through the Portuguese discriminatory school policy was relegated to the rudimentary school provided by the church, or assigned to no school at all because there was no other colonial education structure in the region. Therefore, is not strange that most of PAIGC's pupils were concentrated in the first and second grade. However, it is odd that there is no information concerning the number of students attending the sixth grade during the school year of 1971-1972. It is important to keep in mind that by this time the Party had two boarding schools – *Escola Piloto* and *Escola de Teranga* who was responsible for the fifth and sixth grade. Such absence of numbers is another aspect that makes PAIGC statistical analysis difficult.

Entering the domain of the international educational network of the liberation struggle, the PAIGC received a considerable amount of international support for the different fronts of the struggle, including for education, during the years of 1963 and 1974. Because of the lack of information about how much this help was in monetary or even social terms, my focus goes to the number of scholarships that foreign countries offered to the Party, which allowed the Guinean students to continue their studies abroad. Scholarship support came mainly from European socialist countries like Bulgaria, Czechoslovakia, Hungary, Soviet Union, Romania or the German Democratic Republic (see Tab. 3)

Tab. 3. Total of PAIGC's students who concluded their studies abroad 1963-1975

Country	Male	Female	Total
Bulgaria	10	4	14
Czechoslovakia	21	1	22
Cuba	24	10	34
Hungary	21	----	21
Yugoslavia	19	----	19
German Democratic Republic (GDR)	64	63	67
Romania	10	----	10
United States of America	1	----	----
Soviet Union	128	38	166
Total	298	56	354

Source: Estatísticas do Ensino from Comissariado de Estado de Desenvolvimento e Planificação 1975

and the non-aligned countries such as Cuba and Ghana. Support came also from non-socialist countries such was the case of Sweden.[182]

According to the table 3, between the years of 1963 to 1975, PAIGC received a total of three hundred and fifty-four international scholarships for the more diverse areas of study with special focus on areas related to medicine, mixed farming, mechanical fields, or social sciences such as history and political science. The data includes the total number of scholarships received, two years after the independence. However, documents dated from 1973 reveal a larger number of PAIGC students studying abroad. According to these documents by 1973 there were four hundred and ninety-seven PAIGC students attending schools abroad (see Tab. 4). Yet when this number is compared with the other Party numbers of trained health professional from the previous year (see Tab. 5), which was a total of four hundred and forty-nine people, it is possible to conclude that on the collected data from 1975, that health personnel were likely not included and were treated separately. To add to this, during the years of 1966-1974 PAIGC had in the territory an adult military center – *Centro de Instrução Politico-Militar de Madina do Boé*- CIPM,[183] where military personnel apart from military training

---

182 For more information on the Swedish support to PAIGC liberation struggle as well to Southern African Liberation Movements, please consult Tor Sellström, *Sweden and national liberation in Southern Africa: solidarity and assistance 1970-1994*, (Uppsala: Nordiska Afrikainstitutet, 2002).

183 Translation: Political and Military Instruction Center of Madina do Boé. The *Centro de Instrução Política e Militar de Madina do Boé* administration was composed by a

Tab. 4. Total of PAIGC's students trained abroad 1963-1975

Level	Male	Female	Total	Data 1973 (total numbers)
Professional Training	183	44	227	241
Middle Training	62	12	74	46
University	53	-----	53	36
Political and trade union cadres	-----	-----	------	174

Source: Estatísticas do Ensino doComissariado de Estado de Desenvolvimento e Planificação 1975

Tab. 5. PAIGC's number of trained health personnel in 1972

Activity	Year 1972
PAIGC doctors	18
Medical assistants	20
PAIGC medical technicians	11
Fully trained nurses	25
Sanitary assistants	95
Auxiliary nurses	215
Military nurses	65
Total	449

Source: PAIGC's - La République de Guinea Bissau en chiffres, 1974

also received political education as well as alphabetization classes. The number of people who were alphabetized in this Center is unknown and most likely their alphabetization results were not included in the Party statistics as part of their achievements in the Party educational achievements.

From all these aspects that were presented, one can draw some conclusions. The first conclusion is that PAIGC statistics, and although agreeing with Lars Rudebeck's conclusion that the Party was "still far from having achieved the goal of universal education for the children of liberated Guinea-Bissau",[184] the focus solely on children's education limits an understanding of the larger picture of

---

group of five members (one chief, one chief assistant, three effective members and a non-specified number of trainees)

184 Lars Rudebeck, Guinea Bissau. *A study of political mobilization*, 209.

PAIGC educational initiatives and achievements of the educational efforts during the liberation struggle by ignoring the data relative to adult education. Another conclusion, if we want to expand the concept of education to a broader scale and not only to the skills of reading and writing, and if we take into consideration the political education and consciousness work developed in the territory the Party statistic fails to represent them as part of the educational policy.

To conclude, in order to better understand the PAIGC liberation struggle in the domain of education and its achivements, quantitative data must be viewed and analyzed with a broader and transversal approach (and include also qualitative information), taking into account the dimensions and accomplishments of the struggle in the very different areas of activity. In short, to understand PAIGC's data and its shortcomings, one has to read and understand them in the general context of the liberation struggle.

3 Militant education. Ideas and practices during the liberation struggle (1964-1974)

> *The primary purpose of education is the liberation of man. But a man can be physically free from restraint and still not be free if is mind is restricted by habits and attitudes which limit his humanity. Education has to liberate both the mind and the body of man. It has to make him more of a human being because he is aware of his potential as a human being, and is in positive, life-enhancing relationship with himself, his neighbour, and his environment. Education has therefore to enable a man to throw off the impediments to freedom which restrict his full physical and mental development. It is a matter of attitudes and skills- both of them.[185]*
>
> Julius Nyerere, 2004

1 Militant education: the emergence of concept

Derived from the Latin word '*militant*,' the term 'militant,' was first related with the military field, meaning "to serve as a soldier." Adopted by the church during the middle ages, the word gained importance in the religious vocabulary as in the "Christian Church Militant."[186] Later, between the eighteenth and twentieth centuries the word "militant" was gradually transferred to the political lexicon, used to characterize the individual who actively participates in an associative movement, in a political party, popular educational associations, in a syndicalist organization, etc., linked to an ideology.[187] The 'militant' became the person who struggles to defend an idea or ideology, with the will to change the society where

---

185 Elieshi Lema et al., *Nyerere on Education* (Dar es Salaam: The Mwalimu Nyerere Foundation, 2004), 125.

186 Pierre Daled, "Une définition des termes: la 'laïcisation' du militant au 19e et au début du 20e siècle" in Militantisme et militants, coordinated by José Gotovitch et Anne Morelli, (Bruxelles: EVO, 2000) 8–9.

187 Axelle Brodiez, "Militants, bénevoles, affliés, affranchise,…: de l'applicabilite historique des travaux sociologiques." (2004), URL. https://halshs.archives-ouvertes.fr/halshs-00174309/document (accessed August 3, 2017).

he lives.[188] In the contemporary world, the militant is a combatant, "the one who seeks by action to triumph his ideas, his opinions, who actively defends a cause, a person."[189]

The second half of the twentieth century is marked by the African independence, African liberation movements – FRELIMO, MPLA, PAIGC influenced by the communist and socialist ideologies adopted the term 'militant' to characterize those who followed a ideological, political, social and armed movement, adhered to the struggle and were engaged in the struggle to achieve independence and liberation from the Portuguese colonial government. In 1974, Samora Machel, a military commander, politician, leader of the liberation struggle FRELIMO in Mozambique and a socialist in the tradition of Marxism-Leninism, provided his definition of militant and militancy:

> The militant is the one who lives the concern of the organization and who, in the detail of everyday life, by the creative application that makes our line of thought, becomes for all a model server of the people, the edifier of the new society. The task entrusted to him/ her is fulfilled with the sense that the task is at the service of the people, and receiving its mission from the people to everything it consecrates including its own *life*.[190]

In the PAIGC liberation struggle, militant was used as an umbrella term for all those who consciously adhered the struggle – combatants, commanders, political commissars, responsibles, nurses, doctors, civilians, etc.. The Party considered the militant as being the vanguard of the struggle, the one that:

> (like a good citizen) … does his duty properly [and] in addition to doing his duty, succeeds in improving himself each day so as to be able to do more and better to do more and better[191], [the one that is] ready to put an end to Portuguese colonialism and ready to follow the party watchwords and to respect and carry out the orders of our party leadership. […] those who have exemplary moral conduct, as men and women worthy of our land. […] who work and have work[…] Those who dedicate themselves body and soul to the programme of our Party in our land, ready to fight the enemy.[192]

---

188 Jacques Ion, "Militant, militantisme" in *Dictionnaire de sociologie Le Robert*, (Paris: Seuil, 1999), 341.

189 Pierre Daled, "Une définition des termes: la 'laïcisation' du militant au 19e et au début du 20e siècle", 9–10.

190 Samora Machel, *Fazer da escola uma base para o povo tomar o poder*, (Lisboa: Nova Aurora, 1974), 18. For more information on Samora Machel ideas on militancy, please consult Samora Machel, *Produzir é um acto de militância*, (Maputo: Departamento do Trabalho Idelógico, 1979).

191 Amílcar Cabral, *Unity and Struggle*, 244.

192 Ibid., 89.

In the "service of the liberty and the progress"[193] of the Guinean people, the militant in PAIGC words should "defend at all costs the conquests our people are making through their struggle"[194]. The militant should "live among the people, before the people, behind the people … must work for the Party in the certainty that they are working for the people in our land."[195] To become a PAIGC militant should be a conscious act. Therefore "some specific evidence that one satisfies certain requirements"[196] should be given to the Party leadership, namely the knowledge about the Party program, the agreement with the Party principles as well as what they were seeking to achieve from the liberation struggle.[197]

To achieve this goal, this militant vanguard or what the PAIGC called the *militante armado*,[198] in order to distinguish them from simple soldiers or military, a political education about the struggle, the Party history, its principles and the independence struggle should be put in practice not just for the armed militant (military, soldier, commander) but also other adult civilians, Party members and more specially the children and youth, who the Party considered would be the forged instrument created by the Party[199] and would lead and reconstruct the country after independence. The creation of such vanguard according to the Party, should be "constantly more honed, more sharpened, more perfected, and our people must constantly embellish it."[200]

It was in this context that the PAIGC developed their concept of *educação militante* - militant education. Militant education, as a term is not expressed much in PAIGC archive documents. Before independence, the term appeared on an undated document related to the school curriculum plan for students from the first to fifth grade, initially as a class title for the first and second grade, and was later substituted by the term *educação política* - political education for students attending the third to fifth grade. Only in 1978 was the term used as a concept as a form to characterize the education system developed during the struggle.

A close analysis of PAIGC ideas on education and training of their militants allows a description of militant education as an education system looking for

---

193 Ibid., 75.
194 Ibid., 78.
195 Ibid., 97.
196 Ibid., 103.
197 Ibid., 103.
198 Translation: Armed militant.
199 Ibid., 87.
200 Ibid., 87.

liberation and independence, and with one of the aims to "train cadres to serve tomorrow, the future of [the] struggle... cadres may be military or political, electricians or industrial workers in any branch, doctors or engineers, nurses or radio operators or any specialty."[201] But also to train cadres that would "satisfy the aspirations, dreams, and desires [the Guinean] people: to lead a decent and worthy life, as all the people in the world want, to have peace in order to build progress in their land, to build happiness for their children,"[202] to struggle against misery, suffering, and disaster and against all injustices[203] and to "guarantee for the children in [Guinea] today and tomorrow a certainty that no barrier or wall should be put in their way"[204]

Militant education as an idea was applied to the training of three groups. They were the training of the "militant teacher," the training of the "armed military militant" and finally the formation of the "militant student."

As it emerged in specific historic moment of the mid of the twentieth century, militant education was deeply influenced by the African liberation struggle and their anti-colonial and decolonial positions, the pan-African movements and the African unity principle, the cold war and the ideological blocks, the non-aligned movement and the international solidarity, the period of armed conflict in the Guinean territory and the international human rights struggle of the liberation movement in the realm of the United Nations. All these are aspects contributed to the formulation of PAIGC militant education (as a concept) and militant school (as a space and practices).

Militant education or militant school is a term that I define as being a committed, engaged and conscious education, grounded on anti-colonial and decolonial principles focused on an ample concept and goals of the liberation struggle. In 1978, PAIGC used the following definition to describe its undesratnding of militant education:

> The pedagogical role of the militant school comprised three aspects. Political learning, technical training and the shaping of individual and collective behaviors. Rooted in its community, the school was the privileged site where the armed militant's farmers and young students gathered together and learned among the people and their daily life, everything that could be useful to the progress of the struggle. [205]

---

201 Ibid., 111.
202 Ibid., 77
203 Ibid., 99
204 Ibid., 77.
205 PAIGC, Comissariado de Estado da Educação Nacional, *Educação, Tarefa de Toda a Sociedade*, 1978, República da Guiné-Bissau.

The concept and praxis of militant education aimed that pupils, civilian population and military militants in a combination of political teaching, technical training and the shaping of individual and collective behaviors, were supposed to be guided toward the development of the *Self* as a liberated African citizen whose work was to give their conscious contribution to the sustainable development of the newly independent liberated country, integrated into the international system of states.

For the practice of such objectives, PAIGC militants and trained teachers developed a diversity of materials that ranged from school regulation, school curriculum (for pupils and adults) and school manuals and magazines. However, despite the intentions, the PAIGC concept and the practices of militant education was not exempt from conflicts between the ideas and practices. These conflicts are most evident when these four elements - school regulation and rules, the curriculum, the school manuals, and the classroom environment are put in conversation. These conflicts will be discussed more deeply in the following pages.

1.1 The school regulations and the establishment of routines

Between the years 1966 and 1971, and the growth of schools and students within that period that attested to the importance of education in the liberation struggle, the Party and teachers realized that it was important to provide a regulation that would secure their activity in that field. Therefore, as a result of the first teachers meeting - *Centro de Aperfeiçoamento Reciclagem de Professores*[206] that took place in Conakry July- September 1966, the regulation that was produced in the meeting was later in the same year replaced by the document - *Regulamento das Escolas do Partido*[207]. Both documents were elaborated by PAIGC teachers and were based on their "lived experiences of several years of activity."[208]

Roughly a total of 200 teachers attended the meetings, most of them coming from the liberated areas. The goal of the meetings was to "improve the level of education provided. [...] to raise the level of participation and knowledge of teachers activity. [...] in order to raise their pedagogical level and discuss the main problems of our teaching."[209] In 1971, influenced by the Cuban regulation

---

206 Translation: Center for the improving and retraining of teachers. See Annex 9 at the annexes section.
207 Translation: Regulation of the schools of the Party. See Annex 4 at the annexes section.
208 PAIGC, Regulation of the schools of the Party (Conakry: 1966), 1.
209 Between 1965 and 1973, during the summer vacation period, a total of eight meetings took place in Conakry, at *Escola Piloto* and in the facilities of the Conakry lyceum or others structures provided by the Guinean government. See Annex 10 at the annexes

on education, PAIGC teachers produced a specific regulation - *Regulamento das Regulamento Interno dos Internatos das Regiões Libertadas*,[210] that targeted their boarding schools in the liberated areas, but that was also extended to the Party extraterritorial schools, namely the *Escola Piloto* and *Escola Teranga*.

The regulations approached themes that ranged from the school furniture (teacher and student tables, blackboard, classrooms disposition), to the school hygiene (the waste paper basket, the classroom cleaning, the latrine), and the school garden, and school organization (enrollment, class breaks), and it regulates the student school routines. With a workload that began at 6.30 am to 9 pm during the week and from 7 am to 9 pm during the weekend, the student's schedule started in the morning with formation and gymnastic, followed by breakfast and classes. The working day was interrupted with the lunch and rest period that lasted from 1 pm to 3 pm. The afternoon period was occupied with study classes followed by dinner and cultural activities. By 9 pm all students should be in their rooms.

Despite this schedule, the school routine varied from school to school, and class schedules were adapted according with their local situations. Such adaptation was more visible in boarding schools located in the liberated areas. In the liberated area's school started a bit later and lasted until 4.30pm. The afternoon time that should be used for rest and the study groups was substituted by "shopping" and preparing the meals. The night period was dedicated to the study groups. Weekends were used for hunting or other activities like sports. Lassana Seidi, a student in the *Internato de Móres*, recalled this school routine in the boarding school:

> Our day to day was like that. We would wake up around eight, eight thirty in the morning and then go to school. In that time we would only have one *tiro*. One *tiro*, means one meal, we used the military language. That means you had one normal meal per day, but this during an already advanced phase of struggle, because when the struggle started, you would not have even that. We stayed in school until 4.30pm. Then, we would search for rice, in the armazéns do povo[211] nearby. [...] We would file a request with the person

---

section. "Magazine PAIGC Actualités from 1972" making reference to the teacher course that took place in that same year (not translated).

210 Translation: Internal regulation of the boarding schools of the liberated areas. See Annex 11 at the annexes section.

211 *Armazéns do povo*, means 'people's stores', was an important feature of the PAIGC economic programme for the liberated ares. They intended to replace the " old Portuguese commercial network and to compete with private shops in the Portuguese-held zones. The decision to establish new forms of trade, taken at the Cassacá Congress, underlined Cabral's belief that the 'economic war' with the Portuguese would have

in charge, and he would say 'Look, there are these kilos of rice in this population, so you can go there'. [...] most of the times the rice was paddy rice, and we had to peel the rice during the night. Every week we had a *grupo de serviço*.[212] For example, each day a group of eight to twelve people would find firewood, fetch water, peel the rice. This was made daily, by a group of six boys and four girls for example, but it was not rigid. You should be in groups, and we have made various groups because we were so many. Everybody worked. Sometimes even eight or nine o'clock in the evening we were peeling rice. [During the war] each of us had a lunch box. If you did not eat all your meal, you would keep it. The next day you would warm it quickly, eat and go to school. This was our life in the wood. We studied even at night. When it was your work day, you do not go to class study during the night. Because you already prepared the food, washed the dishes, and when you finished, it was already late. But the others, after dinner would go to the study groups. There was no electricity. We would make a fire so that we could read. At that time, we were kids, so we had good vision, sometimes when it was full moon, we could read. This was our life for four years. In our free time, Saturday and Sundays, we created hunting groups. People use to hunt. Between us, there were people who were very good hunters, and sometimes they would kill a gazelle, a wild pig, things like that. Because it was a war situation, most of us at the time, although we were still small, we could handle a gun. There was old military, very good hunters too, but we didn't wait for anyone. [When new school supplies were neeeded] The population and the military would organize a military column to pick up all these materials in the line borders and bring it to the country's interior. They would choose the older students to take part in those columns. They would go from the country's interior and then would walk to the borders and then carry in hands or arms all the military material, books, medicines, etc. I went once to Camjambara, and I brought 26 books. At that time that was so heavy for me! I brought twenty-six books, but there were also others who would carry notebooks, blackboards, chalk packages, and all the didactic material. The *responsável* for education received the material, would check and wrote down everything and then he would distribute to the schools.[213]

---

a determining influence on the development of the struggle. The first store was set up in 1964, and by 1968 there weer 15)five in the north, seven in the south, two in the east, and one on the border with Guiné). The stores were designed to serve as trade centres where the villagers could exchange their surplus agricultural production for other essential commodities such as oil, soap and cloth. [...] The system of the *armazéns do povo* was also ontended to achieve some form of economic justice by keeping prices lower that those of the Portuguese stores in the non-liberated areas (to which the villagers would have had easy acess)." In Chabal, Patrick. Amílcar Cabral. Revolutionary leadership and people's war. (New York: Cambridge University Press, 1983, p. 112).

212 Translation: service group. It was a weekly group in charge of the school organization.
213 Interview with Lassana Seidi, June 6, 2014.

In the extraterritorial boarding school, namely the *Escola Piloto* Maria da Luz Boal, school director and a collaborator in the writing of the regulations recalled the school schedule and how the regulation was put in practice:

> The day started early. At six in the morning, the teacher rang the bell. The students would get up, and all organized in a row, we would do gymnastics. [...] If Cabral was in Conakry, he would come to visit the *Escola Piloto*, to see the students practicing gymnastics, to talk with them, to call their attention to this or that attitude or for their clothes and how they dressed, this kind of care that normally parents give to their kids. After the gymnastics, the students would go for a shower and then have breakfast. After that, the teacher would ring the bell, and the classes would start. Every student would go to their classroom and stayed there until midday. At mid-day, there was a lunch break. The teachers had their canteen, and the students had theirs. When the bell rang again, they had to be present to eat. During the meal, there was always a teacher. We called him/her the *professor da semana*,[214] who accompanied the students in the canteen, and give some guidance, on how to sit at the table, how to eat, which was really important. They accepted and internalized that with much humor, sometimes even playing with the teacher, when he called their attention, "It's not like that a person eats. It's not the mouth that goes to the food, it's the food that comes to the mouth," and on the next stay, you would find that on the class blackboard. After the lunch, there was a resting period. In the afternoon, there were also classes, such as handwork, music, singing. Normally the singing classes were more at the end of the day. There were all these parallel activities, like dancing and theatre. We had theatre classes, and we did several theatre plays, that represented situations of struggle and its problems. [...] All the school functioned through the work of the students and teachers. Each was in charge of his room, clothes and school cleaning. Every week there was a group of students – *alunos de serviço* who were in charge of the school cleaning. The meals and the kitchen service was made by the students, boys and girls. There was a division of tasks. For the small ones, we gave the small tasks like dish washing. The older ones prepared the food. This was not easy because they had to cook for more than one hundred people, excluding the teachers, it was something like one hundred and twelve to fifteen people.[215]

From both testimonies, it is possible to understand the differences between student lifestyles in school. In *Escola Piloto* where the regulation was more strictly applied, students had less room for maneuver to escape teachers supervision and control. However, in the liberated areas students were more exposed to the side effects of war on their life, for example in Lassana's testimony, the fact that students had to travel from one *tabanca* to another in order to get the rice to prepare the school meals. Another aspect that is important to highlight from

---

214 Translation: Teacher of the week.
215 Interview with Maria da Luz Boal, September 2, 2013.

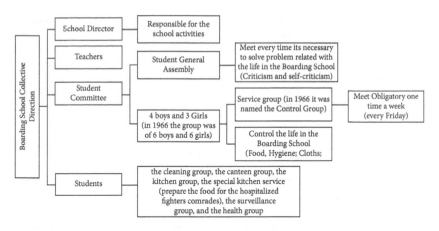

Fig. 5. *Escola Piloto* school organization. *Source: own elaboration based on the conducted interviews, and PAIGC's documents: "A nossa luta pela formação de quadros" (1965) and* "Regulamento interno dos internatos das regiões libertadas."

Lassana's testimony was the contact with the war and how it interacted with the school routines, namely with the contact and handling of firearms for basic activities such as hunting, but also the participation in military columns to travel to the border, to get school supplies and also the military ammunition, not to mention the risk of ambush and the existence in the school of bomb shelters.

Just with student transfers to the extraterritorial boarding schools, a safe environment and a more comfortable life and stable school routine could be provided so that the student could concentrate more on their studies.

1.2 The 'collective' school administration and the socialist influences

The school regulations established that schools should be collectively administrated based on a collaboration between teachers and students (see Fig. 5). The testimonies from the student Lassana Seidi and the director and teacher Maria da Luz Boal revealed a student participation in the school administration through the organization of the *grupos de serviço*. PAIGC education report from 1965 described how students were involved in this process:[216]

---

216 Later this organizational structure and practice was institutionalized in the document "Internal regulation of the boarding school of the liberated areas," from 1972. See Annex 11 in at the annexes section.

The school Direction is based on self-organization management. [This] It is ensured by a *Comité Misto de Direcção dos Internos*,[217] composed by six elements [three boys and three girls]. This group is then divided into two sub-committees, for the execution of tasks - one for boys, other for girls - working in coordination. The Committee is the highest instrument of school management. It takes all the decisions on the administration and operation of the boarding school. The teachers of the school and one permanent person appointed by the Party, guides and watch over the activities of the Committee. The Directing Committee is composed of two groups responsible for the rooms, one for boys and one for girls. Each group is formed by many students as there are rooms on the basis of one boy student or one girl student per room. Group control: There is also a "control group" (Mixed), consisting of two boys and two girls. The aim is to monitor the life in the boarding school (meals, hygiene, gates, etc.). This group responds to the steering committee, to whom it has to report about the life and the activities in the boarding school. [...] The Steering Committee obligatorily meets at least once a week, and extraordinarily if necessary. In the case of poor performance, the Committee may be collectively dismissed and substituted by another responsible body. ... All students 'rotary' participate in the implementation of different services. The main services are: the cleaning group, the canteen group, the kitchen group, the special kitchen service [prepare the food for the hospitalized fighters/comrades], the surveillance group, and the health group. The surveillance service works uninterruptedly, day and night [....] The health service has a small first aid post. One of the girls with more expertise in nursing and small emergencies is responsible.[218]

During the liberation struggle, the PAIGC developed a collective administration of the school in a partnership between the school director, the teachers, the student committee and the students population. Although the hierarchical organization (see Fig. 5), central to this collective administration was the work of the Students Committee through the work of the *grupos de serviço* and their weekly meetings and the Student General Assembly that met every time that it was necessary to solve a problem with the life in the school.

It was during these meetings that the Party introduced in the school educational system the practice of criticism and self-criticism, a behavior already in practice in other fields of the liberation struggle, as well as in educational systems in other countries such as the USSR[219] and China under Mao Tse Tung's regime.[220] With inspiration from the Soviet, Leninist socialist practice, criticism

---

217 Translation: Mixed Internal Steering Committee.
218 PAIGC, *A nossa luta pela educação das massas e pela formação de quadros* (Conakry: PAIGC, 1965), 9.
219 Wolfgang Leonard, *Child of the Revolution*, (London: Collins, 1957).
220 Martin King Whyte, *Small groups and political ritual in China*, (London: University of California Press, 1974).

and self-criticism can be understood as a ritual instrument whose intentions are to improve the execution of broad national policies and also self-improvement at the most personal level. The practice of criticism and self-criticism implied a group participation a clarification of the rules of the process, namely the what rules, norms, or values were violated by a certain person and why this was "repugnant to those upholding the norms, rules, and values in question."[221] After the initial criticism or problem was presented, it was expected that others would join and contribute with thoughts for the discussion. For the one criticized it was his duty to engage in the self-criticism based on the criticism made by his colleagues.[222]

The practice, which implied a sort of exposure in front of the group by exposing one's behaviors, can be understood in the educational context as a form of developing in students an awareness about the school and community problem, exercising in this way their consciousness. Also, it can be understood as strategy to incorporate students in the school routine not just as educational receivers but also as active participants, and in this way develop in them the ideas of living in a democratic and free society and their role in this process. However, a such practice could develop some negative side effects, namely the development a strict and public social and behavior control. Such behavior control was not absent from the school regulation as will be shown in the following section.

1.3 Military influences in militant education: regulating behaviours of teachers and students inside and outside the school

Apart from regulating the school routines, the produced school regulations also tended to regulate relations and behaviors of students and teachers inside and outside of the school facility. The Party expected teachers to "have a political education and be a good militant"; to "always intend to increase their knowledge"; to "not miss class without justified reason"; to "live the daily routine of the student [and] to make them feel better, the better assistance that they are dispensed"; their behavior inside and outside the school "should need to agree with the pedagogy rules and principles of the party."[223] According to the first school regulation from 1966, teachers also had the responsibility to oversee and be vigilant toward

---

221 Paul Hollander, *The many faces of Socialism. Comparative sociology and politics* (London: Transaction Books, 1983).

222 Ibid.

223 PAIGC, Internal regulation of the boarding schools of the liberated regions. See Annex 11 at the annexes section.

the student by following their activities inside and outside the classroom. They should be "ambitious with his students [and needed] to accustom them to a rigid discipline" but with no exaggeration.[224]

For the Party, it was important that "students [didn't] find an environment of a caserne or a prison. There [had] to be a discipline, but not a military one. [the student needed] to feel at ease, free without, however, breaking the rules of discipline."[225] It was the teacher's responsibility to "create a joyful ambiance, disciplined and attractive this is what stimulates the students for the classes. A pleasant environment where they feel content and happy. It's the teachers challenge to create this certain environment of respect and happiness."[226]

This environment of respect and happiness somehow contrasted with obligations that students were expected to fulfill. Signs of good student behavior and education included the show of respect and obedience to "the teachers inside and outside the school"; to be always "properly uniformed"; to be present in every morning formation; their obligatory and punctual presence in the canteen for the meals; to always "stand up when someone enters the classroom." It was also required from students their presence in formation during the hoisting and lowering of the flag.[227]

The regulations defined penalties and punishments for teachers and students who did not follow the rules. In the case of teachers, if "after being criticized in an internal meeting of the boarding school with the comrade director and teachers"[228] they could be objected, suspended or dismissed from their work. For the student, the penalty could go from collective reprehension in front of other students, expulsion from the class, work outside of the boarding school and in extreme cases expulsion from the school. The Party forbade the application of any kind of corporal punishment, although testimonies reveal that they happened from time to time, and these cases were investigated by the Party officials.

One important aspect of the incorporation of military aspects in the PAIGC educational practice is the introduction of military training in the program.

---

224 PAIGC, Center for improvement for teachers, (Conakry:1966), 2. See Annex 9 at the annexes section.
225 Ibid.
226 Ibid.
227 PAIGC, Internal regulation of the boarding schools of the liberated regions. See Annex 11 at the annexes section.
228 Ibid.

Photo 17. Children in a military posture, with sticks in the place of guns.
Source: Arquivo & Biblioteca Mário Soares Foundation - DAC - Amílcar Cabral
Documents

The above photo is representative of the militarization of students body. The photo can be seen from two perspectives, namely from the perspective of a military training, or from the perspective of preparation for a theater play, as some of the PAIGC's militant interviewed mentioned.

In 1965 PAIGC's documentation established as part of the school activities a class called *"preparação militar"* - military preparation/training. The training was aimed at children above 12 years old, and included gymnastics, how to use weapons, and the cleaning and conservation of weapons (see Photo 17).[229] The year 1965 corresponds with the great increase of PAIGC schools in the liberated areas and the introduction of this class might correspond to a strategy of teaching self-defense methods to children due to the attacks that they could face at any moment.

PAIGC expected an exemplary behavior from all Party members, that included 'responsibility;' 'discipline;' and 'respect for the Party principles and regulation.' This same language can be read throughout the school regulation, as

---

229 PAIGC, A Nossa luta pela educação das massas e pela formação de quadros (PAIGC: 1965), 5.

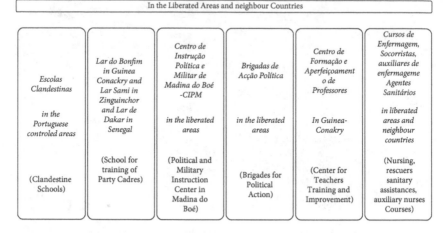

Fig. 6. *PAIGC Educational structures for Adults.* Source: own elaboration based on the conducted interviews, the diverse PAIGC's documents and the magazines: *Blufo*; *PAIGC actualités* and *Jornal Libertação*

well in documents oriented to soldiers. The introduction of military elements, the hierarchical school direction although with the attempt to introduce a democratic practice of collectivism and participation through the concept and practice of socialist elements – the critique and self-criticism, but at the same time implying for students obedience is a conflict present in PAIGC concept of militant education.

1.4 Militant education for adults. Becoming a PAIGC militant teacher

Between 1963 and 1974, PAIGC developed a body of educational structures (see Fig. 6) targeting the adult population. The Party established three multifunctional centers in the Republic of Guinea and the Republic of Senegal, namely the Party representative offices, as recovery centers for those injured in the fight, and the educational centers. They were the *Lar Sami* in Ziguinchor and the *Lar de Dakar*, both in Republic of Senegal, and the *Lar do Bonfim* (also known as *Lar de Conakry*) in Republic of Guinea. In 1966 the Party created the *Centro de*

Reciclagem e Aperfeicoamento de Professores[230], and in the same year of the *Centro de Instrução Política e Militar de Madina do Boé*- CIPM.[231]

Under the watchword, "all those who know should teach those who do not know" launched in the Cassacá Congress, PAIGC opened space within the struggle where everyone could be not only a potential student but most importantly, a teacher. The slogan did not make any reference to reading and writing skills, but simply to the transmission of knowledge in any area that could be relevant for the ideals and development of the liberation struggle. PAIGC's political commissars' work among the population, had the function of conscencializing the community about colonialism and the reasons and the need for a liberation struggle and the need for mobilization and organization. The work of these political commissars can be considered as the first PAIGC's militant teachers' in the struggle, despite the different name that was applied to them.

PAIGC teachers came from different backgrounds, namely from the "working class" (tailors, carpenters, etc.), including also the peasant class (farmers) and some of the "petty bourgeoisie" (former primary teachers, former employees, and students), who abandoned their daily lives to join the struggle. Their ages varied from 15 to 25 years old. Students who had left the Portuguese colonial schools to join the struggle due to their knowledge were also trained to become PAIGC militant teachers.[232]

From the previous testimonies and school regulation presented in this work, some details about the process of becoming a teacher have already been provided. Such can be reinforced by the following passage from 1978, "during the struggle, a teacher, warned that he had to open a school, immediately carried his backpack, and reached the chosen region. He would enroll students and prepared a mission to go to the border in order to get the books and other school supplies. With the participation of adults and children, schools were constructed in tents/barracks with sticks and palm trees."[233]

However, opening a school and teaching the skills of reading and writing were not the main characteristic of the PAIGC teacher. The Party saw the teachers work as a crucial factor in the process of liberation. The teacher was seen as "an

---

230 Translation: Center for Improving and Retraining of Teachers.
231 Translation: Political and Military Instruction Center of Madina do Boé.
232 PAIGC, *A nossa luta pela educação das massas e pela formação de quadros* (Conakry: PAIGC, 1965), 3–4.
233 Comissariado de estado da educação nacional, *Educação tarefa de toda a sociedade* (Guiné Bissau 1978), 13.

educator, and as an educator, he [was] also a politician."[234] Their work was seen as "the frontline of [the] struggle, the vanguard. [A work whose] outcomes might not be visible immediately, but it brings great consequences for the future of our land."[235]

According to the Party, it was the teacher's responsibility to educate the future generation of the country, and therefore teachers should be the prime example for its students, as the following excerpt reveals:

> [The teacher] It is he who designs the future of the man, of the country. We know that a grown-up is the result of all that he learned as a child. [...] When a child goes to school, the parents entrust the future of their child to the leadership of the teacher. He will do what he learned as a child. This is why the teacher has responsibility for his country. Each of those men whom he will bring to graduation will be a part of the state. Those men will bring the ideas, the habits or the education that they learned in school. [...] Also, that all he teaches the children will stay for a whole lifetime.[236]

It was in the process of becoming this Party teacher that the teacher him/herself transformed into a militant teacher, the one whose profession and work was more than to prepare classes, teach the curriculum content and grade students. The transformation implied a change of behaviors, habits, overcoming past experiences, the re-thinking, and production of new knowledge and to adapt to the world and the demands of the liberation struggle. Maria da Luz Boal who also went through this transformation described the process:

> It was a transformation, a change of behaviours. Because can you imagine, a person leaving Lisbon, the university. And then arrives in [liberation struggle] that context, where everything was different, the way of leaving, the habits. Can you imagine a person used to living with a scholarship, arriving the struggle, without a penny? And still had to work, do hard working, with commitment. That was a radical change of attitude and behaviour, of acceptance.[237]

It was within this commitment to independence and liberation that students who studied in Portuguese colonial universities, and teachers trained during the struggle became militant teachers during the struggle. Although the Party

---

234 Amílcar Cabral, *Sobre alguns problemas práticos da nossa vida e da nossa luta* (PAIGC: 1971), 3.
235 Boé, 1967 extract from the film *O Regresso de Cabral* (The Return of Cabral), 1976 from Sana N'nada, Flora Gomes and Josefina Crato.
236 PAIGC, Center for Improvement for teachers (Conakry: PAIGC, 1966), 1.
237 Interview with Maria da Luz Boal, September 2, 2013.

developed training courses for teachers where themes like pedagogy and the acquisition of pedagogical skills was approached, most of the process of becoming militant teachers was learned from a re-investment and re-evaluation of their on their own education and knowledge, and through a *in loco* apprenticeship in the classroom together with their students. Agnelo Regala, a Guinean who had done all his school education in a boarding school in Portugal and continued until graduate studies, left his graduate studies in economy to join the PAIGC liberation struggle in 1970. It was during the struggle that following the Party orders he became a militant teacher in the Party boarding school *Escola Piloto*.

He recalled his apprenticeship in loco in the classrooms or in conversation with his peers. He also recalled the many difficulties that he had to overcome, such as linguistic barriers with his students, his process of teaching history of the country in a decolonial perspective, his fears and insecurities as a teacher, and even his process of deconstruction and re-Africanization of the knowledge he acquired as a student in Portugal. All this was a result of the teacher engagement in the learning and teaching process within an interactive and mutual practice with his students:

> When I arrived in Conakry, I presented myself in the Party headquarters. I said who I was and my student level. They asked me 'what do you want to do here?' [To what] I answered, 'I'm available for the Party, I came here for the struggle, and I'm available to go to the front.' They replied saying, 'Here we have several fronts. You have the military front of direct combat, but we have the education front. That is as important front as the others, because it is not worth to freeing the land if we are not ready to assume the responsibility of independence.' So, they decided I should go to education. And it was like that. I was sent to *Escola Piloto*. [There] I taught geography and sometimes history, and I substituted for other teachers whenever it was necessary because we had to substitute for teachers who went to a Party service mission.
>
> To become a professor! One learns. It's a demand of the struggle. […] We had to prepare and to study the appropriate language because the problem was how do you use a language to transmit the knowledge. And that was complicated. It was a necessary training to simplify the language, to make it more comprehensible and accessible to students. [This was particularly important] when the class was taught in Portuguese, especially for groups of students who had a poor command of the Portuguese language. Sometimes for a better comprehension, it was necessary to translate some things into Creole, and to explain in Creole. First to speak and teach in Portuguese and then translate to Creole, so that everybody could have access to knowledge. It was a rewarding experience.
>
> At the beginning, there was always that fear, the insecurity, because I never gave classes. 'How I'm going to do it?' But after that, with some efforts, and with the experience from the others – we learn from the experience of other colleagues who were teaching in the school for a longer time. Especially from Lilica Boal, because that was her field. Many

times there were discussions. The people would debate in the meeting, what were their problems and difficulties. It was an apprenticeship in loco.

In my case, I had to learn to be able to transmit. In this way, my first phase [as a teacher] was a study phase, and it was a done every day.

I could learn things that I could not learn during my studies in Portugal. I also needed to be able to better translate, to translate the knowledge, the information that was in the PAIGC's school manual. That was the thing.

I had never been a teacher, but at the end I became a teacher, so to say. I learned to be. [...] We had a history book. It was not the colonial history, not the history that we learned [in my school years]. It was not about Vasco da Gama, Dom Afonso Henriques and the Portuguese independence or about Dom Sebastião. It was more something that had to do with our African reality. A new vision of what were the *guerras de pacificação*.[238] [Learn] what happened, how did it happened, [learn about] the people's resistance, the resistance of the people of Guinea Bissau to the colonial presence, which culminated in the process of the liberation struggle, that congregated different groups, and created the conditions for an armed opposition against colonialism. The geography was more focused on Africa, it was a geography that had more to do with knowledge about the civilizations, but that had an emphasis on the African continent, because about the African continent hardly was known. We [teachers] knew better about the Portuguese railways because in our time we had to know them by heart from Portugal, Angola, Mozambique, we were also forced to know every river and all the affluent. Our education [during the liberation struggle] had nothing to do with that. It was centred on Africa.[239]

In 1988 Henry Giroux coined the term of teachers as "transformative intellectuals," meaning that teachers possessed the knowledge the skills and the attitudes to question, understand and interrogate and eventually even act as agents of change.[240] A result of the liberation struggle and emerging from the acquired experience in the Party schools, the militant teacher could be characterized also as a "transformative intellectual", and a militant combatant engaged in the struggle for independence and liberation - whose task was not only to teach the basic skills of reading and writing but to consciously train and politically educate the future generation that would lead the country to liberation.

---

238 To demonstrate Portuguese "effective occupation" of the Guinean territory, whose borders were defined in the Berlin Conference, the Portuguese colonial government developed a brutal 'pacification' campaign against the Guinean people, between 1913 and 1936. The period is know to today in the Portuguese historiography as *'guerras de pacificação'*, meaning pacification war.

239 Interview with Agnelo Augusto Regala, June 5, 2014

240 Henry Giroux, Teachers as intellectuals: toward a critical pedagogy of learning (London: Bergin&Garvey, 1988).

In this process, it was the teacher responsibility to develop the pedagogy, the material and emotional conditions that would lead to the principles and goals designed by the Party.

1.5 The militant teacher and the elaboration of the school manuals

Talking to the PAIGC militants, Amílcar Cabral approached some of the elements that should be part of the teaching materials as well the pedagogy that should be adopted, and these should be grounded in scientific knowledge and should incorporate contents dedicated to the Party and the liberation struggle, to critically exclude from the material everything that perpetuated the colonial ideology:

> Our culture in the school or outside the school we must put in the service of the resistance, in the service of the accomplishment of the Party Program. It must be like that, comrades. Our culture must be developed at the national level of our land. But without despising the culture of the others and with intelligence taking advantage of other people's culture, everything that is good for us, everything that can be adapted to our life conditions. Our culture must be developed with a scientific base. It must be scientific, so to say, not believe in imaginary things. […] Of course, in our schools we have to exclude everything that it was done by the colonialist and that show the mentality of the colonialist. We started doing it already, editing new books that speak about our Party, our struggle, our land, the present and the future of our people, the rights of our people. There are comrades who think that we should not talk about our Party while teaching. What a fairy-tale! The pedagogy that wants that is not a pedagogy at all. For us pedagogy is what we teach our children about the struggle, the rights of our people, the Party, the anthem of our Party, the value of our Party, besides the A, B, C, D, the Cat and the Fox, the wolf and Chibinho, etc., but the Party must be present; the Party organization, the Party leaders; the strength of our struggle, the strength of our people, the strength of our Party, the duties of people. In my school time, teachers would teach about the birth of Jesus Christ, of Virgin Mary that had a son even being a virgin, and I would repeat that, and even seem that I understand that in that time. The miracle of the ascension adapted in the books of that time, the miracles, as the Roses miracles, and so on. Why in that time we would teach the miracles to children, and we cannot teach these great miracles of our land: men and women who unite to mobilize our people for the struggle, to end the suffering, the misery, the disgrace, the slaps or kicks, forced work, etc.?[241]

As a pedagogic resource and a mirror of the ideals of the liberation struggle, the militant teachers were responsible for developing the school manuals that would be part of the PAIGC education universe. Until the publication in 1966 of

---

241 Amílcar Cabral, *Análise de alguns tipos de resistência* (Bolama: Imprensa nacional, 1979), 85–100.

the first school manual, PAIGC teachers had to work with colonial manuals or other material, such as the spelling manual João de Deus, from which the student would learn the alphabet. During this alphabetization process, teachers had a double task. Apart from teaching the alphabet, it was also their work to critically interpret the message that the Portuguese books transmitted and reformulate the message in a way that it could be part of the student universe. Therefore, the school manuals were developed in a way that reflected the student and the liberation struggle, as Corsino Tolentino recalled:

> We wanted something different and in some cases contrary (to Portuguese teachings). We wanted right equality between all the citizens, and we wanted sovereignty, we didn't want that feigned thing that we belonged to the empire from "Minho to Timor." We want just to be Guinea Bissau, just Cape Verde, Angola, Mozambique, etc. And therefore we had the obligation to change the image of the discourse there where it was indispensable [...] In those years, the PAIGC organization, with their objectives, the minor and the major program, etc., was situated in the context of the African struggle for liberation and against colonialism and against all that weight of the past of slavery and exportation, etc. [...] so we recover the images of human figures, from the past, or from the 50's or from the African empires of some African regions and all the mystique. That dynamic, those set of texts and images, tended to replace that image organized and hierarchical empire based on racist theories.[242]

Between 1966 and 1974, PAIGC developed four school manuals from the first to the fourth grade (see Fig. 7), and four other manuals for the fifth to the sixth grade. These included one manual of general African history, one manual focused on the history of Guinea Bissau and Cape Verde, one manual on political lessons, and finally a translation of "The Pre-Capitalist formation" by D. Mitropolski (see Fig. 8). PAIGC school manuals were elaborated collectively, where teachers and other militants worked together. Maria da Luz Boal recalled some episodes how the meetings and discussions went during the elaboration of the manuals:

> I became director the *Escola Piloto*, in 1969. It was Cabral who nominated me. Before I would go there [to *Escola Piloto*], but the director was Domingos Brito. We would go there, talked and worked with him during the vacation period, and we would help in the Teachers Improvement Centre, and we would discuss the necessity of elaborating the school manuals. There was also an extraordinary comrade, Amália Fonseca, who also had a great sensibility for education. We would go to Conakry, do the teachers training and see the needs and we would return to Senegal [because she was also in Senegal], and we would research concerning material (information) for the elaboration of the school manual. We consulted the books that we had in Senegal, and from there

---

242 Interview with Corsino Tolentino, August 21, 2013.

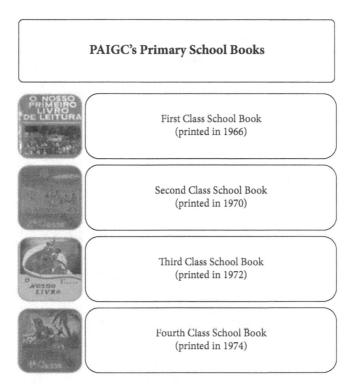

Fig. 7. PAIGC's primary school manuals. Source: own elaboration based on the conducted interviews and PAIG's schoolbooks

we would discuss and tried to adapt those methods and content to the reality of our country. It was an extremely interesting work. We would research school manuals, especially those from France because we had more access in Senegal. Sometimes we would buy some others that seemed to have interest for us. And there we had the study of the language, mathematics, history. But if there were French History, we would substitute with the history of Guinea and Cape Verde. If it were French, we would introduce the Portuguese and at the same time Creole; it was a kind of bilingual teaching. Consulting other school manuals, we would create the school curriculum – Math, physics, universal technical and scientific knowledge. And returning to Conakry with this information, in *Escola Piloto*, we would sit in a classroom, and we would inform others about the results of our research and what we thought about it. The others would give their opinions and based on that we would create and write the texts. Texts that later would be evaluated by other comrades. Before we sent the text to print, we would give them to Cabral. After that, we got the support from Sweden for the printing of the books. I and the comrade Amália Fonseca went to Sweden to do the text correction. [...] The

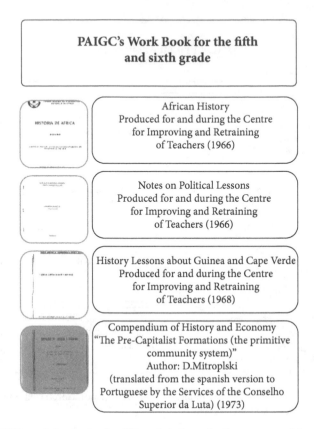

Fig. 8. PAIGC's work books for the fifth and sixth grade. Source: own elaboration based on the conducted interviews and PAIGC's archive material

production of the school books was phased. First, we did the first class and then the others, but always adapted to our reality. That for me was the greatest value of those books, especially the reading. (concerning the book illustration) - There was always a discussion, we were not always in agreement (with the illustration) for the reading texts. Because the theme was based on the struggle, [Tino the illustrator] would draw war wounded, bombings. And we thought that the manuals should have more soft images. We would argue with him, and he would not say anything, and at the heat of the discussion we would think we had convinced him –"well we convinced him." But the next day he would present the drawing as he wanted, so you can find in the books war wounded being transported in a hospital gurney. [...] For everything we had done a study because we had never done that work, it was new for us. And that was really a pleasure. Sometimes we would work just with manuscripts. I remember one time, we have done the meeting in the Conakry Lyceum, and me and Maia [Amália Fonseca], stayed in the same room. In the middle of the night, we felt that it was raining heavily, and our instinct was to get up and run to grab the school manuals so they could not get wet. The rain was so heavy that when we stood, we violently hit each other's head, just in the eagerness to protect the school manuals. This is just to show how important that work t was for us.[243]

Apart from the first school manual that was typewritten and circulated in PAIGC schools, in 1966, the Party published the first color school manual "*O nosso primeiro livro de leitura*",[244] through its department – *Secretariado, Informação, Cultura e Formação de Quadros do Comité Central do PAIGC*.[245] This was followed by a provisional black and white edition of the school manual for the second class. In 1968-1969, with the support of the Swedish government led by the Social Democratic Party of Olof Palme, as well with the support of student organizations like the Swedish African Group and the Democratic Youth League that together launched the campaign "ABC for PAIGC", funds were raised for the printing of more editions of the school manual from first to fourth grade.

After being analyzed in partnership with the Swedish psychologist and pedagogues, the school manual was printed in Uppsala by the printing house - Wretmans Boytryckeri. Ana Maria Cabral, who went to Sweden to follow the printing of the school manual, recalled her experience with the education professionals who analyzed the material:

I was the first to take the school manual to Sweden. When I arrived, I was welcomed by psychologists and pedagogues. I got mad when they said 'How do you people want to educate your children, and already in the first book you had so many color tonalities. That will mess the children head. You see, you have here one kind of red, and here you have other kinds of red.'
But it was the ink, and the gouaches that we got in Conakry, in Dakar from several brands and each one had a different tone. They wanted me to do all those drawings

---

243 Interview with Maria da Luz Boal, September 2, 2013.

244 See Annex 15 "PAIGC's official information about the publication of the school manual for the first class", at the annexes section (not translated).

245 Translation: "Secretariat, Information, Culture and Cadres Train of the PAIGC Central Committee". In what concerns to other support to PAIGC's received in the terms education, in 1968 some support from the WCC (World Council of Churches) although its unknown the grant. In 1972, UNESCO Through the United Nations Development Projects funds granted to PAIGC's *Instituto Amizade* a grant of non-specific value that according to PAIGC's made possible the publication of school book of the fourth class and Mathematics manual for the second class.

again, to which I replied, 'But I cannot do that because it was not even me who drew them. You are the specialists. To us it was something that it didn't cross our minds.'

They argued again, 'But you had done these drawings for yourselves, not for the children. The children cannot see so many colors in the book, they need to be integrated slowly, slowly, and each color must have only one tone.'

They wanted to send the material back, but at the end they made the colors balance, and when I returned I explained that to my colleagues.

And the manuals arrived, and it was the first time that the students received the coloured books,[246] because before everything was black and white. For the more advanced classes, we had to print them with our mimeograph machines that the Soviets offered us.[247]

In total, nearly forty-six thousand school manuals were printed for the first and second grade. The school manuals for the third and fourth grade were also printed in Uppsala, however there it was not possible to find any record of the number of copies that were made.

1.6 The militant teacher and the armed militant.
The school curriculum for adults

Political training was obligatory in every struggle fronts, and it was highly defended by Amílcar Cabral as the following excerpt reveals:

> We have to fight with political consciousness in the head. We must be conscious that is the consciousness of man that guides the gun and not the gun that guides consciousness. The gun is valuable because there is a man behind her, clinging to her. And it is worth as much as the conscience of the man, and much more when this conscience serves a just, well-defined and clear cause.[248]

Besides the teachers training course, PAIGC developed a second center for adult training namely the *Centro de Instrução Política e Militar de Madina do Boé - CIPM*. Inspired by the Cuban military training model, the center was created in 1966 by the commander Pedro Verona Pires, who in previous years received military training in Cuba. The purpose of the creation of the Center was the training

---

246 Although I could not confirm, I believe that Ana Maria Cabral, refers to the reception of book on some areas, because according to the printing date PAIGC's first manual dated from 1969 were already printed in colour. The black and white manual that Ana Maria Cabral refers, the only copy that I found during the research in different countries, was in the personal documentation of Birgitta Dahl, in Uppsala.

247 Interview with Ana Maria Cabral, September 5, 2013.

248 Amílcar Lopes Cabral 1979, p. 13–14.

of military for the armed struggle. Following PAIGC directives it was important that their military had a political consciousness of the struggle, which means to know the reasons why the struggle was happening and what the expected outcomes were.[249] Therefore, political lessons about colonialism and the principles and goals of the liberation struggle were an integral part of the training (see Photo 18).

Due to the high illiteracy rate in Guinea Bissau, the center also promoted literacy classes for their military. The importance of teaching reading and writing skills was a crucial aspect in the military, not only because those skills were necessary so that the military could be able to read the Party political propaganda, but also because the same skills were required for the development of the military logistics, preparation of attacks, for communication between fronts and the Party headquarters, and for the reading and understanding of military coordinates and technology.

The *Centro de Instrução Política e Militar de Madina do Boé* - CIPM instruction curriculum *Programa para a formação do soldado FARP,*[250] had a total of one hundred eighty hours, during a thirty days period. Sixty hours of the total training were dedicated to 'political preparation' which according to the course description should:

[E]nsure that the fighters know the history of our Party, our homeland, as well as the history of the National liberation struggle, learning the cornerstones of PAIGC Program and fundamental political notions. [...] In addition, the fighters daily receive a total of two hours of cultural preparation, which makes a total of 60 hours of the course, in

---

249 As a continuation of this political and ideological work, PAIGC created in 1968 the *Brigadas de Trabalho Político* (Brigades for Political Work), reorganized in 1970 under the name *Brigadas de Acção Política* (Brigades for Political Action). Described in its Statutes from 1971, "as an instrument of the *Comité National das Regiões Libertadas* (National Committee of the Liberated Regions), the main work of the Brigades was strengthening the political work of the party [...] strengthening and development of the political consciousness of the militants, combatants and populations, the explanation and the popularization of the watchwords and other directives of the Party in all fields of our activity [having as] materials for the realization of its function (Party documents, newsletters, press releases, photographs and other audio-visual media) that are provided by the party leadership. [their work should be] among the people." in document: PAIGC, Para a reorganização e a melhoria do trabalho das Brigadas de Acção Política (PAIGC:1971), 1–6.

250 Translation: Training program for the FARP soldier.

Photo 18. PAIGC's adult class in the liberated area in Guinea Bissau. Source: Nordic Africa Institute - Knut Andreassen.

The photo portrays an adult class in the liberated areas (possibly the CIPM). The classroom, constructed with the traditional raw material used in the construction of shelters and houses in the bush in Guinea, is somehow a strange element in this environment due to the arrangement of the classroom, which sharply contrasts with the constellation already presented in photo 1 on page 58. Here a hierarchy dominates, it is represented with the teacher standing in front of the class, transmitting knowledge, and the rather passive attitude of the sitting students who 'receive' the message. The blackboard is the intermediary in this hierarchical relation. The circle and the equality that the photo 1 transmits no longer exist here. Another element important to notice here are the military clothes that symbolize the transition from militants to the political militant soldier. The interviews conducted with Commander Agnelo Dantas in Cape Verde and Ana Maria Cabral in Cape Verde (2013) provided us with some examples of soldiers who learned to read and write during the struggle using PAIGC's school manuals, Cabral speeches, but also lost books, texts and newspaper that were found after the seizure of Portuguese barracks. PAIGC stressed the importance of military people learning how to read and write, also for the purpose of recognizing and selecting important military material found in the Portuguese barracks.

which we should be able to at least give a reading base to those fighters who are illiterate. The combatant preparation must be carried from the level of the man with less cultural preparation and should go from the easy to the difficult, from the simple to the complex.[251]

251 PAIGC, Escola para a formação de combatentes (PAIGC: n.d), 1–2.

The center's political curriculum can be divided into seven sections (see Tab. 6). The first section was dedicated to the history and Party ideology -principles and program, where issues such as colonialism and oppression, and the history of PAIGC and programs were approached. Here, is important to note the presence of socialist and Leninist concepts such as criticism and self-criticism, democratic centralism and revolutionary democracy, which reveal the political influences that the Party received from other ideologies and how it intended to adapt them to the Guinean context.

The second section was dedicated to international issues. The purpose here was to contextualize the PAIGC liberation struggle in the broader context of struggles that were happening around the world and to establish the links between them, therefore the presence of international themes such the decolonization struggle in Africa, Asia and Latin America; the Cold War and imperialism; or the anti-colonial organization around the world which might have included the non-aligned movement.

The third section had its focus on the sociological and ethnographic aspects of the present and future of Guinea Bissau. From this section, is important to highlight the focus on religion, tribalism, and racism. The reason why these issues were important was the strong influence that the religious leaders combined with military religious beliefs could create situations that could jeopardize the struggle's development.

The last section of the program was focused on the training for the militant civic behaviour of the militant military. This included gender equality rights, as well the expected behaviour between the combatants and their discipline and organization.

In addition to this program, the Party developed a range of media information, newpapers for adults, such as *Jornal Libertação*, or the international newspaper *PAIGC Actualités*. They also developed a youth magazine – *Blufo. Orgão dos Pineiros do Partido*, that was widely read by adults. Cabral's transribed speeches and his writtings were used and teaching materials (see Fig. 9). The Party also founded the *Rádio Libertação*, a radio station with that daily broadcasted the news about the struggle, which also contributed to the PAIGC adult education program.

1.7 From adult to pupils education. The education of the Party Pioneer

In 1966, simultaneously with the inauguration of the boarding school *Escola Piloto*, PAIGC created the youth organization *Pioneiros do Partido*[252] (see

---

252 Meaning The Party Pionners.

Tab. 6. CIPM political education curriculum

Study area	Content
History and Party ideology - principles and program	▪ The exploitation of our people by the Portuguese colonial government and its consequences; ▪ How they create oppression and exploitation; ▪ Differentiation between Portuguese colonialism and the Portuguese people; ▪ The necessity to struggle for the liberation of our countries; ▪ History of PAIGC (Mobilization, the beginning of the armed struggle and its development, difficulties and actual situation, the party as the legitimate representative of the nation); ▪ Party program ▪ Party principles (criticism and self-criticism; collective leadership; revolutionary democracy; democratic centralism) ▪ Some of the struggle's weaknesses
International Issues	▪ Africa and our struggle (our allies and enemies) ▪ African Unity; ▪ The contemporary liberation struggle and decolonization (Portuguese colonies; South Africa, South Vietnam; Latin America); ▪ The Cold War and the imperialism (Imperialism; Socialism; the third world and the liberation struggle against imperialism); ▪ The need of fraternal collaborations with other nations; ▪ The help of the socialist countries; ▪ Anti-colonial organizations; around the world;
Sociology and Ethnography	▪ The world's technical and scientific achievements; ▪ Organization, work, and planning methods; ▪ Economy (national reconstruction, need of industrial and handicraft development, collective property, private property, agriculture and modernization, social assistance, economic independence, and neo-colonialism); ▪ Religion (God, *Iran*, *Djambacosos*); ▪ The importance of protecting the unity of the nation; ▪ Condemnation of Racism and tribalism;
Militant Civic behavior	▪ Who is the Party combatant; ▪ What are the right behaviors of a militant with his comrades; ▪ Discipline and organization; ▪ The relation between the combatants (comradeship and discipline); ▪ The relationship between the combatants and the people; ▪ The relationship between the combatants and the *responsáveis*; ▪ The emancipation of woman as a sign of liberty, justice, and progress; ▪ The duty to respect the hymn, the flag, the emblem and the leaders of the Party; ▪ Explanation of the fighter oath;

Source: own elaboration based on PAIGC's Programa Escola para Formação de combatentes 1971. For a complete program, please consult the Annex 12 "CIPM curriculum. School training of Combatants" and Annex 13 "School for the training of Combatants" in the annex section.

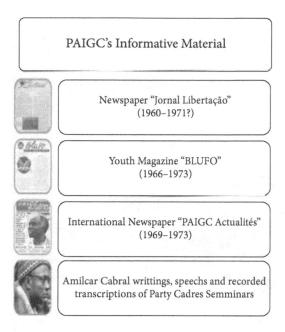

Fig. 9. PAIGC's informative material used for teacher's political information actualization. Source: own elaboration based on the conducted interviews and PAIGC's diverse published magazines and newspapers

Photo 19). The goals behind the creation of what was defined as an "organization of vanguard" for students between the ages of 10 and 15 years old who had concluded the first year of primary education, according to their statutes - *Estatutos do Pioneiro do Partido*,[253] were to contribute to a good education for children, based and acting on the principles of the Party. Other goals included the reinforcement of the children's love for the Guinean and Cape Verdean people, their dedication to the struggle, respect for the family and schools, and the student "fondness for justice, work, progress, and liberty."[254]

These goals and the activities designed around these key words, had the aim of making all members of this youth organization "worthy militants" of the Party and "conscious citizens" with great responsibilities in the future construction of

253 Statutes of the Party Pioneers. See Annex 14 "Statute of the Party Pioneer" in the annexes section.
254 Ibid.

Photo 19. PAIGC's Party Pioneers in Moscow 1973. Source: Teresa Araújo personal archive Cabo Verde 2013

In the photo above, you see the Party Pioneers, July 1973, an image taken at the exit of the hotel where they were staying in Moscow. The visit came as an invitation of the Soviet Union Delegation (the Army National Orchestra) after their presentation in the International Festival of Youth and Students in Berlin. Dressed in rigor, with the Pioneers' uniform inspired in the last verses of the Party anthem, their grey trousers and skirts, symbolizing the morning dawns, announcing the new day, the blue shirt, symbol of the blue sky clear of clouds, and the yellow kerchief representing the sun complemented with the traditional *Sumbia* hats, they walked together, proudly holding their bags with a joyful face, a self-confident posture. The picture represents the achievement of PAIGC's goal of transformation of their students (boys and girls), confident and proud of their identity, and ready to assume the national reconstruction of their country. Source: Luís Cabral, *Crónica da libertação*, 257.

the country and the "uncompromising defense of the conquest of the revolution."[255] It was under the slogan "Education – Work – Struggle" and the salutation "By the PAIGC, strength, light, and guidance for our nation,"[256] that the Party

---

255 Ibid.
256 Ibid.

started to train what it would consider to be "the best sons" of the nation, namely the pioneer and militant student.

Considered the future vanguard of the struggle, the Pioneers characteristic included the love for "justice, work, progress and freedom"; to be a good student that seek to be better through the every day activities, disciplined, responsible and organized and "a good friend of his comrades [that] seeks friendship every day with all the children of his school, of his land and of the world."[257] Besides work to become a good student, other tasks of the Pioneer, militant student included to "discuss everything that concerns [the] struggle, [the] school and [the] land. They should meet with parents, ... leaders, officials, militants, fighters, foreign friends and all those who are interested in Pioneer work. They should organize sports competitions, drawing, games competitions, singing, handwork, etc., both with school students and with other Pioneers."[258]

The developed curriculum for the education of the for pupils comprised several courses that ranged from math, Portuguese (as language), gymnastics, artistic education, geography, science, cooking, theater, choir, etc., represented on as Fig. 10.

From the curriculum program, is important to highlight the 'militant education' course for the first and second school grade, and the 'political education' to pupils from the third to the sixth grade. These two courses, corresponded to the core of the PAIGC militant education. The lectures are a combination of history, geography, sociology and Party ideology and organization, as one can understand from its program described in Tab. 7 "Teaching Program for the schools in the liberated region".

Strongly inspired by the Party political and ideological orientation, and as a product of the world circumstances at the time, the PAIGC curriculum for the courses "militant" and "political" education reveals an emphasis on political themes from the period when it was developed. The complexity and diversity of the subjects can be extracted from the above table, with themes ranging from the Party history and its administrative structure, and organizations, to the international issues of the liberation movements in other African territories colonized by Portugal such as Angola and the MPLA movement, Mozambique and the FRELIMO movement, São Tomé and Príncipe and the CLST movement, and the international organization that combined all these movements the CONCP. Other international themes included socialist revolution, the Great War, the

---

257 PAIGC, O nosso livro 4ª classe (Uppsala: Wretmans Boytryckeri AB, n.d), 20.
258 Ibid. 20.

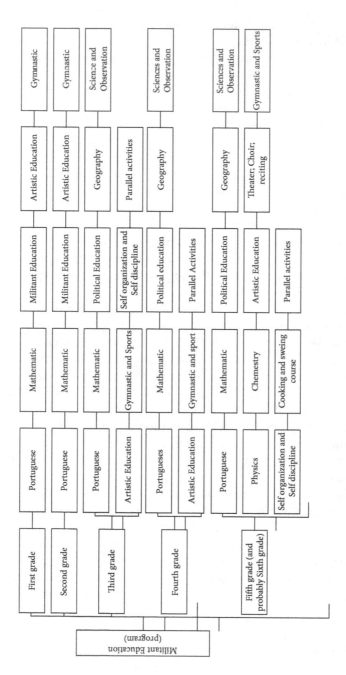

Fig. 10. Militant education. Distribution of PAIGC's school disciplines by school class year. Source: own elaboration based on PAIGC's curriculum documents "*Programa de ensino para as escolas das regiões libertadas*" and "*Programa de ensino 1° à 4° classe*" both with no reference of year date

Rome conference, etc., were also approached in the lecture. The question that emerges from such an extensive curriculum is how teachers were able to transmit this dense information to school pupils in a pedagogic and understandable way.

The writing of school texts was central for transmission of the ideas defined in the school curriculum. From the first to the second grade, the teachers who were entrusted to develop the school manual developed a great diversity of school lessons transforming the liberation struggle of daily life, politics and ideology into short stories. From the first to the fourth grade, lessons included titles such as "The major program of our Party" revealing the Party principles for first grade pupils, or "The great patriot" approaching the theme of the militant combatant for second graders, or "The past or our people" and "Centuries of pain and hope" concerning the history of Portuguese colonialism for third grade pupils, and "The poem of one militant" and "The objectives of our struggle" for fourth grade pupils, are some examples of how political and ideological themes were adapted to school texts (see Tab. 8).

Political and ideological themes were intertwined with other texts that expressed the liberation struggle goals. These themes were about the geography and social life and organization of the territories where the struggle for liberation was taking place, with special emphasis in Guinea and Cape Verde. Here text titles such as "The life in the tabanca"; "The professions" reveals the local social structure and organization, is intertwined the Party organization such as "The Friendship Institute." There was also a special and scientific focus in explaining the pupils about the natural elements and events that occurred in nature, with lessons approaching themes like "The sea"; "The marvels of nature"; "The richness of the vegetable world" (see Tab. 8).

The goal was to explain and demystify natural phenomena to pupils, but at the same time be very careful not to put in question the students' religious beliefs. Another goal to introduce themes about nature was too provide pupils with knowledge of how one could use natural resources in a sustainable form for the country's development. To complement the political and militant curriculum a set of stories were developed, as well as the incorporation of fables with the intent to explore human and militant civic behaviors.

1.8 The school manual: messages in the lessons

As a document that represents the educational practice of PAIGC's as well as the experience, and the practices of the liberation struggle, PAIGC's school manuals as pedagogic materials provide a great source for understanding how the liberation struggle principles and program were transmitted to pupils through texts

Tab. 7. "Teaching Program for the schools in the liberated region"

	Militant Education	Political Education
First Class	▪ Topics about our struggle and our lives; ▪ The love for our fatherland, to the Party, our leaders; ▪ The Hymn of our fatherland;	
Second Class	▪ Topics about our struggle, our lives, and our environment. Tales with moral and patriotic background; ▪ The comradeship, discipline, moral courage; ▪ The love of the fatherland, our Party, our leaders; ▪ Important dates that have to be memorized by the students; ▪ The foundation of our Party; ▪ The massacre of Pidjiguiti; the day of the women; the day of the children; ▪ Portuguese Africa; the movements of liberation (P.A.I.G.C.; M.P.L.A.; F.R.E.L.I.M.O. - C.O.N.C.P.); ▪ Guinea and Cape Verde: the unity of the people of Guinea and the Cape Verde within our Party; ▪ Singing: The Hymn of the Party – the International Hymn.;	
Third Class	▪ Introduction: notion of history - its importance - its purpose; ▪ Exemplary figures of national history - the heroes of our people: ▪ Amílcar Cabral: the man and his work ▪ Domingos Ramos: the patriotic sense of his life; ▪ Aerolino Lopes Cruz: founder of the first school Party; ▪ Titina Silá: example of dignity of women of our land; ▪ Vitorino Costa: the martyr; ▪ Osvaldo Vieira: one of the initiators of the armed struggle; ▪ Pansau Na Isna: its role in the Battle of Komo;	▪ Constitution of the Party Pioneers; ▪ Creation of the organization of the Pioneers- structure, and goals; ▪ Conditions for being a pioneer. The group: its formation and activities; ▪ Fundamental notions of our Party: the constitution, its goals; ▪ The achievements; its constitution; its goals; ▪ The achievements of the Party: Friendship; (The Escola Piloto, The Kindergarten; the Boarding school);

- The schools of our liberated areas. Center for Improvement of teachers. Seminars. SEP[a]. Introduction of the constitution of the Party-program.

- testimonies Na N'ttuge: the role of women in the liberation struggle;
- Simão Mendes: health responsibility during the struggle;
- Madna na Isna: a revolutionary example;
- Key members of the government;
The symbols of our country: the flag; the national anthem and the head of state;

Fourth Class	

- Africa before the colonizers: The great African Empires;
- The origin of colonization of the Portuguese in Africa, Guinea, and Cape Verde. Slave trade;
- The resistance Struggle: Portuguese military occupation: Reasons of why it was possible; colonial economy. Racism. The Origin of the current struggle of national Liberation;
- The socialist Revolution in October 1917: the anti-colonial movement in Portugal and in the colonies. The Great War and the syndicalist struggle in Africa.
- The first Independences;
- The foundation of our Party; Studies of some fundamental points of the Party-Program;
- The Party Principles. History: Period from 1956 to 1959, from '59 to '61 and from '63 to Cassacá Congress; from 1964 until today;
- Our struggle for uniting our people in Guinea and Cape Verde;
- Our struggle and the struggle of the other Portuguese colonies – MPLA, FRELIMO, CLST and the CONCP;
- Our struggle and Africa;
- The UN and the Portuguese colonies;
- Our struggle and the working class in the world;
- The achievements of our Party in political- social and cultural manners.

- The duty of improving the usual work techniques as a way to obtain higher yields;
- Basic idea of regional and national life regarding the respective authorities and their functions
- The authorities' hierarchy
- The great achievements of the Party for the training of the youth: - Friendship Institute; schools in the liberated areas; teachers improvement center, seminars, SEP. Youth JAAC- Juventude Africana Amílcar Cabral (latter in 1973 JAAC- Juventude Africana Amílcar Cabral)[b]
- The role of youth in the liberation struggle and the construction progress of our land, need for young people prepare themselves to continue the great work of national reconstruction. Love (respect) for work and for the workers. The Youth as a guarantee of the future of our people.
- The exploitation of our people by the Portuguese colonialists
- Oppression. What is exploitation, oppression? The Portuguese people do not want exploitation of our people. The distinction between the Portuguese people and the Portuguese colonialism. The condemnation of the Portuguese colonialist crimes by all peoples of the world. Our people and our friends
6. The help of our people to freedom and progress. What progress is? Need to struggle to keep the freedom and progress of our people.

(continued on next page)

Tab. 7. Continued

Militant Education	Political Education
Fifth Class	▪ The history of the people of Guinea and Cape Verde; ▪ Notions of social structure of the Fulani, Mandingos, and the reading; ▪ Studies about the colonial society in Guinea and Cape Verde.; ▪ The history of our people and our struggle; ▪ Studies of diverse types of resistance; ▪ Detailed studies about the Party-program. The U.N.T.G (*União Nacional de Trabalhadores Guineenses*)ᶜ its formation and goals; ▪ The realities of our Party and the goals of our struggle, ▪ The national and international liberation struggle; ▪ Our struggle as expression of our culture; ▪ Our culture as contribution to the development of the African culture; ▪ Our Party in Africa and in the world; ▪ Our struggle as a contribution to peace in the world; International conferences. The Rome conference; ▪ Support of the people in Portuguese Colonies;

ᵃ Meaning *Secção dos Estudantes do Partido –SEP* (Branch of the Students of the Party). The *Secção dos Estudantes do Partido –SEP* founded in Moscow on September 2, 1962, was a youth organization of PAIGC students studying abroad, located in different countries. This organization should meet locally every month to study and discuss the Party directives; the students school success, problems, and needs. The gathering of this information should be them reported to the Party headquarters by the group's responsible person. Every year PAIGC students from *Secção dos Estudantes do Partido –SEP* and different countries should organize an international meeting between the students studying abroad. The organization of this meeting (such as time, day, place and logistics) was decided internally by the student's commission after the arty approval.

ᵇ Meaning: African Youth Amílcar Cabral (JAAC).

ᶜ Translation: National Union of Guinean Workers.

Source: Based on PAIGC's document "Programa do ensino para as escolas das regiões libertadas" and the PAIGC's Programa de ensino from first to fourth grade

Tab. 8. PAIGC's school manual content from first to fourth class

	1) Militant and Political Education (Political and ideological History)	2) Militant and Political Education (geography, social and political organization)	3) Militant and Political Education (evocation and commemoration of people and important events achieve during the struggle)	4) Militant and Political Education (civic education – Body and behaviors)
First grade "Our First reading book."	■ The old N'bunde goes to school; ■ Kalungo ■ *Morés* ■ The major program of our Party; ■ Our Party ■ Congratulations, dear Student.	■ The Fruits ■ Brinsan's Mother; ■ Fishing; ■ The donkey; ■ The animals; ■ My *Tabanca*; ■ The family ■ The *mancarra*; ■ The dangerous animals; ■ The professions; ■ The lack of rain; ■ Let's light the fire; ■ The week. The month. ■ The year; ■ Travels; ■ The sea; ■ The doors.	■ The liberation of Komo;	■ The class; ■ Little *Kondé* goes to school; ■ The truth; ■ The games; ■ Hygiene; ■ The human body; ■ The tooth.
Second grade "Our second class book"	■ *Bandêra di Strêla Negro* (The flag with the black star); ■ The great Patriot; ■ Let's learn this song: Africa;	■ Our school; ■ In the playground; ■ *Morés*; ■ The life in the tabanca; ■ The Pioneers; ■ Aliu, the fisherman;	■ The woman's day; ■ Comrade Amílcar Cabral. General secretary of the Party.	■ The first school day; ■ In the classroom; ■ The little chicken goes to school; ■ What Brinsan's does during the day;

(continued or: next page)

Tab. 8. Continued

	1) Militant and Political Education (Political and ideological History)	2) Militant and Political Education (geography, social and political organization)	3) Militant and Political Education (evocation and commemoration of people and important events achieve during the struggle)	4) Militant and Political Education (civic education – Body and behaviors)
Third grade "Our Book"	• *Lala Quema* (Burn land) • *Aviso* (The Advice); • The past of our people and we; • Ended the night, the dawn has dawned; • The other people who struggle against Portuguese colonialism; • When the wolf colonized the animal republic;	• The mothers work; • The domestic animals; • The savage animals; • Brinsan's family; • The African boy; • The professions; • The history of a plant; • Our land; • The Friendship Institute; • The marvels nature; • Lai discovers the sea; • The rivers and the bank; • The forest is our friend; • The richness of the vegetable world; • The animal kingdom; • house construction; • Bissau; • The cinema session; • The first cosmonaut;	• "This is our beloved land." The party anthem, the anthem of our people; • The best son of our people (Amílcar Cabral); • Comrade Amílcar Cabral;	• Let's play: let's learn how to say very quickly • Our body; • Neatness; • The wolf returns to hunt; • We should not lie; • Guess, Guess, but guess it right; • The elephant, the turtle, and the snake; • Give me your hand comrade; • The new school year; • Neatness; • Be clean and organized; • Food hygiene; • The vitamins; • Football in the school; • Healthy body, healthy spirit; • The medical inspection; • The Doctor sees the patient; • The Party pharmacy; • *Maria ka ta cuda, Maria komporta* (Maria is not careful, Maria need to behave)

Fourth grade "Our Book"	The poem of one Militant Why do we love our fatherland; The long Way The hour arrived; *Hora dja Tchiga* (The hour arrived); How the armed struggle started; It's necessary to plant The famines in Cape Verde; Departure for the *Contracto* (to St. Tome and Principe); The best friend of the children of Guinea and Cape Verde; The objectives of our struggle; The major programme of our Party.	The Cape-Verdean Islands; *Baía do Porto Grande* (São Vicente island); The work; The sea; The lion; The water drop; The discovery of the fire; The house; The plants; *Batuko* (Capeverdean traditional dance). *	The people's Hero (Domingos Ramos and others comrades); The women (March 8th); The *Komo* Battle; The Worker day (May 1st)	The water comfort; The electricity; The media The hare and the wolf; Our people; The weapons of our people; *O lobo e o chibinho;*	To speak; To read; To write; An exemplary girl; The turtle's bet; The hare and the jaguar; The lazy bee; The hare and the turtle; ** All children of the world must love each other; Negligence; The bet; Hygiene. The Party Pioneers;

Source: own elaboration based on text titles from PAIGC school manuals from first to fourth grade and images. To illustrate some aspects of how PAIGC's liberation struggle was taught and described in school manual lessons, a selection of texts and image were chosen with the aim to illustrate some of the aspects of PAIGC's militant and political education.

Written for third-grade pupils, the following texts "Our People" and "The weapon of our people" were written with the goal to transmit to pupils about the ideals of the struggle, its process, and outcomes.

Our people

Our people are and always will be our greatest richness. The people the all over the world love Justice and Liberty, they know and admire the struggle of the People of Guinea and Cape Verde. Our people, under the direction of our Party, proved its great capacity to build a new life in our land, after we had conquered freedom with weapons in hand.

The power of the guns is great, but the power of the Man is even greater. And the power of the men and women is enormous!

The great victory of our People is that they understand that unity is a strength and that diversity is a richness. We say diversity when one people are formed by different races, each one with its culture, each one with its experience.

We will seize each others' experiences, we will learn with each other and, in this way, our people will increase their knowledge and their experiences. And the richer experience a People has, more capable they will be to develop his land.

And our people must rise each day higher on the strength of its unity, in the richness of its diversity, to open new paths, wide and bright. Paths of Peace and Progress.[259]

The weapon of our people

Our people have modern and powerful weapons, weapons that serve to expel the colonialists from our land and to defend the conquests of our struggle.

But the P.A.I.G.C. Combatants, well trained and well-armed, are above all politicized. We are armed militants. Politics is also a great weapon.

Today and tomorrow, the work of our People is our main strength. To build progress in our land, it is necessary to have productive weapons. The hoe, with which our people work the land, and all work instruments, are weapons that give us the guarantees for the development of our land, and the well-being of all.

Our People, at the same time we conquer our freedom and our dignity, struggle against ignorance. The book is our weapon. By giving the People the weapon of knowledge, the Party opened a big door to the children of our land. This door will take us to the marvelous world of science and technology.[260]

Celebration and valorization of Guinean richness and diversity, the embracement of local forms of knowledge and experience is the message in the core of

---

259 PAIGC, *O nosso livro 3ª classe* (Sweden: Tofters Tryckeri AB, 1974), 115–116.
260 Ibid., 117.

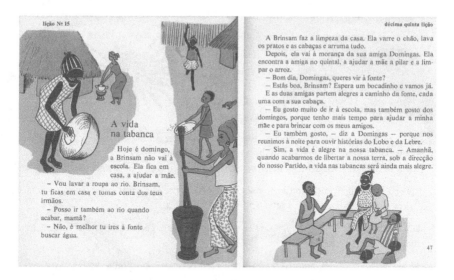

Photo 20. PAIGC school manual lesson for second graders. Source: PAIGC, O nosso livro 2ª classe (Uppsala: Wretmans Boytryckeri AB, 1970), 46–47.

the first text. Throughout the text, terms like 'justice', 'liberty', 'freedom', 'peace and progress' are the political messages that PAIGC transmitted all along the liberation struggle, and now also present in school manuals. From both texts, is clear the importance placed on people and their power. By people here, the text is referring to the general oppressed population of Guinea Bissau. The people in the general sense of the word being them well trained and well politicized, they would become the main "weapon" of the liberation struggle. Instruments like the hoe as a representation of the working group, or the book as a representation of the intellectual work are presented in the text as equivalent knowledge artifacts of the struggle. With this message, PAIGC equalized the role of physical and intellectual work during the process of liberation and national reconstruction.

Teachers and militants who contributed for the elaboration of school manuals recalled from their school manual experience during their education under the Portuguese educational system, the complete absence in a positive and dignified form, of images and daily activities that they could relate with. The text "Life in the Tabanca" (Photo 20) combined with images portraying some of the daily activities is not only a reaction to the colonial school manuals but is also a sign of the Africanization and representation of Africans and their daily activities with a positive image, giving students the opportunity to relate themselves with the lessons and images.

Life in the Tabanca

Today its Sunday, and Brinsan is not going to school. She stays at home, helping her mother.

- I am going to wash the clothes in the river. Brinsan, you stay at home and take care or your siblings.
- Can I also go to the river when I finish mom?
- No, it's better if you go to fountain get water.

Brinsan cleans the house. She sweeps the floor, washes the dishes and the calabashes and arranges all. After that, she goes to the *morança*[261] of her friend Domingas. She finds her friend in the house yard, helping her mother to pound and clean the rice.

- Good morning, Domingas, do you want to come to the fountain?
- How are you Brinsan, wait a little, and we go in a minute?

And the two friends leave happy on the way the fountain, each of them carrying their calabashes on their heads.

- I like to go to school, but I like the Sundays too because I have more time to help my mother and to play with my friends.
- I like it too, says Domingas – because we gather at night to hear the stories of the wolf and the hare.
- Yes, life is happy in our *tabanca*. Tomorrow when we free our land, under the direction of our Party, life in the *tabanca* will be much happier.[262]

Although living in the context of war, and images reflecting this reality are not absent of the school manual (see Photos 21 and 22), the above text, this text transmit the message of freedom, happiness and hope, having in the background the implicit concept of unity and collective resistance, being the tabanca the space where this resistance took place.

One of PAIGC's struggles within the liberation struggle was the fight against the fears and suprestitions that surrounded knowledges about natural phenomena. In a round talk with teachers and others militants in the liberated area, Amílcar Cabral spoke about the struggle against the superstitions disseminated by religious leaders and practices. In the meeting, Cabral spoke about the dangers of superstitions and the work that needed to be done in order to combat this form of "ignorance", emphasizing the role of teachers in this process:

Comrades, to tell you the truth, I am very pleased we are gathering this year in Boé. Comrade teachers, maybe some of you might doubt your real contribution to the

---

261 Translation: Group of houses of a family household.
262 PAIGC, *O nosso livro 2ª classe* (Uppsala: Wretmans Boytryckeri AB, 1970), 46–47.

lição Nº 23

Um grande patriota

Vocabulário:

um patriota é alguém que ama muito a sua terra, a sua pátria e que luta por ela.

— Mamã, hoje o professor falou-nos muito do Domingos Ramos. Parecia que eu estava a vê-lo a gritar para os combatentes.
— Fogo! Vamos avançar, camaradas!

74

Photo 21. PAIGC School manual lesson n. 23 with the title "The great patriot". Source: PAIGC, O nosso livro 2ª classe (Uppsala: Wretmans Boytryckeri AB, 1970), 74.

liberation of the land. But those who doubt still fail to understand our struggle, or our life, or our party. Weapons are not sufficient to liberate a country. It is not only military or political work that frees a land. The greatest battle we must engage in is against ignorance. Only when men and women understand this can they overcome their fear. Fear of flooded and fast running river, fear of thunderstorms, fear of lightning, fear of thunderbolt, fear of the kapok tree, free of the dark path, fear of the Cobiana bushland, fear of Quinara bushland, fear of the fortune-tellers, fear of sorcerers, fear of healers, fear of spies, or the police, fear of any political leader, fear of men, fear of the forces that lie ahead. Only with a clear understanding is the man is able to lose these fears. As you know, our people lived too long in fear. The biggest liberation is to free our

lição Nº 27

O dia da mulher

Naquele dia, o professor entrou na aula e disse.

— Meninos, amanhã é o dia 8 de Março, dia das mulheres. Não há escola. Todos nós ficamos contentes com o feriado.

— Hoje, nós vamos falar do dia das mulheres. Estão de acôrdo? — perguntou o professor.

— Sim, sim — gritámos todos.

— Todos os anos, o dia 8 de Março é feriado porque é o dia das mulheres. Nós amamos as mulheres porque são as nossas mães, as nossas irmãs, as nossas esposas e as nossas companheiras de trabalho e de luta. Elas sacrifi-

88

Photo 22. PAIGC school manual Lesson n. 27 with the title "The woman day". Source: PAIGC, O nosso livro 2ª classe (Uppsala: Wretmans Boytryckeri AB, 1970), 46–47

people from fear. To liberate our people from fear, we must liberate them from ignorance. This is fundamental, comrades. That is why the teacher's work is the frontline of our struggle, the vanguard. Its outcomes might not be visible immediately, but it brings great consequences for the future of our land.[263]

Therefore, a school manual based on scientific information that could demystify the natural phenomena but that at the same time could incorporate traditional

263   Amilcar Cabral, Boé, 1967 exerpt from the film O regresso de Cabral, 1976.

knowledge was central to PAIGC educational program. The school manual lessons "The forest, our friend" and "The richness of the vegetable kingdom," are two of the examples that attempted to deconstruct and demystify superstitions and to lead the pupil and the country to the "marvellous world of science and technology."

The forest, our Friend

Not so long ago, you were the mysterious forest to our people, and our People were afraid of you.

The struggle came and, although feared, you offered to our People a natural shelter against the bombs. The people learned how to overcome the terrible fear they had of you, the People learned to love you.

Forest friend, forest our ally.

The day will come based on our study, based on the strength of our work. We will discover all your secrets, and you will not be mysterious anymore. Our people will look at you in a different way, with the new eyes that the struggle gave to them.

What will remain from the forest when the fear and the mystery completely disappear? What will remain the poetry of the forest?

And in the poetry of the forest, there will be no fear. There will be the beauty of the forest for the charming of our eyes, there will be the richness of the forest for the progress of our beloved land.[264]

The richness of the vegetable kingdom

In Guinea, there is huge forest, which is one of the richness of our land.

What can the trees of our forest offer us?

On the first place, timber: *in particular for gro*ups, *teca, pau-sangue, bissilon.*

The timber is good to build canoes, houses, and furniture that we use in our houses, schools and work places. Still this year, in the 3° class, you learned, or you will learn, that the paper is produced with the paper paste and that we obtain this from the forest.

Equally, we use the sap of some trees: palm wine is the sap from the palm tree. Rubber articles are fabricated with the sap of the rubber-tree.

The main medical plants, those that heal certain diseases, are the *buque*, the *macete*, the cola.

Another great richness; the *palmares*. The palm tree it's a tree of great utility. Do you know, that from the palm tree fruit we produce the palm oil for our food, but also from the *coconut* that gives an oil that is used in the soap industry.[265]

The forest in the animist tradition in Guinea Bissau represents the house of the ancestors' spirits and the other spiritual forces. It's the house of the *irã*. Without making any direct mention of religion and beliefs or going against it

---

264 PAIGC, *O nosso livro 3ª classe* (Sweden: Tofters Tryckeri AB, 1974), 64.
265 Ibid., 69.

in a pejorative way, the lessons approached this theme through the lens of the benefits that one could find in the forest, not just for the economic development, but also for health, by making use of the African traditional medicines. The demystification of forest might have another implicit message, which is the limitation of the power of spiritual, traditional figures the *Djambakus*, the *Baluberu* and the *Moro* (Islam).[266]

These religious figures were considered to be religious intermediaries between the *Iran spirits* which caused a great respect and fear in the population. To maintain their power and prestige these traditional figures installed in the population the fear ofthe liberation struggle particularly defending their practices as most of them were against the principles defended by the PAIGC.

1.9 Militant curriculum: between the ambitions, resources and tensions

PAIGC's militant and political education can be characterized as an anticolonial, decolonial and African-centered education in its objectives. Anticolonial in the sense that it aimed to dismantle the biased, hierarchical and oppressive educational system and practices inherited from Portuguese colonial education. Decolonial in the sense that critically it deconstructed and produced new knowledge, brought experiences of social life to school manuals and curriculum.[267]

PAIGC African-centered education has a special emphasis on teaching about colonialism and colonization, and the violent relations that emerged from its practices, but also to teach about the need for resistance against such practices. Its intentions were to teach about people's experiences, their past, present, and future and to integrated into the school curriculum their forms of knowledge from local communities. With these new variations of knowledge, it intended to cultivate in the learners a personal sense of obligation to oneself, one's peers and community.

The African-centeredness of the curriculum was approached through the presence of Africa and Africans as critical subjects. African-centeredness was defended by Amílcar Cabral already in 1949 when reporting on the agricultural situation of the Cape Verdean territory, arguing that to defend the land in the

---

266 Moema Parente Augel, *O desafio do escombro: nação, identidade e pós-colonialismo na literatura da Guiné Bissau* (Rio de Janeiro: Garamond Universitária, 2007).

267 Molefi Keti Asante, *The afrocentric idea* (Philadelphia: Temple Universty Press, 1998); George J, Sefa Dei, *Teaching Africa: Towards a Transgressive Pedagogy* (New York: Springer, 2010).

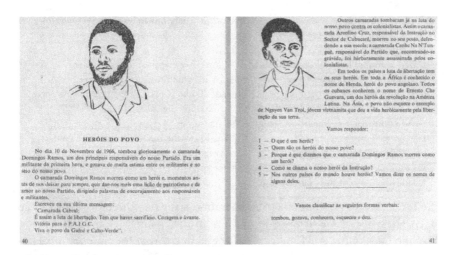

Photo 23. PAIGC school manual lesson with the title "Our people heroes".
Source: PAIGC, O nosso livro 4ª classe (Uppsala: Wretmans Boytryckeri AB,
n.d), 40–41.

sense of learning and understanding how to use and to consciously improve the
benefits and profits taken from the soil was also to defend the people, in the sense
to better their life conditions.

Despite these goals for education, PAIGC school program and school texts
were not completely achieved, namely in school manuals from first to third grade.
The absence of African history and culture in the school manuals is notorious.
The great focus on celebrating the struggle, its battles, and heroes, left almost
unexplored in the school manual themes related with traditional culture or local
history. One example of this aspect can be seen in a almost complete absence
of the diversity of social groups and their cultures, that existed in the territory
of Guinea Bissau. The school texts "The people's heroes" (Photo 23) written for
fourth-grade pupils is one of the examples.

The people's heroes
On November 10, 1966, Comrade Domingos Ramos fell gloriously, one of the main
people responsible for our Party. He was a militant of the first hour and enjoyed much
esteem among members and within our people.
Comrade Domingos Ramos died a hero and moments before leaving us forever wanted
to give us another lesson of patriotism and love for our party, addressing words of
encouragement to the leaders and militants.
He wrote in his last message:

"Comrade Cabral: so is the struggle for liberation. There has to be a sacrifice. Courage and onwards. Victory for P.A.I.G.C.

Long live the people of Guinea and Cape Verde."

Other comrades have fallen in the struggle of our people against the colonialists. So, the comrade Aerolino Lopes Cruz, responsible for instruction in the Cubucaré Sector he died at his post, defending his school; Comrade Canhe Na N'Tunguê responsible party who, being herself pregnant, was brutally murdered by the colonialists.

In all countries, the liberation struggle has its heroes. Across Africa is the name of Henda, well-known Angolan hero. All Cubans know the name Ernesto Che Guevara, one of the heroes of the revolution in Latin America. In Asia, the people do not forget the example of Ngunyen Van Troi, Vietnamese young man who gave his life heroically for the liberation of their land.[268]

The text refers to six figures of the liberation struggle. Three of them related to PAIGC's liberation struggle in Guinea Bissau, namely Domingos Ramos, Aerolino Lopes Cruz and Canhe In N'Tungue, and three other international figures, the Angolan hero Henda, Che Guevara in Latin America and Ngunyen Van Troi from Vietnam. Although PAIGC's objective is to show and encourage the links between the liberation struggles around the world, as it was already mention there is valorization of the military figures, that contrast with the almost absence of the local African figures.

The presence of military heroes in the school lessons is a tension often found in the school manual, which perhaps reveals the limitations to fulfill the PAIGC's proposal of Africanization – in the sense of a more broader perspective on history and the diversity of culture and social groups in the African continent. However is important to highlight PAIGC's reference to the role of the women in the liberation struggle by the figure of the Na N'Tunguê referring to her as a militant freedom fighter in an equivalent way as the male counterparts. By doing that, the school text brings to the discussion the role of women in the struggle and issues of women emancipation and gender equity.

Hygiene and cleanness were a very recurrent topic on PAIGC's curriculum and school manuals lessons. The text "Hygiene" and the reference to the issue one of the examples possible to find throughout the PAIGC school material.

Hygiene

All of us are born equal.

We have the same possibilities of living with health and die of old age. Unfortunately, there are some factors that can decrease these possibilities. One of those factors are diseases.

---

268 PAIGC, *O nosso livro 4ª classe* (Uppsala: Wretmans Boytryckeri AB, n.d), 40–41.

The health is a normal condition in all of us, but the disease it is an abnormal condition, an incident in our life.

Therefore, we have the duty to preserve our health, not only for our well-being but also in order to be able to produce and help build our country.

We must bathe every day, wash hands before eating, wash our clothes, combing hair, cut the nails and keep our house always clean.

We must avoid by all means the existence of places where mosquitoes and flies might appear. These insects are great transmitters of disease.

So, we should not spit or throw fruit peels, food scraps and papers on the floor.

It is so easy to put waste in a garbage can! And how good it is to be in a clean place!

In short, all the rules of hygiene should be followed carefully. The health of a home and healthy people are of great importance for the construction and life of a country.[269]

In the text the issues of hygiene and cleanness are linked with the themes of health care, society good manners, and development. The link between hygiene and health, alert the student about the dangers of poor hygiene can directly cause in a person's body. There is also a concern with the body presentation such as cloths, nails, and hair, but also with the social spaces such as the house. All these aspects are resumed in the text the last paragraph when linked with the country development. Despite the importance of the theme for the liberation struggle, the image that the theme represents and the almost extreme presence in the curriculum makes it almost impossible to dissociate it from the Portuguese colonial campaign for the civilization of the indigenous. Such concern of how one takes care of its hygiene, how to dress and act, can be interpreted as an inherited residue of the colonial education received by those who wrote the lesson.

Also important in the text is how PAIGC's starts the presentation of the theme, by referring the equality between all the human when they are born. The Party message can be interpreted as such "all men are born equal, but their future depends upon of people's attitudes during their life" which again raises the issue of responsibilities toward the collectivity and the community.

The use of Portuguese idiom – the colonizer language, as a writing and teaching language was the aspect from which PAIGC had been most criticized and its one of the most visible tensions on PAIGC practice of militant education.[270]

Due to the context of the liberation struggle PAIGC's had to take the difficult decision on what language to use in the school manuals and classrooms. The

---

269 PAIGC, *O nosso livro 4ª classe* (Uppsala: Wretmans Boytryckeri AB, n.d), 92.

270 Paulo Freire, *Cartas à Guiné Bissau. Registo de uma experiência em processo* (Lisboa. Moraes Editores, 1978); Paulo Freire and Sérgio Guimarães, *A África ensinando a gente. Angola, Guiné Bissau, São Tomé e Príncipe* (São Paulo: Paz e Terra, 2003).

Party opted for the pragmatic solution and adopted the Portuguese language, which was, in fact, the only common written language that most of the teachers knew. The Creole language although it was used, disseminated and even written during those years, was envisioned as a language to be developed after the struggle until it would be designated as country's official national language. However, this decision for the Portuguese idiom did not complete exclude local languages form the school environment as we will see more later.

The pragmatism of the decision to teach in Portuguese might also have another cause, namely the stronger possibilities of the groups that knew Portuguese well to prevail over all those groups to whom Portuguese was a foreign language. By giving access to Portuguese to all the population, PAIGC granted the principle of equality and the democratization of knowledge, "It's courageous political decision" in André Corsino Tolentino's words.

Nonetheless, critical Africanization, celebration of all cultures in and outside the country, demystification of the natural world through the application of scientific knowledge, the principles of non-discrimination and non-oppression, the valorization of the Party work and the meaning and ideals of liberation struggle, the political preparation of the future generation and their work and responsibilities towards the collective community in a independent country, although the tensions between the struggle ideals and the representations in the school books, are themes that constitute the core of the messages of PAIGC's school manuals, in their work to politically, conscious and emotionally prepare a political, conscious and responsible citizens that would be able to develop the country and active participate in the construction of the democratic, independent and liberated society.

1.10 The life inside and outside the classroom.
Being love in times of war

In *Teaching to Transgres: Education as practice of freedom*,[271] the educator bell hooks defined the work of teaching as a performative act. hooks described teachers, not as performers in the traditional use of the word in the spectacle world, but instead used the word performers to characterize the teacher as a "catalyst that calls everyone to become more engaged, to become more active participants in learning."[272]

---

271 bell hooks, *Teaching to transgress. Education as a practice of freedom* (New York. Routledge Taylor & Francis Group, 1994).
272 Ibid., 11.

Classrooms are the most common stage where the teacher and the teaching performance took place. It's the place where the process of becoming an teacher takes place. It's also the space of challenges, inventions, spontaneity, reconceptualization and the teaching of experiences.[273] During the liberation struggle, classrooms could also be perceived as a sharing space where emotions from teachers and pupils were in constant exchange, the liberation struggle being the common ground that linked both parts. In 1966, PAIGC documents described the responsibilities of the militant teacher:

> Therefore, teachers have responsibilities: 1) for the child he is teaching; 2) for the parents of the child; 3) for the country [...] The teacher needs to be very conscious of those responsibilities to fulfil his mission excellently. [...] the teacher needs to have this in mind. Being a teacher is difficult. It is not enough to know a lot of things, nor to study hard. It helps, but you will need vocation – a tendency, a preference to and manner to lead children to teach and educate them. [...] The teacher needs to be open-minded towards children. He has to live for/with them, figure out that certain way that is indispensable to educate children. This requires a bigger effort of the teachers, but we have to make it possible if we want to create a country capable of acting.[274]

War conflicts forced children and adults to live through traumatic and stressful experiences. Developed and integrated into the context of a guerrilla war, the PAIGC militant school was the stage where emotions and feelings like stress, anxiety, trauma, anger, fear, loss and death were part of the daily life and environment in the classroom (see Photo 24). All these inevitable sentiments were manifested from both sides – teachers and pupils. Lassana Seidi, who studied in the liberated areas and recalls the episode that marked his life as a student during the liberation struggle:

> I still remember the first time that I witnessed a bombardment in Morés. I confess that it was on that day that I felt, that understood what death was, and what it meant to die. I saw people dying, and I even got some shrapnel, and my sister too. I was seated in one place, and I saw many people dying, and a bomb exploded over our heads. There was a big tree, and we were hidden under a big tree. The airplane dropped a bomb and that fell on top of that tree with much smoke and all that. That was in 1964 if I'm not wrong. I was a child in that time, and it was then when I started to understand what the war really was. I saw people dying. People who minutes before I saw walking, doing their life, and in that day, they died around me. This scenario marked me a lot, even today almost fifty years later. It was my first day of the war, my first big trauma.[275]

---

273 bell hooks, *The pedagogy of hope* (New York: Routledge, 2003).
274 PAIGC, *Centro de aperfeiçoamento de professores* (Conakry: 1966), 1.
275 Interview with Lassana Seidi, June 3, 2014.

Photo 24. *Escola Piloto* view from inside a classroom. Source: Arquivo & Biblioteca Fundação Mário Soares Foundation. DAC- Amílcar Cabral Documents

The picture of a classroom in *Escola Piloto* represents an environment very different from the one in the liberated areas. Here we have a stable structure with blank walls, doors, and windows. The disposition of the classroom is the same. The teacher's desk is at the front and students are distributed in a row, following the regulation established in the Teacher Course. However, is important to emphasize three new elements. The first is the charts hanging on the walls, two of them about the human body, and a third one on the African continent. The second element is the teacher's civilian clothes, although it was also possible to find teachers with military clothes. This element also includes the way students are dressed, the shirt and the skirts or trousers represent a sort of ritual of passage from the liberated area to the *Escola Piloto*, revealing a new posture. The third element, is teacher's traditional hairstyle, that here symbolizes the full integration and affirmation of one´s African identity in the classroom.

Teachers could not ignore these aspects in the life of their students. It constantly happened, and therefore, it was necessary to teach pupils what was happening, why it was happening, and how this could be handled by the teacher community. Maria da Luz Boal recalled how teaching politics was part of the teaching performance as well as it contributing to the process of healing.

> Some [students] were orphans. Other the parents were on the war front. And it was difficult because sometimes one comrade would arrive with his backpack and say "I'm going to the country interior." He goes, but he does not return. And constantly we received the

news that the comrade went and stayed [died]. And so, there was this environment of living the struggle, and the will to be free. It was so strong that those kids would draw the airplanes, rifles, bombings. That was their world. [...] We were politicians in that situation, it was difficult not to be. A child who comes from the liberated areas, who hears the bombings, you have to explain why there were bombings about colonialism, that he didn't see but that he was feeling it. You had to explain why the people decide to fight to be free from the colonial oppression.... Politics was so evident, that they had to know and understand.[276]

But, if the classroom was a part of these healing process through the practices of militant education, the classroom was also a space of challenges, were the teacher and pupils developed and grow together as collective-individuals. Although the existent hierarchy and discipline that the Party wanted from teacher as well as students, it also desired the practices of love, respect and care between the two. Classrooms were also spaces where despite obligation, the practices of freedom was a constant presence, a space where everyone could learn and where education was a practice of freedom that enabled moments for transgression, moving beyond boundaries of a predefined curriculum.

Militant education was not merely a sharing of information from teachers to pupils. Paraphrasing bell hooks, education in the classroom was also the sharing of intellectual and spiritual growth, where the empowerment of students also meant the growth and the empowerment of the teacher in the process of learning-teaching.[277] The testimonies of teachers and pupils allow us to understand some of these intellectual and freedom dynamics in the classroom where all were parts of a collective of forces and where everybody was at the same time student and teacher.

Recovering the criticism on the use of the Portuguese idiom as a teaching language, mentioned already, the preference for this language did not invalidate, completely erase or forbid in the school environment the use of local languages. Actually, they were necessary for communication between the school community, and pupils did not always accept passively the use of Portuguese, which sometimes posed sometimes problems and challenges to the teacher. Ana Maria Cabral, who also taught Portuguese recalled one of the many episodes when she was confronted on this matter by her pupils:

The Portuguese class was very difficult for them. They hated it. None of them liked it. Because in the Portuguese lesson I had to explain to them the "r," like "R" from rua [street]

---

276 Interview with Maria da Luz Boal, September 13, 2013.
277 bell hooks, *Teaching to transgress. Education as a practice of freedom*. 1994; bell hooks, *Teaching Community. A pedagogy of hope*, 2003.

that should be read like "rr," and they would say "Oh teacher, that hurts my ears!" [...] The "lh" was also difficult, because there was the "h" and you have to read the "h," and they would say "Oh no teacher, Portuguese no!". And the students answered "Pamodi qui nu ka sa ta studa krioulo?" (why are we not studying Creole?). I spoke with Cabral about those situations, and he would answer, "if they understand that one of the influences, the roots of the Creole language is the Portuguese, you will see that it will be more easier for them." And then I discovered one book that was published in the nineteen century written by a priest about the Guinean Creole language. So, there it were some stories in Creole of Bissau, and Creole of Bolama which is different. And I took this book to my classes, and I wrote some phrases when I arrived. And it was my best class. They loved it. "Yes teacher, this is the way it should be." I gave them all the freedom that was possible, and we would discuss everything in the class.[278]

In the liberated areas where the diversity of languages was even greater. The teacher inability to speak most of the local languages meant pupils who could manage several languages became official translators in the classroom, and therefore second teachers of their peers. Faustino Pok recalled how he since his early age in school became the official translators in the class, translating between three languages, namely Manjaco, Creole and Portuguese:[279]

I, as the older student was chosen to do the translation of the lessons to other students, for those who were school beginners, in order for them to participate in the school, you have to know how to speak Creole. If he does not understand, then you would move to the local language to make him understand that 1+2 was equal to three. You would have to transfer this information to his own language so he could understand that 1 in Manjaco language is plóló, 2 is kedow, "ó qui u djunta plóló cu kedow, dava quajes" (when you join 1+2, it was equal to 3), that means it was 3. You would explain this with small sticks, in the desk, so he could follow the class. After two, three months he could follow, but in Creole, not in Portuguese, it was from Manjaco language to Creole, and then from Creole to Portuguese.[280]

Both testimonies of Ana Maria Cabral and Faustino Pok allows us to think how local languages were not completely excluded from the classroom, but integrated

---

278 Interview with Ana Maria Cabral, September 5, 2013.
279 About the learning of languages in Guinea Bissau and its problematics Ibrahima Diallo wrote two important studies in this area, namely, and the work of Ibrahima Diallo, *Em torno da problemática da língua de ensino*. (Bissau: Agencia Sueca para o Desenvolvimento Internacional (ASDI), 1996); and Ibrahima Diallo, *L' incidence des facteurs sociolinguistiques sur l' usage et l' apprentissage des langues en Guiné-Bissau-Une étude des classes expérimentales CEEF avec créole comme langue d'enseignement dans la région de Catio*, (Bissau: Agencia Sueca para o desenvolvimento Internacional (ASDI), 1995).
280 Interview with Faustino Pok, May 16, 2014.

into the teaching process. Such did not happen only in a verbal form in the classroom, but also was exemplified in the school manuals, through the introduction of a bilingual system with in the Cape Verdean/Guinean Creole and Portuguese. The incorporation of these idioms in the school manual were a clear official recognition and attempt of PAIGC in developing even during the struggle the project a bilingual education system.

Pupils attitudes and curiosities, challenged routines in the classrooms, and forced teachers to review their class program and make them conscious of other issues that somehow teachers omitted from school manuals, but that were part of the pupils daily life. Ana Maria Cabral recalled how some situations created by pupils inside and outside the classroom forced teachers to rethink other themes such as age, sexuality, and taboos in the liberation struggle and the integration of these for the development of militant education:

> One day they found some charts that were there in the school, and the rascals found the chart about the urinary tract. That day I was not supposed to teach that in the class, but the rascals hung the chart the wall. We had already studied the lungs and the heart, and before I went to the next lesson, I always like to repeat the lesson for two to three classes, because I wanted them to learn well. When I got in the classroom, and I saw the chart about the urinary tract, I thought, "Rascals! Well, it's better to leave it, since they put it there, we are going to study the urinary tract". And I ask them "who had hung the chart. That was not the lesson for today". And they replied, "Please teacher let's study this." So, I started and when I said the word 'Pee' they started to laugh. And I said "it does exist or not? You boys and girls don't have the necessity to urinate?" I used this word 'urinate' not 'pee' as the children would use. "It's part of the human body. There is no reason to be ashamed. So, let's discuss it." I presented the class, although I was not well prepared. But as everything was explained in the chart, I just had to follow and explain and answer their questions. The human body was a seven-headed hydra for them. But in my classes we would discuss everything; inclusively we started to introduce, although it was a difficult issue between the teachers, the sexual tract. I said that that was not a taboo. For example, there was a student that was always sick, so I went to the boys' room to see what his sickness was. He was honest and said, "teacher, I in the forest was already married, and here I'm forced...., well I have my problems." I said to him, "Well, I cannot help you much, but go and talk with professor Brito. He is a man, and he can give you better advice on that matter. Because here in the school you cannot solve this problem". They could flirt, some kisses here and there, but it could not go beyond that. In the boarding school it was not possible, although we knew that child development in Africa is different than in Europe. But I allowed these issues to be addressed, including girls and boys, I spoke about the pill and contraceptives. It was an issue that the Party organization had to deal with.[281]

---

281 Interview with Ana Maria Cabral, September 5, 2013.

The diversity of themes approached in this chapter are representative of the PAIGC militant education project. But they also reveal the several tensions that existed within such project and their struggles for a equilibrium between the idealized environment and the teaching, within a war situation in which these educational ideas and ideals were developed. Nonetheless, PAIGC's militant education was not a finished top-down project ready to be implanted. Instead, due to the complexities of the time it was an experimental process in development. Therefore, tensions and difficulties and inconsistencies or ambiguities between the written projects, its practices and the daily challenges, are factors that one needs to have in mind in order to understand the development and practice of educational projects within the context of the liberation struggle.

4 The conception of an educational structure after the independence. The Bissau meeting in 1978 and the perspectives for a pan-African education

> *This first meeting allowed us to know the experiences and projects of one another and realize that although the historical and social constraints of our diversity play out in one or another aspect, there is a remarkable convergence of guidelines and solutions to the problems that we face. We can without fear affirm that the project, in general, is common, applied to the specific case of each country. This means that people united by a common ideology and history always affirm the same principles of social liberation when their voices can finally express and create.*[282]

> *Marcus Arruda, 1978*

1 The extended militant school in Africa's liberated areas: the case of Angola and Mozambique

In the context of the liberation struggles against the Portuguese colonial structure, Guinea Bissau was not an isolated case. In 1961/1962 the MPLA in Angola and the FRELIMO in Mozambique began their respective liberation struggles for independence in their territories. Although economic interests and profits of Portuguese investments and cultural prejudices about the colonized territories played in favor of the development of more educational facilities in these territories, the colonial educational system and ideology in practice was very similar with the one practiced in Guinea Bissau.

With the beginning of the struggles, the development of educational facilities and school curriculum became central tenets of the liberation movements, and therefore as with PAIGC example, MPLA and FRELIMO also invested during the struggle in the development of education in their territories.

---

282 Marcus Arruda, "Uma educação criadora para as sociedades africanas independentes," *Economia e Socialismo- Revista mensal de economia política*, (1978): 29.

Starting with Angola, a summary of the statistics of education in Angola for the school-years of 1965/66 published by the Angolan Statistics Department, reveal that in that year the territory had enrolled in their 2 819 educational facilities (from primary school to teachers training for school-post and primary schools), approximately 255.690 pupils, with a total of 6.708 teachers. The primary education reform of 1964 that abolished the former adaptation schools and established a uniform primary school in the territory in practice did not fully integrate every pupil in school. The rural schools-post in the rural areas continued to apply for the Indigenous Statute and the school program and material. One example of the existent discrimination in school policies was the fact that "in January 1967, in Luso (Moxico district), children who already could speak Portuguese were not admitted to take the pre-primary exemption because they came from a different environment and therefore required to go through the pre-primary adaptation class."[283]

The Angolan liberation movement was aware of the need to develop educational infrastructures during the liberation struggle. There is not so much information on how exactly this was developed and what were the outcomes during the struggle, but the experience of education structure developed by the MPLA was partly documented by The International Youth & Student Movement for the United Nations – ISMUN, in their Nineteenth General Conference that took place in Sweden.

With the help of the Cuban government, the MPLA founded the *Centro de Instrução Revolucionária*,[284] located in the northern part of the territory in Dolisie region in Congo Brazzaville[285] and later also established near Cabinda.[286] The report describes the Center as including more than 200 militants men, women, and children, and it had three different programs, namely "primary level program, middle-level program and secondary level program. There was also a

---

283 UNSA. The educational systems of the liberation movements and the Portuguese in Angola, Mozambique, and Guinea-Bissau. A Report to ISMUS:S nineteenth general conference by UNSA of Sweden. (n.d), 9.

284 Translation: Revolutionary Instruction Center.

285 Paulo Freire and Sérgio Guimarães, A África ensinando a gente, 122.

286 Edward George, The Cuban intervention in Angola, 1965-1991. From Che Guevara to Guito Cuanavale (New York: Frank Cass, 2012), 28. See also, Christine Hatzky Kubaner in Angola. Süd-Süd-Kooperation und Bildungstransfer 1976-1991 (München: Oldenbourg Verlag, 2012).

teacher course which administers a literacy campaign and also teach at the primary level."[287]

The Center was organized around three different programs, namely, "the primary level, the militants are divided into three groups according to the degree of education they need: 1) literacy classes; 2) first and the second year of primary schooling; 3) third and the fourth year of primary schooling."[288] The primary classes took children up to 14 years old whereas the middle and secondary level programs were designed for adults. Very similar to PAIGC, the report mentions that the base for all the courses was focused on political and military knowledge. The political training was based on the MPLA liberation and independence program.

Colonial education in Mozambique was not different from those in Guinea or Angola. The Mozambique statistics concerning Portuguese education in the territory for the year 1965/66 report the existence of 473.004 pupils, distributed for 4730 schools, from primary to higher education, and the total of 8604 teachers. Following the same pattern of PAIGC and MPLA, the FRELIMO in Mozambique also developed their educational structure. The *Instituto Moçambique*[289] founded in 1963 with a grant from Ford Foundation, and with headquarters in Tanzania, Dar-es-Salaam was the institution that in cooperation with FRELIMO, coordinated the education structure. In 1968, the *Instituto Moçambique* fall under the head of the Department of Education of FRELIMO.

The original purpose of the *Instituto Moçambique* was, "to give supplementary education to the Mozambican youth who had a chance to getting scholarships from abroad, but did not yet have the educational background necessary to enable them to follow a program of higher education."[290]

In 1968 according to UNSA report, Frelimo launched six different courses:

1) Normal 4th class.
2) Normal primary education. These courses both have the same content: writing, reading, Portuguese, history of Mozambique (pre-colonial, colonial and that of the liberation movement), the political constitution of Mozambique (the colonial one and Frelimo's), mathematics, geography, and drawing.
3) Accelerated primary education. This course contains subjects as do 1. and 2., but is for adults and therefore has more intense teaching. It is primarily for those adults actively

---

287 UNSA. The educational systems of the liberation movements and the Portuguese in Angola, Mozambique, and Guinea-Bissau, 11.
288 Ibid.,11
289 Translation: Mozambique Institute.
290 Ibid., 16.

working with Frelimo, who need further education to be able to carry out their work within Frelimo in a satisfactory way. This point also contains the "Campaign against illiteracy program," a program aiming at teaching all Mozambicans how to read and write.

4) Teacher course. The contents are still the same, but in this course, the education is conducted on a considerably higher level. It also included some pedagogies.

5) Political course. These courses is primarily for those who work with political information within Frelimo. Contents: history of Mozambique (pre-colonial, colonial and that of Frelimo), the Portuguese colonial administrative and political structure, Frelimo's policy (i.e., what countries support and what countries counteract Frelimo).

6) Agricultural school.[291]

FRELIMO's educational programs were carried out mainly in Dar-es-Salam, where the party secondary school was located, providing an education that would enable students to study at university levels. The Institute, also worked with a diversity of other school programs, such as primary schooling located in the regions of Bagamoyo and Tunduru, Cabo Delagado, Niassa and Tete and the refugee camp in Rutumba, the literacy training in Mozambique and in various refugees centers in Tanzania, the administrative training three-month courses, where history, geography of Mozambique, basic economic concepts necessary to an independent nations, and simple accountancy was taught, and finally medical aid that the Institute supported through a clinic wherever there was an educational program.

In the year of 1969, the number of students enrolled in these educational programs was 23.220, from which 110 students were receiving education to become teachers. They also developed a literacy campaign that reached 7.000 people. In total around 275 teachers worked in this project.[292] Along with the Guinean case, Angola's and Mozambique's are two other examples of efforts and investment in education during the armed liberation struggle and the educational ideology and goals that these movements developed despite their very limited resources and difficulties in the terrain.

1.1 Guinea- Bissau: re-building education after independence

The PAIGC's self-proclamation of independence on September 24, 1973, signaled the achievement of one of the struggle's goal, which was the political and territorial independence. With the seizure of power in Bissau, all the PAIGC's

---

291 Ibid. p.16.
292 Ibid., 16–17.

structures located in the neighboring countries were transferred to Bissau. The students of boarding schools were transferred to Bolama and then distributed by the several schools within the territory.

In Bissau where the colonial educational system was in practice, the education curriculum and concepts developed in PAIGC-schools during the struggle clashed with the educational structures left by the Portuguese. The 1978 meeting report revealed some of the problem that the Party had to face in the education field after independence:

> "Children are the flowers of our struggle and the main reason of our combat", said Cabral. "Education is a right, and a duty of every citizen" affirms PAIGC. Stimulated by this slogan, immediately after independence tens of thousands of children and young people flow into schools seeking the instruction that the colonialists had always denied. In the four years following the full liberation, more than 50 thousand new students had access to school. This means that the approximately 45,000 enrolled in 1973/1974 rapidly went to over 100 thousand. This gigantic explosion of schools presents extremely difficult problems: how to immediately meet the pressure of the population who demand access to the masses to school and at the same time radically transform education to adapt it to the exigencies of building a new society? The lack of material resources, the lack of teachers and their insufficient qualification, the absence of programs and materials, all these difficulties do not allow us to extend nationwide the educational experiences in gestation in the liberated regions. To correspond to the population expectation and given to the need to quickly train technical cadres indispensable for national reconstruction, the only alternative is to run the school inherited from colonialism despite all its deformations, and gradually and safely transform them, having in mind the model of the school as a democratic center to exchange experiences.[293]

The difficulty of introducing in the daily life of the school a system where students could learn through the elements of their social environment and apply the newly acquired knowledge in the transformation of their surroundings was the most difficult reform to put into practice. The PAIGC's report to the III Congress postponed this reformulation for a future "second stage" of national reconstruction.[294] However, the results presented in the III PAIGC-Congress report, despite delaying the school deep transformation project, note that the PAIGC was able to put into practice between 1974-1978 some of the experiences of the militant schools, with the establishment of a new education system, where the rural and

---

293 PAIGC, *Educação tarefa de toda a sociedade*, 12.
294 Aristides Pereira, Relatório do C.S.L. ao III congresso do PAIGC (Mindelo: PAIGC, 1978).

the urban world interacted, and the school should be connected with Guinean socio-cultural reality.

After independence, PAIGC created new school structures, but it also adopted others some from the Portuguese colonial regime. The Party established kindergarten education with the institution named after the Mozambican Josina Machel (1945-1971), who had co-directed a residential education center for Mozambican students in Tanzania. A number of middle and high schools and *Internatos* (boarding schools) followed the same pattern of names in tribute to other figures from liberation struggle.[295] They clearly aimed at pursuing transformative goals that strongly resembled elements of socialist pedagogies with the "introduction of productive work in the school curriculum, [the valorization] of manual labor linked to theoretical teaching and practice, to enable students and teachers to overcome the distance between knowing and knowing-doing."[296] These last goals also included the participation of students in community service.

Institutions for technical and professional training were established. One example was the creation of the *Centro de Educação Popular Integrada - CEPI*,[297] an educational facility for adults, whose aim was:

> To respond to the challenge of ... education in rural areas [by] raising the level of political knowledge, science and scientific knowledge of rural populations, so they can improve their living conditions, increase production and productivity, and create a greater social and economic balance between the countryside and the city. In CEPI we combine the tasks of training teachers in theory and in pedagogical practice for primary education in the rural areas. This includes trying out new programs that meet the needs of the development of our farmers. Because what we want with the new school in the rural areas is to train open-minded peasants to experiment in all fields of life and the rural economy, so they could be able to permanently raise their technical level and incorporate innovations to their way of farming.[298]

As usual in these particular situations of establishing new policies, adult education was a central piece in the PAIGC's strategy. It was about the:

---

295 Within the tributes the Party created the National Lyceum Kwame N'Krumah; Regional Lyceum: Hoji Ya henda in Bafatá; Ho Chi Minh in Cantchungo; José Martí in Boloma; Escola Piloto in Bolama; Internato Fernando Cabral and Internato Tetina Silá in Bissalanca; Internato Saco Vaz in Pelundo; Internato Aerolino Lopes Cruz in Empada; Internato Osvaldo Vieira in Morés; Internato Domingos Ramos; Internato Abel Djassi in Boé; Internato Frantz Fanon em Bór; Internato de Morés.

296 PAIGC, *Educação tarefa de toda a sociedade*, 18–20.

297 Translation: Center for Popular Education.

298 *Ibid.*, 22.

mobilization of the population for literacy in Portuguese, in cultural circles. [...] Since Portuguese is a foreign language to the people and the possibilities of using it practically are non-existent, culture circles revealed a slow development in learning to read and write. In addition, some participants applied the concepts they learned in writing Portuguese to write Creole. This and other literacy experiences in rural settings led the people in charge of education to intensify the effort to make Creole a written language.[299]

One specific, but all-important segment of adult education concerned the training of teachers. The combatant teachers of the struggle period had to be systematically integrated into the new structures, which was part of the role of the *Centro de Capacitação e Recuperação de Professores Máximo Gorki*[300] in Có-Cacheu. The Center developed pedagogical methods with the perspective of developing a closer relationship between teachers and students, through the process of gathering historical testimonies to create a narrative collection archive. The principle behind this center was the fact that his defenders were:

> Convinced that the people are the unique and authentic creator of history the teachers-students collect testimonies. Stories and narratives that serve to reconstruct the history have to be collected [...] The narratives are registered in recorders and then submitted to a team of various groups of students and teachers to study the collected material and produce it in writing/written form. Finally, there is a seminar with the population where the document is discussed together, modified and approved in its final form. This collection of oral tradition gives the people the opportunity to 'write' their own history and, at the same time, allows students and professors to re-encounter their roots, and to rediscover African culture.[301]

One particular feature of the efforts in the post-independence years that show the strong international impact of the Guinean case was the participation of the educator Paulo Freire in the period after independence. Between 1975 and 1977, Freire together with his wife Elza Maia Oliveira, worked as an advisor for the education reform in Guinea-Bissau. The experience of the work in Guinea-Bissau was registered in a series of letters that Freire addressed to Mário Cabral, the person responsible for the *Comissariado de Estado da Educação Nacional.*[302]

The letters, published in 1978 under the title "Pedagogy in Process - The Letters to Guinea-Bissau," and "Amílcar Cabral. O pedagogo da revolução" (1985)[303], reveals how the knowledge that he gathered in conversation with

---

299 Ibid., 23.
300 Translation: Maximo Gorki teacher training Center.
301 PAIGC, *Educação tarefa de toda a sociedade*, 21.
302 Translation: National State Education Commissariat.
303 Freire, Paulo. *Amílcar Cabral. O Pedagogo da Revolução*. http://forumeja.org.br/files/amilcar.pdf (accessed November 18, 2016).

PAIGC militants about education during the liberation struggle, his experience and involvement in the PAIGC reconstruction of Guinea Bissau in the period between 1975-1978 as well as the educational initiatives developed in the territory during this period informed his thoughts and writings on liberation and education. A more intensive consideration of the cross-Atlantic entanglements of the leftist Latin American educational movements and the processes of decolonization in Africa is still a future direction of research. Freire's participation shows that the attraction of militant education as a concept developed by PAIGC's *in loco* in the terrirory were noticed and valorized by some political forces of the time.

1.2 Institutionalizing of pan-African militant education? The Bissau meeting in 1978

The establishment of an underground network of schools and educational facilities following the idea of a militant education took place in a very particular context, the pan-Africanism. In the 20th century, a series of transnational, yet not universalist movements like pan-Slavism, pan-Arabism, and pan-Africanism gained momentum and shaped political identities. Not all of them left significant traces in the field of education. Pan-Africanism seems to have been the movement with a particular impact – at least at the level of common goals and projects – on educational agendas.[304]

In its most direct version, pan-Africanism can be understood as a political project calling for the unification of all Africans into a single African state to which those in the African diaspora can return to their countries of origin. In its general and more cultural form, pan-Africanism has pursued literary and artistic projects that bring together people in Africa and those that were in diaspora.[305]

---

304 John Karefah Marah, "Educational adaptation and pan-Africanism: development trends in Africa." Journal of Black Studies, (1987):...., and Kenneth James King, Pan-Africanism and education: a study of race philanthropy and education in the southern states of America and East Africa (Oxford, Clarendon Press, 1971).

305 For more information on pan-Africanism, please consult the works of George Padmore, *History of the Pan-African Congress* (London: Hammersmith 1947); Hakim Adi and Marika Sherwood, *Pan-Africanism History: Political figures from Africa and the Diaspora since 1787.*(London: Routledge, 2003); Kwame Anthony Appiah, Appiah, *In my father's House: Africa in the Philosophy of Culture* (New York: Oxford university Press, 1992); Olisanwuche P. Esedebe, *Pan-Africanism: The idea and Movement, 1976-1963* (Washington D.C: Howard University Press, 1994), Ronald Walters, *Pan-Africanism in the African diaspora* (Detroit: Wayne State University Press, 1993) and

In the twentieth century, the African American W. E. B Du Bois organized the Pan-African Congress in 1919, to bring together Africans and leaders of nations involved in the African diaspora, and to promote the cause of African independence. The term was challenged at the end of the Second World War in particular by African intellectuals born in the continent such as Kwame Nkrumah of Ghana, Gamal Abdel Nasser of Egypt, or Haile Selassie from Ethiopia, appropriated the term and developed it further into a more geographical, nationalist and political idea of an African unity and identity, that gave origin to the Organization of African Unity - OUA founded on May 25, 1963.

The two primary aims of the organization were: 1) to promote the unity and solidarity, cohesion and cooperation among the people of Africa and African states and act as a collective voice of the African continent; 2) the eradication of all forms of colonialism, by defending the interest of the independent countries and helping those still colonized to pursue independence. Concerning education and colonialism, where Africans were largely left outside of decision-making concerning formal school education, on the continent as well in the diaspora, the emergence of liberation movements and independent countries enabled African countries to develop a pan-African approach to education. African voices started to emerge against colonial education,[306] defending a mass "political" and "African" education.[307] Joseph Ki-Zerbo, approached the issue of the need to for a curriculum reform while defending a decolonial Africanization of African school curriculum:

> Education is the very core of development in Africa. It is one of the main levers for speeding up its progress in all spheres: in the political sphere, by the institution of a minimum standard of education, without which democracy is a meaningless word; in the social and human sphere, because it develops man's awareness of his dignity and his powers of expression and creation and opens the way to freedom [...]; even in the economic sphere, since education is, in the long run, the most valuable of investments; in the international sphere, because it helps people to know about other peoples and therefore to appreciate their qualities. Education thus has a strategic position in the great

---

Imanuel Geiss, *The Pan-African Movement: A history of Pan-Africanism in America, Europe, and Africa*, (New York: Africana, 1974).

306 John Karefah Marah, Educational adaptation and pan-Africanism: development trends in Africa, 471–473.

307 Ahmed Sekou Touré, *África: ensino e revolução* (Lisboa: Via Editora, 1977) ; Kwame N'Krumah, *Africa must unite* (London: Panaf Books, 1998); and Kwame N'krumah *Neocolonialismo. Último estágio do imperialismo* (Rio de Janeiro: Civilização Brasileira, 1967) and Lema, Mbilinyi e Rajani (Julius Nyerere) 2004.

battle for progress. Now, if it is to fulfill its many functions satisfactorily, education in Africa must be African; that is, it must rest on a foundation of specifically African culture and be based on the special requirements of African progress in all fields. Africa's progress would undoubtedly demand less effort if the continent had not inherited the heavy burden of the past, so familiar to all, and did not suffer from that great handicap which can be overcome only by 1) "decolonizing" or "Africanizing" education; 2) adapting education to the situation in which an underdeveloped country that has to catch up with the rest of the world within a certain space of time finds itself. [...] African education of course involves a problem of quantity; but the problem of quality, relating to the content of education and the nature of the curriculum, is of more revolutionary significance in this context.[308]

The Guinea Bissau independence opened a new period for the prospects of militant education. Inspired by the results of a prior Conference of African States on the Development of Education in Africa that took place in Addis Ababa, 15-25 May 1961, ministers and educators from Angola, Cape Verde, Guinea-Bissau, Mozambique and São Tomé e Principe gathered in Bissau in February of 1978 for the first time, with the aim of share their educational experiences during the liberation struggle, and to think the future of education in each country based on previous experiences, and finally to define a common educational ground principles and program:

> [E]xistence of a common history, forged in the process of resistance and struggle against the same enemy; the existence of a common project, which aims at the complete sovereignty and economic, social, technological and cultural independence, the existence of several common problems inherited from colonial domination and, finally, the need, that in the specific context of the national reconstruction of each country, to redefine education (seeking) through critical debate and creative experimentation to train the people for the immense and urgent task of building new liberated societies.[309]

Their experience in education during the respective liberation struggles was clearly at the center of the discussion. However, they were significant as far as these could inform new lines of action after independence. Utopian aspects still prevailed such as the search of a common and "new education." The meeting was organized around four major themes and divided into four working

---

308 UNESCO, Conference of African states on the development of education. Final report 1961. (Adis Ababa: 1961) http://unesdoc.unesco.org/images/0007/000774/077416E. pdf (accessed May 12, 2016), 55.
309 Marcus Arruda, "Uma educação criadora para as sociedades africanas independentes", 20.

group1) Education and knowledge; 2) Education and economic development, 3) Education and social inequality; 4) Education and cultural identity.

From each workgroup, there was a list of recommendations that each country should adapt to their own realities. From the first group - **education and knowledge**- it is important to highlight four recommendations. First, the concern to develop the conditions for the progressive and effective inclusion of the school in the community, considering the introduction of the productive, socially work as an important element for the achievement of objectives. Second the creation of conditions for the rehabilitation of the work taking into account the important role that this plays in the connection between the theory and interdisciplinary practice. The third recommendation refers the importance in the curricular contents of the teachers training with aspects linked to political training, pedagogical and scientific training. The fourth aspect was related to the evaluation methods. Here the recommendation was to develop the conditions for the introduction in the evaluation of all the non-quantifiable elements that were linked with the pupil's personality so that the evaluation method could be systematic and continuous considering the pupils environment.[310]

The second workgroup – **education for the economic development** – in general, recommended that each country's educational structure must correspond to their development phase. Within the recommendations the group defended a progressive generalization of a primary and popular educational education that should be proportional to the human, material and economic resources of each state, taking into account the rural and urban specificity of each state. It also recommended that popular education should contemplate the following domains: politics, productive and sanitary conditions, the learning of reading, notions of calculus and management, overall culture as a support for the access to the advanced level of knowledge. To close, the main sectors of the national economy should be linked to the progressive reformulation of structures and programs of technical and professional training, adequate to the realities, resources, and objectives.[311]

The third group – **education and social inequality**, recommended as priority the population have access to education and the gradual extension of education, according to the developmental rhythm of each country. It also defended a radical transformation of the curriculum content in a way to adapt them to the national reality as a way to guarantee the country's cultural identity and

---

310 Ibid., 20-22.
311 Ibid., 22- 24.

to critically incorporate data of modern science, also including a new attitude towards works such that the work to become an essential component of learning, in sum through the method learning by doing.[312]

The last group – **education and cultural identity**, recommended a major attention to stimulate, research and incorporate into the educational structure of the positive values of the African culture. Among the proposed activities were the collection of data on dance, music, oral traditions, medical plants, and linguistic diversity. Here is important to highlight two important aspects, first the defense for an adoption of Portuguese as a foreign language, and second the development of strategies against the incursion of the capitalist ideology through the media and of models of production and consumption, as a way to safeguard the cultural identity and the country's independence.[313]

From the recommendations outcomes of the 1978 meetings, one can understand that some of the liberation struggles aims developed during the struggle continued to be part of the educational program after independence. Education continued to be seen as a political act and a central piece for the socio-economic development. The post-independence educational project continued to defend the need for political education, and defended of the Africanization of the school curriculum adapted to national reality and cultural identity of the country in a more systematic form. Linguistic diversity continued to be the one of main barriers that the educational structure had to face.[314]

However, from this meeting emerged a new concern about which direction education should move. Liberation struggle ideals were still present, and this meeting lets us understand an educational project more focused toward work and socio-economic development of the country. The relative emphasis on the economic development somehow obscured the importance of militant education developed during the struggle. However, such a change of direction is characteristic of transition states, whose education post-independence apart from being a legitimized mechanism that defended a fundamental connection among knowledge, social change and power, and deemed essential that everyone should be educated, gave a high priority to adult education. There was, therefore, a special need to focus on work trainings that allowed adults and young people to

---

312 Ibid., 24-26.
313 Ibid., 26-29.
314 Cleghorn, Ailie. "Language issues in African school setting: problems and prospects in Attaining Education for All." in Issues in African Education. Sociological perspectives, by Ailie Cleghorn and Ali A. Abdi, (New York: Palgrave Macmillan, 2005, 101–122).

enter the labor force with appropriate skills, in order to develop the recently independent country.[315]

Some of the meeting's outcomes such as the analyses of the struggle's results and the formulation of recommendations for the future of education were short-lived. From five participating countries in the 1978 meeting, only São Tomé e Principe and Cape Verde were able to maintain a reasonable political stability that would allow them to follow the recommendations for educational development. In 1977 Mozambique was plagued with a long and violent civil war between the opposition forces of anti-Communist Mozambican National Resistance -RENAMO rebel militias and the FRELIMO regime, that lasted until 1992. Although the Angola participated in the 1978 meeting, the country was living since independence in 1975 through political instability and power struggles between two major political movements, namely the MPLA and the National Union for the total Independence of Angola - UNITA. Eventually, the country was in a civil war with some interludes from 1975 to 2002.

In late 1980, the Guinea Bissau post-independence government was over-thrown by the Prime Minister and former forces commander João Bernardo Vieira, a situation that led the country to a great political instability and a civil war in 1998. The political instability that emerged from that period is still today present in the territory.

This political instability, as well as many other difficulties in the economic and therefore social sector, that these countries face daily, to which we may add the globalizing education politics that has been defended by the international program under the umbrella "Education for all", has thrown to the backstage of history the innovations developed by the liberation movements and their defense for the need of an African-centered curriculum. In this way PAIGC militant education, its history, practices, outcomes and the future of a possible development of a pan-African militant education in those territories in specific, and Africa, in general, are still worthy of examination today.

---

315 Joel Sammoff, Socialist education? Comparative Education Review, Vol 35, No. 1, Special Issue on Education and socialist (R)evolution (1991), 1–22.

Final considerations

> *Everywhere in the world education is the fundamental*
> *basis that underpins the work of emancipation of every*
> *human being, the consciousness of man, not according*
> *to the needs of every individual or class conveniences but*
> *in relation to the environment he lives, the needs of the*
> *community and the problems of the mankind. [...] Today,*
> *education aims at the goal of the full realization of man,*
> *without the use of races or origins, as being conscious*
> *and intelligent, useful and progressive, integrated into the*
> *world and its environment (geographic, economic and*
> *social) without any sort of subjection. For this reason*
> *and therefore the problem of education cannot be treated*
> *separately from the social-economic one, as a mere*
> *resultant of the turbulence or the licentiousness of the*
> *times.*[316]
>
> Amilcar Cabral, 1951

1 Liberation struggles and the PAIGC militant education 'for revolution'

In this book, liberation struggle (or liberation movements) is used as a general term to refer to a social and political phenomenon that I define as an individual-collective process-response of people who, becoming conscious of the racialization, dehumanization, oppression and exploitation through which they are subjugated under colonial-oppressive governments inside and outside their 'country', organize themselves to dismantle or destroy the institutions and practices to which they are subjugated, employing towards this end any means at their disposal, including violent acts (such as an armed guerrilla struggle) and nonviolent acts (such as strikes, educational projects and programs, or cultural and civil resistance, or any combination thereof).

The second half of the twentieth century was marked by the emergence of popular liberation movements throughout the world. In the African context besides the PAIGC, some of these African movements like the FRELIMo in

---

316 Amílcar Cabral, "A propósito da educação," Boletim de Propaganda e Informação, (1951): 24–25.

Mozambique and the MPLA in Angola were already explored in previous pages of this book. To these cases we may add the Tanzania's struggle for independence from the British government in 1950's and 1960's against; the South Africa liberation struggles against apartheid[317]; and the Zimbabwean liberation struggle (also known as the second *Chimurenga*) against the British during the 1960's and 1970's.[318] Such liberation struggle was not exclusive to the African continent. Other cases can be found in Asia: for example the chinese Cultural Revolution which took place in the 1960s and 1970s under the Mao Zedong regime. Across the Atlantic other liberation struggles were taking place, in including the Cuban revolution in the 1950s, the Black Panther Movement in the US of America between the 1960s and 1980s,[319] and the *Frente Sandinista de Liberación Nacional* happening in Nicaragua between the 1970s and 1990s.[320]

In all of these movements and their political actions, education wasa a common aspect in the struggle and an integral part of the liberation struggles tradition and their projects to develop a sustainable education for revolution. In his work from 1976 *Education for revolution: a study of revolutionary strategies, and leadership from three ideological perspectives,*[321] Maurice Geary clearly distinguishes between 'revolutionary education' and 'education for revolution'. The first is concerned "with new ways to achieve old goals, the old goal of the present political situation[…] that is not deliberately aimed to overthrowing

---

317 Mugomba T. Agrippah and Nyaggah Mougo. *Independence without freedom. The political economy of colonial education in Southern Africa* (Oxford: Clio Press, 1981) and Steve Biko, *I write what I like* (Johannesburg: Heinemann, 1987).

318 Fay. Chung, *Re-living the Second Chimurenga Memories from the Liberation Struggle in Zimbabwe* (Stockholm: Nordiska Afrikainstitutet, 2006).

319 Russel Rickford, *We are African people: Independent Education, Black power and Radical imagination* (New York: Oxford University Press, 2016), and Eldridge Cleaver,. "Education and revolution." The Black Scholar, Vol. 1 Issue no. 1, the culture of revolution (1969): 44–52.

320 Anthony Dewwes and Robert F. Arnove "Education in revolutionary Nicaragua, 1979-1990." Comparative Education Review, vol. 35, Issue no. 1, Special issue on education and socialist Revolution (1991): 92–109. For more information on pedagogies and education reforms around the world please consult the work of Asit Datta and Gregor Lang-Wojtasik, *Bildung zur Eigenständigkeit. Vergessene reformpädagogische Ansätze aus vier Kontinenten* (Frankfurt am Main: IKO- Verlag für Interkulturelle Kommunikation, 2002).

321 Maurice Geary, "Education for revolution: a study of revolutionary strategies, and leadership from three ideological perspectives." (PhD diss., Wayne State University of Detroit, 1976).

the present political economic system and replacing it with a new one that has nothing to do with the values, standards, laws, or government machinery."[322]

The second, "education for revolution," is described as being a permanent and continuous process of reflection and action that aims to organize political consciousness through the:

> development and a reconstruction of ourselves, our thinking and feeling, so that we become conscious of what is happening to us and why it is happening [...] a continuous process of reflection and action that is identical with revolution itself and precedes, accompanies, and follow the actual seizure of power one moment in the revolutionary process. This process of education for revolution leads to the organization of the politically conscious, and to wrenching away of political and economic power from the hands of the owners and managers of our society. [...] Education for revolution is an ongoing process of dialogue between revolutionary leaders and the masses of people from which they come from.[323]

In this book, the PAIGC liberation struggle and militant education shared ideals and practice of Maurice Geary concept of "education for revolution". Throughout this book, militant education as a concept and as a practice is approached from three angles. The first angle, which is explored in the opening chapter and previous to the liberation struugle, analyzes the conditions or circumstances of becominga militant and the first stage of the militant education process. This chapter reflects on the impact of Portuguese colonial education in Africa, and explores the role played by self-re-education in the process of consciousness-raising and militancy in the PAIGC as well as in African students' participation to the liberation struggle. The second angle, which is explored in the second chapter, presents the early accomplishments of the militancy and militant education in the liberation struggle, with the development of an educational structure in the liberated areas of Guinea Bissau and its neighboring countries. Through and analysis of statistical documents, this chapter reveals how PAIGC education efforts were supported by an extensive network in terms of scholarships from socialist countries to PAIGC students that allowed them ro continue their education abroad. The analysis lets us understand how limited the statistical data that survived to today are, in order to understand the accompllishments and extentsion of PAIGC educational efforts during the years of the armed struggle.

The third angle, that is, the praxis of PAIGC militant education, is explored in the third chapter. Here the focus is on the development of an educational

---

322 Ibid., iii.
323 Ibid., 9–157.

curriculum which aimed to train three groups, namely, civilian adults, the military and schoolchildren. This chapter describes the collective organization of schools, the production of the school materials, as well as the political education in the curriculum, school lessons and daily activities. This same chapter explores the tensions inside the militant education system, namely the conflicts between the ideals of the struggle and its actual conditions, as well as the residuals of colonial education received by its participants and their struggles to dismantle them.

The fourth chapter explores how other liberation struggles, such as those in Angola and Mozambique, developed their educational structure during their fight for independence. More importantly, this chapter explores how these liberation movements envisioned the future of education in their countries now independent, opting for a pan-African-centered education systems attentive to local particularities.

The PAIGC militant education emerged in a specific historical moment in the mid-twentieth century and was informed by political movements and ideologies of the time. The African liberation struggles and the anti-colonial and decolonial positions that inspired them; the pan-African movements and the African unity principle; the Cold War and the ideological blocs it created; the Non-Aligned movement and the international solidarity; and the period of armed conflict in the Guinean territory and the international human rights struggle of the liberation movement within the United Nations all deeply influenced the concept, practices, and organization of PAIGC militant education.

The term militant education is inextricably linked to the concepts political education, political freedom, and liberation rather than to the 'military', although disciplinary elements of the latter can be found. Militant education and militant school, as mentioned in chapter three, referes to a type of educational practice that is committed, engaged conscious and grounded on anti-colonial and decolonial principles. It is focused on an ample concept and goals of the liberation struggle. The aim is that pupils, civilian population and military militants receive a education that combined political teaching, technical training and the shaping of individual and collective behaviors, guided them toward the development of the *Self* as a liberated African citizen. The work of this liberated African was to give their conscious contribution to the sustainable development of the newly independent liberated country.

Despite the fact that the PAIGC's militant education existed only for a brief period and within a small territory, it is still an important part of the larger liberation struggle movement This book, forces us to leave the realm of the theoretical, that is, the political ideology and military aspects on which histories of liberation struggles are usually centered. Instead it abandons the romanticism that generally surrounds the theme, to focus on the more pragmatic realm of how the ideals of the struggle were put in practice in the daily life and how they were transmitted to the future generation. Along the way, it also attends to the individual struggles faced by militants during the process of the war. The practice of the militant education explores the liberation struggle as an " powerful instrument on information and political education."[324] It offers a great contribution on how one thinks the links between education, revolution, and liberation, to which the militant education curriculum is crucial for its understanding.

While the book provides useful explanations of political concepts and definitions related to PAIGC militant education, its primary focus is on the production of consciousness and the processes that lead to it. The PAIGC ideological program was the greatest source of inspiration for the militant education curriculum. Political education was the most important way to keep the Party ideology alive, as well as the only way to solidify the roots of independence in order to imagine and create the future.[325] Therefore ideology, education, and conscious politicization worked together in the PAIGC educational project, in a way that allowed me to reveal the liberation struggle as both a process and as an educational praxis in this book.

According to Jacques Depelchin, the actual periodization of African history, and therefore the history of education in Africa, only contributes for the creation of silences. The work, *Silences in African History. Between the syndromes of discovery and abolition*, Depelchin defends the importance of studying what he calls paradigmatic silences, i.e., "silences that are difficult to detect because they are framed in such a way that they evade critical theoretical questions [...] if one looks at the periodization of African history, and how the transitions from one period to another were made, it should be obvious who dictates the terms under which the transformations are carried out."[326] One of these silences lives around the collective and individual histories that fought against colonial oppression.

The present book on PAIGC militant education, give the authors of the liberation struggle the opportunity to break this silence and in this way to open the floor to this long silenced chronological period in the historiography, that I describe as being the long and continuous period of resistance and liberation

---

324 Amílcar Cabral. Unidade e Luta. A Arma da Teoria. (Lisboa: Seara Nova: , 1978, 247).

325 Benedict Anderson, *Imagined Communities. Reflections on the origin and spread of nationalism* (New York: Verso, 2006).

326 Jackes Depelchin, *Silences in African history. Between the syndromes of discovery and abolition*, xiii.

struggles against oppression, exploitation and dehumanization. The responsibility of documenting histories and experiences that had been silent and silenced for four decades was challenging but also enthusiastic in the writing of this book.

Nowadays, as social and student movements around the world are demanding the decolonization of schools curricula, manuals and teaching practices, studies of previous movements carried out in the name of liberation help us to better understand the future of education in Africa and beyond. This book makes its historical contribution exactly on this point, by providing a space for the voices and the experiences of people's resistances against oppression, exploring the use of education as an crucial tool for liberation, and by restoring the the rights and the dignity of the people as politically conscious and militant citizens.

Short biographies of PAIGC militants

Agnelo Augusto Regala Born in 1952 in Quitafene, Guinea Bissau,Agnelo Augusto Regala was the son of small-scale merchants. In 1959, at the age of seven, he traveled to Portugal to start his studies in Tomar at the *Colégio Nuno Alvares Tomar* (College Nuno Alvares Tomar), where he stayed until 1969. From there he went to Santarém to the *Colégio Brancamp Freire*. He continued his studies in economics in Lisbon at the *Instituto Superior de Ciências do Trabalho e da Empresa* -ISCTE (Superior Institute of Business and Labour Sciences) and attended the PAIGC's clandestine study groups in the city. In 1970, he secretly left Lisbon and travelled to Spain and lived briefly in Denmark,and Sweden, before settling in Guinea Conakry. In Conakry, he worked as a teacher of history and geography at the *Escola Piloto* and then as the broadcaster for the PAIGC's *Rádio Libertação* (Liberation Radio). He is the founder of today's *Rádio Bonbolom* and lives in Bissau.

Ana Maria de Foss Sá Cabral Born in 1940 in Canxungo, Guinea Bissau, Ana Maria de Foss de Sá Cabral, traveled with her parents to Angola-Uíge. There she studied in at boarding school in Luanda. After her father's assassination in 1955, the family traveled to Lisbon, where she continued her studies while working as at the *Caixa dos Operários Metalurgicos.*

In Lisbon, de Foss de Sá Cabral got in contact with the organizations of *Casa dos Estudantes do Império* and *Centro de Estudos Africanos*. In 1963, she traveled to Prague-Czechoslovakia, where she studied philosophy on a fellowship offered by the Czechoslovakian government to PAIGC militants. There she was the vice-president of the *União Geral dos Estudantes da África Negra sob Dominação Colonial Portuguesa* - UGEAN (The General Union of Students from Black Africa under Portuguese Colonial Domination). In 1966 she joined the PAIGC in Guinea Conakry, where she worked as a teacher at *Escola Piloto* during the years from 1966-1971. In May of the same year, she married Amílcar Lopes Cabral, PAIGC's General Secretary. Ana Maria Cabral was one of the persons responsible for the publication of PAIGC's youth magazine "*Blufo. Orgão dos Pioneiros do Partido*", and she also worked in the PAIGC's Department of Civil Registration in Conakry.

André Corsino Tolentino Born in 1946 on Santo Antão Island, Cape Verde. In Santo Antão André Corsino Tolentino completed his primary and preparatory studies in his home town before moving to São Vicente to complete secondary school. In 1966, he traveled to Portugal with a scholarship offer by the then Overseas Minister Adriano Moreira. In Portugal, he studied on a two-year course in public administration in the *Instituto de Ciências Sociais e Politicas da Universidade Técnica de Lisboa* (Higher Institute of Social and Political Sciences of the University of Lisbon). In 1968 under pressure from the political police, heobtained a passport authorization by bribing the Portuguese armed forces and subsequently left Portugal for Belgium. authorization.

There Corsino Tolentino studied at the Louvain University in Brussels and continued to participate in PAIGC's clandestine groups in the neighboring countries. In 1970, he received an official order from the PAIGC to travel to Conakry. Between the years 1970 and 1974, he worked for a short period at the *Escola Piloto* (Experimental school), received naval training on the Black Sea in Odessa, and also served as the Assistant Director of *Centro de Instrução Politica e Militar de Madina do Boé*. After the independence, he moved to Cape Verde, where he worked as a teacher and occupied several political positions. He has a master's degree from the University of Minnesota and a doctorade from University of Lisbon. Today he is retired and lives in Cape Verde.

Anselmo Cabral Born in 1945 in Bolama, Guinea Bissau. Anselmo Cabral was the son of a public employee. He completed primary and preparatory school in Bolama and arrived in Bissau in 1959 to continue his studies at the Lyceum. In 1962, mobilized by Rafael Barbosa, he joined the PAIGC and left Bissau to work in the liberated areas. In the liberated areas he was one of the founders and coordinators of the schools in the Morés region, and responsible for running the Morés boarding school and schools in the North of the territory. He also participated in the teacher's course in Conakry. After the independence he worked in several state departments, the most recent in the capacity of Director of the *Casa da Cultura* (House of Culture). Today he is retired and lives in Bissau.

Birgitta Dahl Birgitta Dahl was born in Råda – Sweden. She earned a B.A. at Uppsala University in 1960 and was one of the first students in the African Department there. During her studies, she was politically active in the Uppsala Student Union and the Social Democrat Party. In 1970, she traveled to Guinea-Bissau's liberated areas and was active in the efforts to mobilize of funds to support the PAIGC's struggle. Together with Knut Andreassen, she is the author of '*Guinea-Bissau: Rapport om ett Land och en Befrielserörelse*' (Guinea-Bissau: Report about a Country and a Liberation Movement), published by Prisma, Stockholm, 1971. Today she is retired and lives in Uppsala.

Braima Sambu Auó Born in 1957 in Guinea Bissau. Braima Sambu Auó, the son of Guinean farmers, integrated the first groups of students at *Escola Piloto*. In 1966, he was sent to Cuba, where he continued his studies at the *Escuela Maria del Mar*, where he graduated from secondary school. In 1973, he enrolled at the *Escuela Militar Camilo Cienfuegos* where he studied the tactical command of troops. In 1979, he returned to Guinea-Bissau, but due to the country's political and military situation, he decided to study history and sociology in Lisbon. Today he lives in Bissau, and he is writing a book about the country's history.

Califa Seidi Born in 1956 in Bambadinca, Guinea Bissau, Califa Seidi, the son of Guinean farmers, studied for a short period in the barrack school of Domingos Ramos. Later, he was sent to Conakry where he integrated the first group of students at the *Escola Piloto*. He continued his education in Belgrade, Yugoslavia, where he studied electrical engineering. Today he lives in Bissau, and he is the president of the *Fundação Guineense para o Desenvolvimento Industrial* -FUNDEI (Guinean Foundation for the Industrial Development).

Carlos Alberto Teixeira de Barros Born in 1947 in Bissau, Guinea Bissau, Carlos Alberto Barros was the son of public employees. He attended primary school first in Bissau and then, later in Portugal at the *Colégio Nuno Alvares (College Nuno Alvares)* in Tomar and Coimbra. He officially enlisted in the PAIGC in 1963, but had already been working for them in secret for some time before. He worked in the PAIGC's liberated areas as a teacher at the Campada school, and later at *Escola Teranga* as an art teacher. During this time, he also worked as a soldier in the war territory recognition groups. After the independence, Barros studied art and architecture in USSR and worked in Bissau in the public construction sector. Today he lives in Bissau and is a well-known plastic artists working under the pseudonym Carbar.

Faustino Luís Pok Born in 1957 in Cacheu, Guinea Bissau, Faustino Luís Pok attended the PAIGC's school in the Cobiane region in 1966,. At the age of 15 or 16 Faustino Luís Pok took part in the PAIGC's combat in Pelundo and Cachungo, as an equipment loader (ammunition). After the independence, with the sixth class made in PAIGC school during the liberation struggle, he attended the Merchant Marine course but also worked as a teacher in Bolama, Cachungo, Calequise. In 1984, Pok went to Lisbon to study Accounting. Today he lives and works in Bissau and handles the accounting services of the *Instituto Nacional de Estudos e Pesquisas da Guiné Bissau* –INEP (Guinea Bissau National Institute for Studies and Research).

Felinto Vaz Martins Born in 1934 in Empada, Guinea Bissau to a Cape Verdean father and a Guinean mother, Felinto Vaz Martins started his primary school at a missionary school in Empada, but was expelled because his parents did not followed the catholic church. He continued his studies at home with his father before resuming his primary school studies in Bolama, finally completing his secondary school education in Bissau. He worked for a period as an accountant in the customs services before receiving a scholarship from *Mocidade Portuguesa* (Portuguese Youth). He then moved to Portugal and studied engineering at the *Instituto Superior Técnico* in Lisbon from 1952-1953. In 1961, due to the pressure from the political police, he joined the first group of students that clandestinely left Portugal in 1961. Despite his militancy in the PAIGC, he continued his studies in Switzerland, where he worked until 1973 as an engineer in solar energies. In 1973, after the assassination of Amílcar Cabral, he moved with his family to Conakry, where he was nominated for the position of Director of the *Escola Teranga* in Ziguinchor, Senegal. After the independence, he continued to work in the engineering department in Bissau. Today he is retired and lives in Bissau.

Jose Sambe Born in 1951 in Caboxanque, Guinea Bissau, José Sambe was the son of Guinean farmers. He left home at age 13 to join the struggle. In 1964, dispite his lack of experience, Sambe started teaching literacy and writing classes to the PAIGC's soldiers in *Lar do Bonfim* in Conakry and then in the hospital Simão Mendes (located in Boké region) between 1965-1969. He attended several teaching courses in Conakry, and in 1969 or 1970 he was sent to the Aerolino Lopes Cruz boarding school as primary school teacher. He was also responsible for the organization of the Party Pioneer groups and for the production of theatre plays and songs. After the independence, he worked at the *Instituto Amizade*. Today he lives in Bissau where he continues to work.

Lars Rudebeck Born in 1936 in Lund, Sweden, Lars Rudebeck was active in the Uppsala South Africa Committee/Africa Group. His visited Guinea Bissau first in 1972, and then again in 1974. While working as an Associate Professor of Political Science at the University of Uppsala, Rudebeck published the book *Guinea Bissau: A Study of Political Mobilization*, in 1974 and has since then published several articles on the country's politics and development. Today he lives in Uppsala, Sweden and is a professor emeritus of political science at Uppsala University.

Lassana Seidi Born in 1953 in Morés, Guinea Bissau, Lassa Seidi was the son of farmers. He attended the first years of school in the PAIGC's village school in Canjambare and later he continued his studies at Morés boarding school. In

1972, he was sent to *Escola Teranga* in Ziguinchor. The school moved to Bolama after Guinea Bissau achieved independence and Seidi completed his secondary studies between the years of 1975 and1976. In late 1976, he opted to continue his education in Lisbon, where he studied Law at Lisbon Law University. Today he lives in Bissau and works as a judge at the Bissau Courthouse.

Mamai Badinca Born in 1955 in Farim, Guinea Bissau, Mamai Badinca was the daughter of farmers. At the age of nine or ten years, she left home to join the PAIGC's school in the Farim region in the liberated areas. After a Portuguese attack on the barracks left her wounded she was transferred to the border to receive treatment. By order of Luís Cabral, she was later sent to Conakry, where she joined the first group of students of the *Escola Piloto*. In 1972, she was sent to Czechoslovakia to attend university. There she studied the course in pharmaceutical technology. Today she lives in Bissau works in the pharmacy section of the Hospital Simão Mendes.

Marcelino Mutna Born in 1959 in Quitafene, Guinea Bissau, Marcelino Mutna was the son of Guinean farmers. He completed part of his primary school education in the PAIGC's village school in Tafore and later attende the semi-boarding school in Campon in the liberated areas. From 1972 to1973 he completed secondary school at *Escola Teranga* in Ziguinchor. Between 1974 and1979, he attended university in Czechoslovakia, were he studied industrial chemistry. Today he lives in Bissau and works as a water engineer.

Maria da Luz Boal (also known as Lilica Boal) Born in 1934 in Tarrafal, Santiago in Cape Verde, Maria da Luz Boal was the daughter of Cape Verdean small business owners. She attended primary school in Tarrafal, and moved to São Vicente Island to continue her preparatory studies, and later relocating to Portugal to finish secondary school. Between 1956 and1961, she studied history and philosophy in Coimbra and Lisbon. In 1961, together with her husband the Angolan medicine student Manuel Boal, she joined the group that clandestinely left Portugal to join the liberation struggle.

In the same year, she moved to Dakar where she at the same time that she worked at the PAIGC's office while attending the course "Propaedeutic and African History" for two years at Dakar University. She also participated in the development of the PAIGC's school manuals. In 1969, she was nominated by Amílcar Cabral to be the Director of *Escola Piloto*, a position she held position until 1974. Between 1966 and1973, she worked on the organization of the Teacher's Course in Conakry. After the independence, she was named the General Director of National Education in Bissau. During the coup in 1980, she moved to Cape Verde, where she continued to work in the firld of education. Today she is retired and lives in Cape Verde.

Maria Teresa de Sá Araújo Born in 1961 in Lisbon, Portugal, Maria Teresa de Sá Araújo was the daughter of Amélia Rodrigues de Sá, a broadcaster at the PAIGC's *Rádio Libertação*, and José Eduardo Araújo who was responsible for the PAIGC's justice department. Shortly after her birth, her parents, along with a group of other African students, clandestinely escaped from Portguals and resettled the family in Conakry. Teresa grew up in Conakry, where she attended the PAIGC's kindergarten and the *Escola Piloto*. In 1973, she was sent to the Soviet Union with a group of other Guinean students to continue her education. There she studied child education with a specialization in pedagogy and psychology of childhood. In 1984, Teresa went to Cape Verde, where she has been living ever since. She currently works at the Cape Verdean Education Ministry.

Pedro de Verona Rodrigues Pires Born in 1934 in São FilipeCabo Verde Pedro Verona Rodrigues Pires was the son of farmers. Pires studied in São Filipe and later in São Vicente. In Lisbon, he carried out his obligatory military services and attended the meetings of *Casa dos Estudantes do Império*. In 1961, together with Maria da Luz Boal, he joined the group that escaped the country in secret. In Dakar, Pires worked as a mobilizer in the Cape Verdean community. He then lived in France for a year to continue the same mobilization work in the Cape Verdean community there. He received military training in Cuba. When he returned to Guinea Bissau, he created the *Centro de Instrução Política e Militar de Madina* do Boé, where he was responsible for the training of the military personnel. After the independence, he was nominated for the office of the Prime Minister (1975-1991) and was later elected as the country's President (2001-2011). Today he lives in Cabo Verde.

Rui Néné N'Jata Born in 1958 in Mansoa, Guinea Bissau Rui Néné N'Jata was the son of Guinean farmers. He completed his primary studies in the PAIGC's semi-boarding school in Umol located liberated areas. Between 1972 and 1973, he completed his secondary studies at *Escola Teranga* in Ziguinchor. Between 1974 and1979, he continued his studies in Czechoslovakia in industrial chemistry, and later moving to the US to doa a course in soil and water sciences. Today he lives in Bissau and is the service director of rural engineering.

Segunda Lopes Born in 1950 on Como Island, Guinea Bissau Segunda lopes was the daughter of farmers. She attended primary school in Madina de Baixo in Guinea-Bissau. Later she joined the struggle and participated in several Teacher's Courses. She was appointed teacher for pupils up to the third grade level and carried this role in CIPM and in the boarding school *Escola Colégio Militar Abel Djassi* where she worked as the Director. She continued to work as a teacher after the independence. Today she lives in Bissau and works in the city municipality in the municipal police department.

Teodora Inácia Gomes Born in Quinara in Guinea-Bissau, Teodora Inácia Gomes was mobilized to join the PAIGC by her uncle in 1962, and worked as political commissioner for them in 1963. In September of that year, Gomes traveled to the USSR where she completed a ten-month political internship. She returned to Guinea Bissau and for a short period what came to be the *Juventude Africana Amílcar Cabral*- JAAC (African Youth Amílcar Cabral). Between 1964 and 1969, she studied pedagogy in the pedagogy and psychology Gorka Institute in Kiev, Ukraine. In 1969, she worked as the Director of the PAIGC's kindergarten *Jardim de infância Bellevue*. From 1971 to 1974 she worked in the liberated areas as Political Commissioner. After independence, Teodora Inácia Gomes occupied several positions in the government. Today she lives in Bissau and still is a member of PAIGC.

Annexes

Annex 1. Ethnic groups and subgroups from Guinea Bissau

Ethnic groups and subgroups from Guinea Bissau

Ethnic Division based their antiquity and local	Groups and Subgroups	Tradition Sedentary or nomad	Religion	Structure
Paleo-Sudanese of the coast ('The older habitants of Guinea-Bissau)	Balantas «de dentro»	Sedentary	Animists	Horizontal structure
	Balantas «de fora»	"	"	Division in
	Balantas Bravos	"	"	age classes
	Balantas Cuntohe	"	"	No State
	Balantas Nhagas	"	"	"
	Balantas Mansoancas	"	"	
	Balantas Mané	"	Islamicized	"
				"
				"
				"
				"
	Mancanhas (Brames)	Sedentary	Animist	No State
	Papeis (Bissau)	"	"	"
	Manjocas	"	"	"
	Beafadas	Sedentary	Islamicized	No State
	Bijagós	"	Animists	"
	Nalus	"	Islam-Anim.	"
	Felupes (Djolas)	Sedentary	Animists	No State
	Baiotes(djolas)	"	"	"
	Bainuk (Banhuns)	"	"	"
	(Djolas)	"	"	"
	Cobianas (Djolas)	"	Islamicized	"
	Cassangas (Djolas)			
	Landumas	Sedentary	Islam.-Anim.	No State
	Cocolís	"	Islamicized	"
	Bagas	"	Islam.- Anim.	"

(*continued on next page*)

Continued

Ethnic groups and subgroups from Guinea Bissau

Ethnic Division based their antiquity and local	Groups and Subgroups	Tradition Sedentary or nomad	Religion	Structure
Paleo – Sudanese from the interior	Padjadincas	Sedentary	Islamicized	No State
	Tandas	"	"	"
	Oincas	"	Islam.-Anim.	"
Neo-Sudanese Mandingo-Group	Mandingas	Sedentary	Islamicized	Vertical
	Saracolés	"	"	Structure
	Sossos	"	"	With State
	Jacancas	"	"	"
	Bambarãs	"	"	(no State)
	Jaloncas	"	Islam.	
	Sonnikés	"	(Anim.) Islamicized	
Neo-Sudanese Fulani Group	Torancas	Nomadic	Islamicized	Vertical
	Futadjaloncas	"	"	Structure
	Tuculores	Sedentary	"	Division
	Fulas Forros	Nomadic	"	in social
	Fulacundas	"	"	strata with
	Fulas Pretis	Sedenatry	"	State
Groups that came or were born with the colonization	Cape-verdeans	Sedentary	Christians	
	Mestizos	"	"	
	«Cristons»	"	(Anim.)-	
	Libanese		Christ	
	Sirianos		Christians	
	Mauros		Islamicized	
	Portuguese		"	
			Christians	

Source: CIDAC: Terra Solidária. *Guiné Bissau. Tempo de Mudança.* Vol. 24.
Lisboa: CIDAC, 1990, p.6.

Annex 2. Ethnographic map of Guinea Bissau

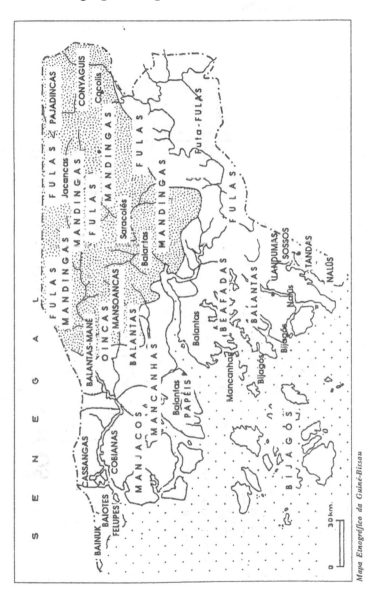

Mapa Etnográfico da Guiné-Bissau

Source: CIDAC: Terra Solidária. *Guiné Bissau. Tempo de Mudança.* Vol. 24. Lisboa: CIDAC, 1990, p. 6

Annex 2.1 Liberated areas in Guinea Bissau 1964 -1966 and 1969-1974

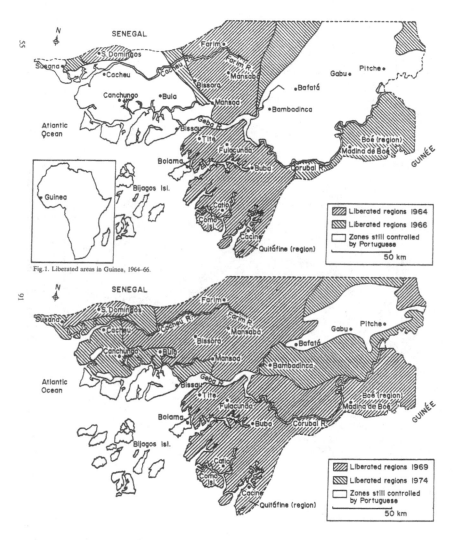

Fig.1. Liberated areas in Guinea, 1964–66.

Source: Patrick Chabal *Amílcar Cabral. Revolutionary leadership and people's war.* New York: Cambridge University Press, 1983, 54-91.

Annex 3. PAIGC's Minor and Major Program

The PAIGC Minor Program

1. Structural union of all nationalist and patriotic forces of "Portuguese" Guiné and the Cape Verde Islands in order to liquidate Portuguese imperialist domination in these two African nations.
2. Structural union of nationalist and patriotic forces of Guiné and Cape Verde at home and abroad in the fight for the liquidation of Portuguese colonialism.
3. Effective alliance with nationalist and patriotic forces organizations with other Portuguese colonies for mutual support and coordination of the fight for liquidation of Portuguese colonialism. Collaboration with African, Asian and Latin American peoples who are fighting against colonialism and imperialism.
4. Effective training based on mobilization and organization of the popular masses to fight against Portuguese colonialism and imperialism
5. Struggle – and only if necessary, armed conflict – for the rapid and total destruction of the Portuguese colonial forces in "Portuguese" Guiné and Cape Verde Islands and for the conquest of complete national independence for the peoples of Guiné and Cape Verde. Fight against imperialism.
6. Structural union of all political, union, and mass organizations in "Portuguese" Guiné and Cape Verde, to build a life of peace. well-being and progress for the peoples of Guiné and Cape Verde. In this union will be the permanent defense of the interest of the peasants and urban workers who make up almost the entire population.
7. During the fight for liberation and after the conquest of national independence, collaboration with all the progressive anti-colonial and anti-imperialist forces of the world for the construction of a life in peace and progress for all peoples.

The PAIGC Major Program

1. Immediate, total Independence

1. Immediate conquest, using any necessary means, of national, total and unconditional independence for the people of "Portuguese" Guiné and Cape Verde.
2. Conquest of power in "Portuguese" Guiné by the people of "Portuguese" Guiné and in the Cape Verde Islands by the people of Cape Verde.
3. Termination of all colonialistic or imperialistic relationships, and end to all the Portuguese and foreign prerogatives over the popular masses, revision

or revocation of all agreements, treaties, alliances, concessions, made by the Portuguese colonialist involving "Portuguese" Guiné and the Cape Verde.

4. National and international sovereignty of "Portuguese" Guiné and the Cape Verde. Economic, political, military, and cultural independence.

5. Permanent vigilance, based on the will of the people, to prevent or destroy any attempts by the imperialists and colonialists to re-establish themselves, in new forms, in "Portuguese" Guiné and the Cape Verde.

2. National unity in "Portuguese" Guiné and the Cape Verde

1. Equal rights and duties, solid union and fraternal collaboration among the citizens, whether considered individually, by social class, or by ethnic groups. Prohibition and extermination of all attempts to divide the people.

2. Economic, political, social, and cultural unity.

In "Portuguese" Guiné this unity will take into consideration the social and cultural characteristics of the diverse ethnic groups, whatever their population.

In the Cape Verde Islands, each island or group of similar Islands in proximity will be able to enjoy a certain administrative autonomy, always within the framework of unity and national solidarity.

3. The return to "Portuguese" Guiné of all emigrants who wish to return to their country. The return to Cape Verde of all exiled emigrants or workers who wish to return to their country. Free circulation of all citizens throughout the national territory.

3. Unity between peoples of the "Portuguese" Guiné and the Cape Verde

1. After the conquest of national independence in "Portuguese" Guiné and the Cape Verde union of the people of these countries for the construction of a strong and progressive African fatherland based on opportunely consulted popular will.

2. The form of union between the two peoples will be established by their legitimate, freely elected representatives.

3. Equal rights and duties, solid union, and fraternal collaboration between the peoples Guiné and the Cape Verde. Prohibition and extermination of all attempts to divide the two peoples.

4. African Unity

1. After the conquest of national independence and if desired by freely manifested popular will, to fight for the unity of African peoples, considered as a whole or by continental regions, always governed by respect for liberty,

dignity and these peoples' right to political, economic, social, and cultural progress.

2. To combat any attempt by any nation whatsoever to annex or put pressure on the people of "Portuguese" Guiné and the Cape Verde.
3. Defense of the rights and the political, economic, social, and cultural gains of the popular masses in "Portuguese" Guiné and the Cape Verde is the fundamental condition for the realization of unity with other African peoples.

5. Democratic, anti-colonialist, anti-imperialist regime

1. A republican, democratic, lay, anti-colonialist, and anti-imperialist regime.
2. Establishment of fundamental liberties, respect for the rights of man and guarantees of the exercise of these liberties and rights.
3. Equality of citizens before the law, with no distinction as to nationality or ethnic group, sex, origin, cultural level, profession, wealth, religious, beliefs, or philosophical convictions. Men and women will enjoy equality in regard to the family, work, and public activities.
4. All individuals or individual groups who, by their actions or conduct, favor colonialism, imperialism, or the destruction of the people's unity will be deprived of their fundamental liberties, by whatever means necessary.
5. General free elections of organs of power based on universal, direct, and secret suffrage.
6. Total elimination of the colonial administrative structure and establishment of a national, democratic structure by the internal administration of the country.
7. Protection of the persons of all foreigners living and working in "Portuguese" Guiné and the Cape Verde who operate with respect for the current laws.

6. Economic independence, a structured economy, and the development of production

1. Termination of all colonial imperialistic relationships. Conquest of economic independence for "Portuguese" Guiné and the Cape Verde.
2. Harmonious planning and development of the economy. Economic activity will be directed according to the principles of democratic centralism.
3. Four types of ownerships: state, cooperative, private, and personal. The natural resources; the principal means of production and communications, social security; the radio and other means of broadcasting, of imparting information, and of spreading culture will be considered as belonging to the nation of "Portuguese" Guiné and the Cape Verde and will be employed in accordance with the need of rapid economic development. Voluntary cooperative

exploitation of the land and agricultural production, of the production of consumer goods, and of handicrafts. Private exploitation can be developed as needs to promote progress, on the condition that it be useful to the rapid economic development of "Portuguese" Guiné and the Cape Verde. Personal property- especially individual consumer goods, houses, and savings earned through work will be inviolable.

4. Development and modernization of agriculture. Transformation of the present system in order to end the one-crop agricultural economy and to erase the obligatory character of earth-nut cultivation in "Portuguese" Guiné and maize cultivation in the Cape Verde. Struggle against agricultural crises, drought, floods, and famine.

5. Agrarian reform in the Cape Verde, with the private rural property to be limited on extend so that all peasants may have enough land to work. In "Portuguese" Guiné, to profit from the traditional agricultural structures and to create new ones that will permit the land to be used in a manner that will most benefit the people's progress.

6. Both in "Portuguese" Guiné and the Cape Verde, confiscation of lands and other possession of proven enemies of the people's liberty and national independence.

7. Development of modern industry and commerce. Progressive establishment of the state commercial and industrial enterprises. Development of an African artisan class. State control of foreign trade and coordination of domestic commerce. Price adjustment and stabilization. Elimination of speculation and unjust profits. Harmony between urban and rural economic activities.

8. Budgetary equilibrium. Creation of a new fiscal system. Creation of national currency stabilized and freed from inflation.

7. Justice and progress for all

A. At the social level

1. Progressive elimination of man's exploitation of man, of all forms of subservience of the human person for the profit of individuals, groups, or classes. Elimination of misery, ignorance, fear, prostitution, and alcoholism.

2. Protection of the rights of workers and guarantee of work for all that can work. Abolition of forced labor in "Portuguese" Guiné and of exportation of forced laborers or laborers "taken under contract" to the "Portuguese" Cape Verde.

3. Just salaries and fees based on the principle of equal pay for equal work. Positive competition in work. Limitation of the length of the workday

consistent with the progress that must be made, but also with the interest of the workers. Progressive elimination of the differences between (working conditions for) urban and agricultural workers.

4. Freedom for union and guarantees for their effective exercise. Participation and creative initiative on the part of the popular masses effective in all levels of national leadership. Instigation and support of both urban and rural mass organizations, principally those of women, youth and students.

5. Social assistance for all unemployed, invalid, or ill citizens involuntary in need. All institutions of public health and hygiene will be directed or controlled by the state.

6. Establishment of social services to be tied to the productive activity. Protection for the pregnant women and infants, Protection for the aged, Rest recreation, and culture for manual, intellectual and agricultural workers.

B. At the educational level:

1. Educational centers and technical institutes will be considered as possession of the nation and, as such, will be directed or controlled by the State. Educational reform, development of secondary and technical education, creation of universities and of scientific and technical institutes.

2. Rapid elimination of illiteracy. Compulsory, free primary education. Formation and urgently needed improvement of technical and professional staffs.

3. Total elimination of the complexes created by colonialism, of the consequences of colonialist culture and exploitation.

4. In "Portuguese" Guiné, stimulation of the use of native languages and of the creole dialect, creation of a script of these languages. In Cape Verde stimulation and a script for the creole dialect. Development of the cultures of the various ethnic groups and of the people of Cape Verde. Protection and development of literature and the national arts.

5. Utilization of all the gains and discoveries of value made by human culture for the progress of the peoples of Guiné and Cape Verde. The contribution of these peoples culture to humanity in general.

6. Support and development of physical education and sports for all citizens of "Portuguese" Guiné and the Cape Verde. Creation of physical education and sports institutes.

7. Religious freedom; freedom to have or not to have a religion. Protection of churches and mosques, of places and objects of worship, of legal, religious institutions. Independence for religious personnel.

8. Effective national defense based on the people themselves

1. Creation of the groups necessary for an effective national defense: army, navy, and air force, tied to the people and led by national citizens. The fighters for the conquest of independence will form the central core of national defense.
2. The Democratic system within the armed forces. Discipline. Close collaboration between the armed forces and the political powers.
3. All the people must participate in the vigilance and the defense against colonialism, imperialism, and the enemies of the people's unity and progress.
4. Absolute prohibition of foreign military bases in the national territory.

9. International policy to be developed in the interest of the
nation of Africa, of peace, and of the progress of humanity

1. Peaceful collaboration with all the peoples of the world, with respect for the principles of mutual respect, national sovereignty, territorial integrity, non-aggression, and noninterference in domestic affairs, equality and reciprocity, and peaceful coexistence.

Development of economic and cultural agreements with all peoples whose governments accept and respect these principles:

2. Respect for the principles of the United Nations Charter.
3. Nonalignment with military blocs.
4. Protection for natives of Guiné and Cape Verde residing abroad.

Source: Lars Rudebeck, *Guinea Bissau. A study of political mobilization.* Uppsala. The Scandinavian Institute of African Studies, 1974, p. 253-257.
(translated from Portuguese)

Annex 4. Regulation of the schools of the Party

Preamble

Ever since its foundation, our party always gave great attention to the problem of the education of our nation. Already at the beginning of our political struggle, the creation of undercover schools was one of the tasks that our leaders had to deal with. In those schools, they not only taught the first writing and reading but also tried to create a nationalistic and revolutionary consciousness in the students.

The tradition of the struggle against ignorance remained over these last years, despite the enormous tasks that were imposed on the party, like the mobilization of almost all the cadres that were directly linked to political and military activities. On the other hand, with the development of the armed struggle and the progressive liberation of large regions of Guiné, the area of which our educational activities is required, is increasing rapidly, demanding from us the extension to populated sectors every day more.

Effectively, when in the school year of 1964/1965 in our territories ran 50 schools, attended by circa 4.000 students, the number of enrolled students in the last school year (1965/1966) ascended to 13.500, which forced us to increase the number of schools over 100%.

Therefore, in the school year 1965/1966, we had 107 schools, of which only three - the Pilot-school and two border schools - worked abroad.

And to highlight also that one of the first schools that we built in the north of the country - the Morés School - was transformed into a boarding school with 100 enrolled students.

These numbers attest the huge importance of the work that has already been realized by the party in the field of education and shows that the moment has come to secure the regulation of our activity in this field.

With that intention, this regulation of the party schools was drafted.

Resulting from a proposal of the head committee of the second center for the development of teachers (Conakry, July/7.9.1966). After a long discussion, in which almost all teachers of our schools participated, the present regulation was elaborated. The basis was lived experiences of several years of activity.

Its application will certainly stimulate the work of our teachers and students, bringing an improvement of the operations in our schools.

It is starting a new stage of the educative activities of our Party.

Regulation of the Party schools

<u>Art.nr. 1</u> - The schools are organized through this present regulation § of exception - The pilot school and the boarding schools will have an own, internal regulation

<u>Art.nr. 2 – Teachers</u>

a) The teacher of the party needs to be politically educated, a good militant and give the oath of the honor of teachers.
b) The teacher's behavior, in and outside of the school has to agree with the pedagogy rules and principles of the party.
c) During the semester the teacher can't miss nor leave his zone if its not for a severe reason.
d) The teachers always need to have the book of registration, the teachers paper, the membership book, the inventory of the school material. All this material, and the flag of the party, need to be kept in a safe space.

c) In case of attacks or any other dangers, the teacher must help the minor students.

f) The teacher is always obligated to improve. Every year he must attend the internship at the Center for Improvement.

Art. nr. 3 - Students

a) The students need to respect and obey the teachers, inside and outside of the school.

b) The students must show good behavior in and outside of the schools, respect their parents and the political responsible of their zone.

c) The students must arrive at school as early as possible.

d) The students must stand up when someone enters the classroom.

Art. nr. 4 - Organization

a) The enrollment can begin in October, but the classes start only in November, after the raining season. The final exams must begin in June.

f) The cleaning group has to be changed every day.

Art. nr. 6 – Supervision

a) The supervisors in charge for education have to inspect the schools regularly under their own responsibility.

b) The head of the party orders periodic inspections to every school in the country.

Art. nr. 7 - Punishments

a) the teacher that doesn't fulfill the regulation of the party schools will suffer the following punishments:
   – reproof
   – suspension

b) Students that show undisciplined behavior will be punished. It is absolutely prohibited to use the cleaning tasks as a punishment, to hit the children or to cane anyone with a stick.

Art. nr. 8 – Emulation

The teacher and the students need to be encouraged to perform their work every day better.

The best teacher and students will be enlisted in "staff of honor." They may also be assigned for material rewards.

For the bestowal of the awards it should be taken into account:

the student: his work and behavior inside and outside of the school year the teacher: his political education, pedagogy, and his assiduity in classes and in the improvement center.

September, 19th, of 1966

Source: The Nordic Africa Institute. Uppsala

(translated from Portuguese)

Annex 5. Statutes of the Friendship Institute

Art. 1 - The "Friendship" institute is an autonomous and non-political organization with educational and humanitarian purposes. It was created by a group of nationals of Guinea-Bissau and the Cape Verde Islands.

Art 2. - The "Friendship" institute is a legal person. Until the total liberation of Guinea-Bissau and Cape Verde, the "Friendship" institute will have two permanent representative offices abroad: one located in Dakar, Rue Marsat Prolongée X Félix Eboué (BP 2319), and the other in Conakry (BP 298). These representations serve as provisional seats of the "Friendship" institute.

Art. 3 - The goals of the "Friendship" institute are the following:

a) Informing, protecting and educating children effected/victimized by the colonial war

b) Educating selected young people in schools in the liberated zones of Guinea-Bissau

c) Training the future leadership of Guinea-Bissau and Cape Verde

d) Studying and developing methods for alphabetization and school education with the aim to help the people of Guinea-Bissau and Cape Verde to liberate themselves from their ignorance.

Art 4. - The "Friendship" institute realizes its goals by establishing and operating Kindergartens, primary and secondary schools, boarding schools, high schools and vocational schools; it acts in close collaboration with the Educational Department of the liberated areas of Guinea-Bissau.

Art. 5 - Eligible for regular membership of the "Friendship" institute are all nationals of Guinea-Bissau and Cape Verde irrespective of their race, social origin, religious persuasion or political opinion.

Art 6. - Any humanitarian or anti-colonial organization is eligible to become a donating member of the "Friendship" institute.

Art 7. - Regular members of the "Friendship" institute are obliged to pay an annual fee stipulated by the General Assembly.

Art. 8 - Donating members are obliged to contribute regularly to the "Friendship" institute in the form of monetary or in-kind donations suitable for supporting the institute and its goals.

Art. 9 - The General Assembly can bestow the title of "Honorary Member" to any individual or organization who has supported the institute in an exceptional manner.

Art. 10 - Membership expires in the following cases:

a) failure to pay membership fees
b) interruption of payment of donations
c) resignation accepted by the Steering Committee
d) deletion on the basis of severe reasons by the General Assembly

Art. 11 - The legal bodies of the institute are:

- the General Assembly
- the Steering Committee
- the Treasury Board

Art. 12 - The General Assembly is constituted by the founders and the regular members and it is the supreme authority of the "Friendship" institute; it holds two regular conventions per year, in order

- to discuss, correct and approve the report and accounts of the Steering Committee;
- to elect new members of the Chair of the General Assembly, the Steering Committee and the Treasury Board;
- to discuss and approve plans for future activities and the budget.

Art. 13 - The Chair of the General Assembly consists of a president, a vice-president and a secretary.

Art. 14 - The Steering Committee consists of 5 members: 1 director, 1 deputy director, 1 treasurer, 1 secretary, 1 assessor.

Art. 15 - The Steering Committee is the executive body of the "Friendship" institute. It applies the decisions made by the General Assembly, directs, controls and coordinates the activities of the institute.

Art. 16 - The Treasury Board consists of 3 members: 1 president, 1 secretary, 1 assessor.

Art. 17 - The Treasury Board controls the financial activities and sees to the correct application of decisions made by the General Assembly concerning the budget.

Art. 18 - The budget of the institute is composed of:

- the membership fees
- the regular contributions from the donating members
- any other donations or pecuniary legacies

Art. 19 - This charter can only be modified by a General Assembly explicitly convened for this purpose and by a majority vote of at least two thirds of the members present.

Art. 20 - The "Friendship" institute can only be dissolved by a General Assembly explicitly convened for this purpose; such dissolution can only be announced with the consent of a majority of at least two thirds of all regular members of the institute enjoying membership rights.

Art. 21 - The Assembly which dissolves the institute must also decide about the liquidation and purposes of the assets

Source: The Nordic Africa Institute. Uppsala

(translated from French)

Annex 6. Domingos Brito original document of PAIGC's schools

Quadros Formados pelo Partido até 1971 (31/12/71)

Curso Superior - 21 ½ camaradas (1 formado por cada 29.000 habitantes)

Curso médio Técnico - 30 " (1 " " " 26.000 ")

_Curso profissional e de
    especialização_
                     -107 " (1 " " " 7.000 ")

_Quadro Político e
    Sindical_   -171 " (1 " " " 5.000 ")

Enfermagem: - 90 " (não estão incluídos os formados
                            nas nossas Regiões Libertadas,)
                        1 formado por cada 9.000 habitantes

Quadros em Formação no estrangeiro (até 1971)

Curso Superior - 31 camaradas (1 em formação por cada 25.000 hab.)

Curso médio Técnico, profissional e de especialização - 259 camaradas,
                        1 em formação por cada 3.000 habitantes

Nota: Foram enviados para estudar no estrangeiro no ano lectivo 1972/73
                184 camaradas, a saber:

Para o Curso Superior -   21 camaradas
    " " " médio Técnico -   84 "
    " " " Prof. e de especialização - 58 "
    " Quadros políticos e sindicais - 21 "

O Total dos estudantes do Partido no estrangeiro até 14/9/72 é
            de 474, distribuídos assim pelos seguintes cursos:

Superior - Direito, História, Arquitectura, Agronomia, Electro-
            tecnia, Química, Medicina, construção civil,
            Geologia e Minas e Economia.

Médio Téc., prof. e espec^ão: Agronomia, Electrotecnia, Química e
        petróleo, Medicina, Música, Pedagogia Infantil com ênfase
        rural, Silvicultura, Zootecnia, Educação física, veteri-
        nária, Rádios por Anestesista, Belas artes, Radioteni-

Curso Superior (27 camaratas) a saber.

Agronomia ———— 5
Ciências Políticas ———— 1
Medicina ———— 8
Economia ———— 3
Ciências Jurídicas ———— 1
Direito Internacional ———— 3
Eng.ª Construção ———— 1
Eng. e dest. jeunes ———— 2
Electrotécnia ———— 1
Física ———— 1
Administração Pública ———— 1

Total ——— 27

Curso médio técnico (30 camaratas)

Agronomia ———— 6
Veterinária ———— 3
Ajudante Técnico Médico ———— 10
Geologia ———— 1
Comércio ———— 1
Pedagogia ———— 1
Construção Civil ———— 1
Constr. de Estradas e Pontes ———— 1
Electrotécnia ———— 1
Agente técnico de máquinas ———— 1
Indústria Química e Petróleo ———— 3
Agente técnico de Reparação e
    Montagem de Centr. ———— 1

Total 30

Ver Verso

Curso prof. e de especialização: (107 cursos)

Construção de estradas _____ 1
Mecânica de carriçanes _____ 2
carpinteiro de construção _____ 2
Tractorista _____ 4
Mecânico motor a Diesel _____ 2
Mecânica de Auto _____ 15
Mecânica de auto e Máq. Agrícola ____ 12
Pesca ____ 1
ANESTESISTA _____ 1
Agricultura Tropical _____ 2
Agricultura e Produção animal _____ 2
Puericultura _____ 3
Imprensa (composição e impressão) ____ 6
Jornalismo _____ 1
Radiodifusão _____ 4
Central Telefónica _____ 2
Radiotelegrafia _____ 34
Electricista _____ 10
Metalurgia _____ 1
Operador de cinema _____ 4
Ortopedia _____ 1
                    Total 107

Quadros políticos e sindicais ___ 171
recuperação   ___ 90

Quadros formados pelo Partido ~~dermos de 14 outubro de 19~~
Depois de 31/12/71 até 14 Setembro de 1972

Curso Superior — (13 formados) a saber

Agronomia _____ 1
Medicina _____ 2
Direito _____ 1
Química _____ 1
Geologia e Minas _____ 2
Arquitectura _____ 2
Ciências Políticas e Sociais _____ 4
Total — 13

Médio Técnico — (12 formados)
Agronomia _____ 1
Veterinária _____ 1
Preparação de couros _____ 1
Laboratorista _____ 1
Construção civil _____ 1
Montador de Ins. Eléctrica _____ 1
Serralheiro de Maq. Agric. e Tractor. 2
Mecânica agrícola _____ 2
Mecânica Industrial _____ 1
Mec. de automóvel _____ 1
Total 12

Profissionais e de Especialização (29 formados)

Enfermagem _____ 1
Enfermeiras-auxiliar _____ 28
Total 29

Formação de Quadros

| Pessoas formadas na Guiné desde a presença portuguesa (1471 - 1961) | Quadros do P.A.I.G.C. EM Formação (1961 - 1964) |

Pessoas formadas na Guiné desde a presença portuguesa (1471 - 1961)

Ensino Superior:

Administração Colonial	2
Agronomia	2
Economia	1
Engenharia	1
Medicina e Veterinária	4
Letras e Direito	4
Total	14

= 1 formado por cada 57.000 Hab.

Ensino Técnico

Técnico Industrial	5
Agricultura	3
Ensino	3
Total	11

= 1 formado por cada 72.000 Hab.

Quadros do P.A.I.G.C. EM Formação (1961 - 1964)

Ensino Superior:

Agronomia	7
Arquitectura e Const. Civil	6
Economia	3
Educação Física	1
Electrotecnia	4
Farmácia e Química	3
Geologia	5
Mecânica	6
Medicina e Veterinária	17
Letras e Direito	7
Assistente Social	4
Soma	63

= 1 em formação por cada 12.000 habitantes

Ensino Técnico:

Agricultura	6
Arquitectura e Const. Civil	9
Comércio	3
Electrotecnia	4
Ensino Técnico Industrial	2
Farmácia e Química	2
Geologia	1
Mecânica	6
Pesca	2
Soma	35

= 1 em formação por cada 22.000 Habitantes

<u>Nota:</u> O P.A.I.G.C. forma, só entre 1961 e 1964, 3 vezes mais de quadros do que os formados sob a dominação colonial em cerca de 500 anos de presença portuguesa.

Saúde

Dados relativos a 31 de Dezembro de 1971

I. UNIDADES SANITÁRIAS DO PARTIDO — 128

  • Hospitais no Exterior .... 3 = 3 ———— 3

  • NAS REGIÕES LIBERTADAS .... 125 ⟨ Hospitais campanha 9
                                           Postos Sanitários 116
                                      Total 128

II. NÚMEROS DE CAMA ——————————— 488

  • UNIDADES SANITÁRIAS EXTERIOR — 223 ⟨ Boké 123
                                           Ziguinchor 50
                                           Kuhngara 5ᴰ 223

  • NAS REGIÕES LIBERTADAS ——— 265 ⟨ Posto Sanit. 165
                                        Hospitais 100 265

                                   Total 488

III. ASSISTÊNCIA SANITÁRIA

  • VACINAS ——————— 20.000 ⟨ Exterior 5.000
                                Reg. Libertados 15.000
                                Total 20.000

  • Transfusões — Hospital Boké —————— 300

IV. PESSOAL EFECTIVO

  • Médicos ———— 5
  • Ajudantes Médicos ——— 8
  • Enfermeiros Instruídos — 1 por cada unidade de combate
  • Enfermeiros auxiliares — 410

        #

Nota: _Não se fez ainda o movimento relativo as consultas, trata-
mentos, intervenções cirúrgicas, etc, referente ao ano de 1972, por
ainda não ter todos os dados necessários._

Annex 7. School enrollment registration document

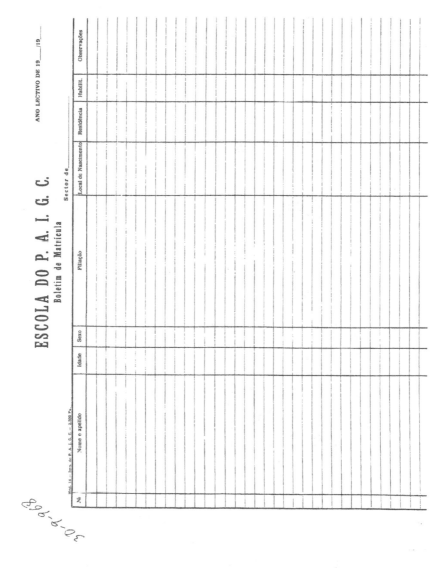

Source: Archive Nordic African Institute. Uppsala 2015

Annex 8. PAIGC's school attendance card

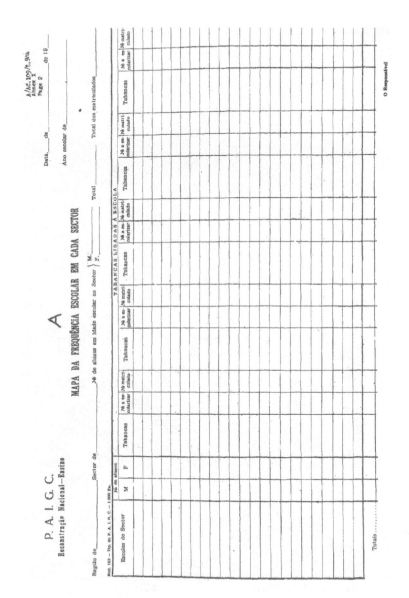

Source: Horacio Sevilla-Borga, "Report of the Special Mission established by the Special Committee at its 840th meeting on 14 March 1972." United Nations-General Assembly, July 3, 1972.

Annex 9. Center for Improvement for Teachers – Conakry July/September 1966

Pedagogy

Responsibilities of the teacher

We have already seen which is the role of the teacher for a man, and so for a whole nation.

It is him who designs the future of the man, of the country. We know that a grown-up is the result of all that he learned as a child.

Therefore, the teacher has responsibilities:

1 for the child he is teaching
2 for the parents of the child
3 for the country

The teacher needs to be very conscious about those responsibilities in order to fulfill his mission excellently.

When a child goes to school, the parents entrust the future of their child in the leadership of the teacher. It will do what he learned as a child. This is why the teacher has a responsibility for his country. Each of that men that he will bring to graduation will be part of the state. Those men will bring the ideas, the habits or the education that they learned in school.

The teacher needs to have that in mind. Being a teacher is difficult. It is not enough to know a lot of things, nor to study hard. It helps, but you will need vocation - a tendency, a preference to and manner to lead children in order to teach and educate them.

It's obvious that in our situation in which we need to teach, without being teachers, we have to make a bigger effort. The teacher needs to be open minded with the children. He has to live for them, figure out that certain way that is indispensable in order to educate children.

This requires a bigger effort of the teachers, but we have to make it possible if we want to create a country capable of acting.

We need to find a way and patience to understand the children and lead them on a better way.

The teacher has to know that his work has a huge responsibility and is of great importance for the construction of our country.

Also, that all he teaches the children will stay for a whole lifetime. There is no rewind. A life of a child only goes forward. That is why we can't erase the good things, or what we learnt in school.

SURVEILLANCE

The teacher has to be vigilant regarding his student. He always needs to be attentive and follow what he is doing. During class he has to make sure that his students are disciplined. the teacher needs to make an effort to learn the students names and has to follow all their movements in order to call attention if one of them is behaving in a undisciplined way. The teacher has to be vigilant regarding his student during and outside of the classes. The whole life of the student has to be of interest for the teacher. It's the totality of the students activities that will help the teacher to get to know better his student and find the best way to guide him.

SCHOOL ENVIRONMENT

We know that the teacher has to be ambitious with his students. He needs to accustom them to a rigid discipline but it's important not to forget that we should not exaggerate that.

It is important that the student doesn't find an environment of a caserne or a prison. There has to be a discipline, but not a military one. He needs to feel at ease, free without, however, breaking the rules of discipline. The teacher has to create a joyful ambiance, disciplined and attractive this is what stimulates the students for the classes. A pleasant environment where they feel content and happy.

It's the teachers challenge to create this certain environment of respect and happiness.

A happy child will tend to be good. And therefore, a child that doesn't feel happy, who suffered injustice, will feel angry and turn into a bad person for its country.

THE REGULATION

Every school must have a school regulation, in other words the rules of life and work in school. The regulation is important to maintain the order, the discipline and the progress of the students. Our regulation needs to be in agreement with the current conditions of our country.

The regulation has to be fulfilled but, however, there are certain exceptions: day of rest, the problem of the work of the fields and gardens, that depend on the different possibilities of every region and every teacher.

The regulation:

1 the discipline of the teacher
2 the discipline of the student
3 the regulation of how the work of the school should be organized
4 school hygiene
5 supervision, means how to work of the school needs to be guarded by the party

6 school penalties
7 emulation between the schools, means to encourage the schools to always improve and the awards that the party gives to the best schools

THE BREAKS

The breaks are very important for the students. They need at least 2 breaks in the morning and two in the afternoon.

The break is a rest for the student. He needs to stretch his legs, play, and do his needs to be able to enter with a fresh mind in class again.

The break is very important, and the teacher must supervise his student during the break. It is in the time of the break that the students feel more at ease and so they will do what they want. Therefore it's the best occasion to get to know better his students. Hence he must supervise and control the student, without making him feel controlled. In order to do so he needs to play with him. To be among them, not to create fear or not letting them play freely, but to get to know them.

That doesn't mean though that the student can show lack of respect for his teacher. To play together doesn't mean to abuse his authority. He should play but with all his respect. It is important not to forget that he is the teacher.

PENALTIES

1 The student should know that he has to respect the discipline of the school, because if he wouldn't he'd receive a penalty. 2 – The penalty should be an aid for the student to work more. Therefore, we can give copies and other scholar tasks as a punishment or as well a collective reprehension, meaning in front of the other students in class. But never with bad language or screaming. The student has to feel that it's for his best.

But we should never only give a punishment. It is also important to reward the good students, the ones that study hard or are very disciplined.

The reward won't always be a present. If the teacher doesn't have any presents he can give praises to him in the presence of the other students.

This is an encouragement that will help the student wanting to work even better.

THE SCHOOL

The school is created in 3 parts:

1 the barrack of the school
2 the latrine
3 the garden.

Barrack of the school

Before we construct the school barrack we have to think about our current situation in our country and of our struggle.

We are in times of war. We still don't have all the possibilities to build a school as it should be done. On the other hand we cannot wait until Independence to raise and educate our children.

We have to find the best way we can to make it happen.

The first thing that we should think about is a good place to build the school.

- what would be a good place?

1 A safe place, protected from the attacks of the enemy
2 Healthy, in the means good for the health. It must be an inclined place, where water runs, to avoid standing waters (breed mosquitoes that can bring illnesses).
3 Cool and pleasant space, that means with a lot of trees and shadow where the students can play.

When the school is situated well, the students will work with more effort.
Therefore, the teacher has to make his school attractive.

4 Furniture: inside of the school building must be:

   1) Student tables
   2) table for the teacher
   3) cupboard
   4) waste paper basket

Student tables

The tables for the student must be constructed accordingly to the student physics.

The part where the student writes must be on the right side. He needs to be in a good position, so he will not tire his few, nor his back. To avoid beach fleas or other fleas in the feet, we have to construct a board underneath the table where the students can put their feet. The table have to be organized in a proper lines. They shouldn't be too close, so the students won't feel squeezed.

That is why the tent has to be big.

Teachers table

The table of the teacher has to be simple and should stand in front of the student tables a little bit higher. So when we build the ground of the tent, we can leave the ground a bit higher there.

Blackboard

The cupboard is very important. It should be situated in front of the student tables, on the side of the teachers table. We use white chalk to protect the children's eyes.

Waste paper basket

Every school should have Waste paper basket where the student can put their waste before leaving to the break.

It needs to be emptied every day.

School material

In our current situation we cannot have a cupboard to keep the school material. The teacher should keep the material in a safe place at his house, in the house of the responsible politician or in the warehouse of the party.

School hygiene

The teacher needs to pay attention to the tidiness of the school. He should find a group of students to clean the school. Every group has a day of work.

At the end of classes those students need to: sweep the floor, clean the tables from dust, the teachers table, the black board and empty the paper waste basket. They should not be burnt, in order to not attract the attention of the enemy. Therefore, they must be buried a little distant from the school.

Garden

The teacher must teach how to cultivate just in the same way he teaches Portuguese or calculation.

Why does the school need a garden?

The school needs a garden because we need to teach our children to respect and love the earth. Even if some of the students are going to be doctors, they should respect the ones that work with the earth. Teaching that the main wealth of our country derives from agriculture. It is very important to develop the agriculture for the progress of our country.

The garden also serves to give food to the teacher, the students and their families.

Source. Arquivo & Biblioteca Fundação Mário Soares. Lisboa
(translated from Portuguese)

Annex 10. PAIGC actualités 1972, n. 47, p. 6

Source: Brochure kindly offered by Arlette Cabral. Bissau 2014

Annex 11. Internal Regulation of the boarding schools of the liberated regions

Art. 1 - The boarding school is depends on the Institute of friendship which is destined for the children of martyrs and fighters of Guinea and Cape Verde. In the boarding school the children receive a preparation necessary to later attend other educational establishments.

Chapter 1 - the organization of the direction

Art. 2 - The boarding school is organized by this regulation

Art. 3 - The boarding school is orientated by a collective management and a committee of students.

Art. 4 - The collective management is constituted by the teachers of the boarding school, with a principal who is the main responsible for the activities of the school institution.

Art.5 - Every initiative of the fellow teachers related of the activities of this institution have to be discussed with the boarding school principal.

Art. 6 - The fellow Principal must perform a general and permanent control of the activities of the boarding school.

Art. 7 - In case of absence or impediment the Principal chooses his substitute.

Art.8 - The committee of students is constituted by 4 boys and 3 girls, elected by the general assembly of students. They decide between those students who have shown best results in politics and work the most.

a) - the committee collaborates with the principal on the execution of the daily tasks.

Chapter 2 - Teachers

Art. 9 - The teacher must have political education and be a good militant

Art. 10 - The teacher's behavior, in and outside of the boarding school needs to agree with the pedagogy rules and principles of the party.

Art. 11 - The teacher can't miss a class without a justified reason.

Art. 12 - The boarding school teacher can't be absent without a license, given by the head principal or the teacher of the week.

Art. 13 - The teachers must always intend to increase his knowledge.

Art. 14 - The teacher should try to live the daily routine of the students to make them feel better the assistance that they are dispensed

Art. 15 - the teacher should have a certain spirit of cooperation and give priority to the tasks that are most important.

Art. 16 - the teacher should perform and ensure this regulation.

Chapter 3 - The students

Art. 17 - The student of the boarding school should be educated and respectful.
Art. 18 - The student of the boarding school should always be properly uniformed.
Art. 19 - The student of the boarding school should perform and ensure this regulation.

Title 4 – The organization

Art. 20 - The general organization of the boarding school is subordinated to the following schedule, which should be rigidly fulfilled by all the teachers and students of the boarding school:

Monday to Friday

6.30 - getting up
6.45 - getting in formation/checking of attendance
7.00 - fitness
8.30 - breakfast
9.00 - classes
13.00 - lunch
13.30 - rest (from 13.30 until 15.00)
16.00 - study class
18.00 - dinner
19.30/21.00 - cultural activities
21.00 - silence

Saturday

7.00 - getting up
8.30 - breakfast
9.30 - washing clothes
13.00 - lunch
13.30/15.00 - rest
15.00 - general meeting
18.30 - dinner
21.00 - silence

Sunday

7.00 - getting up
8.00 - hoist the flag
8.30 - breakfast

9/12.00 - leisure time
18.00 - lowering the flag
18.30 - dinner
21.30 - silence

Art. 21 - Every student has to attend the formation in the morning that is hold to check presence.
Art.22 - Every meal should be taken in the refectory, assisted by the teacher on the week schedule. He is the first to enter, and the last one to leave the room.

a) right after the bell, all the students should gather in front of the refectory. They must be properly combed and clean.
b) The presence in the refectory is obligatory. Only exception is in due of sickness, proven by the health responsible, or in any missions outside of the boarding school.
c) There must be meals saved for the students of the kitchen-service, for the teachers and the students in missions outside of the boarding school

Art.23 - every student must enter the classroom right after the bell, after 9.00 o clock.
Art. 24 - on Sunday and holidays the flag must be hoisted and lowered at 8.00 and 18.00 o clock.
Art. 25 - there is a teacher and two students - one girl and one boy- of service every week.
They are responsible for the fulfillment of this present regulation.

a) there is also a group of cleaning, responsible for the general hygiene of the boarding school each one week.
b) each week there is one group assigned to the services of the kitchen

Art. 26 - every Saturday, after a meeting hold by the teacher of the week and the committee, there is a general meeting for all the students and the teacher of service of the week.
Art. 27 - the teacher of the week needs to inform the Director of the boarding school, and the other teachers of any abnormality verified during the week.

Chapter 5 – Health care

Art. 28 - there's a constant health service led by a comrade doctor or nurse.

Chapter 6 - Penalties

Art. 29 - a teacher of the boarding school that will not follow his duties, after being criticized in an internal meeting of the boarding school with the comrade Director and teachers, will receive the following penalties:

a) objection
b) dismissal

Art.30 - every student that is committing an act of indiscipline receives the penalty of:

a) boarding school service
    1 if student misses the checking of presence without reason
    2 if the student abandons his place of service
    3 if the student mugs or fights with another one
    4 in cases of bad behavior outside of the boarding school
b) expulsion of class
    1 if the student didn't do his homework
    2 if the student disturbs in class
c) with one week of working outside of the boarding school
    1 if the students refuse to obey the teachers orders
    2 if the student takes or steals something from the boarding school or other persons

Art. 31 - every student that is repeatedly of undisciplined character, and so disturbs the general
    Order of the boarding school needs to be expelled.

Chapter 7 - Emulation

Art. 32 - there is a board of honor for those students who reach an average of "very good."

a) those students receive an award which should stimulate their works in school

Chapter 8 – Omission

Art. 33 - every case that hasn't been listed in this present regulation will be solved by the comrade Director of the boarding school.
September 1971
Source: The Nordic Africa Institute. Uppsala
(translated from Portuguese)

Annex 12. CIPM curriculum. School for the Training of Combatants

1. Education of the combatant:

a) What is the combatant for the party? His duties.

b) The relation between combatants – camaraderie and the mutual help
c) The relation between the combatants and the national
d) Revolutionary discipline (of the consciousness)
e) The difference between soldiers of the Party and soldiers of the Portuguese colonizers
f) Secrecy, surveillance and security
g) Honesty, discretion and modesty
h) Word and action
i) The necessity to constantly improve the military knowledge
j) Criticism and self-criticism
k) The worth of the example
l) The relation between combatants and the responsible

2. Brief history of Guinea and Cape Verde

The Portuguese Colonialism

3. Brief history of our Party

Foundation of our party. Mobilization and organization. The begin of the armed struggle. Development of the armed struggle – difficulties in it. Current situation. Perspectives.

4. The Party program

Some principles of operation of the party.

5. Religion. God. *Iran*. *Djambacoso* (Traditional Healer)

6. Tribalism: Limits and its disadvantages

Racism: The causes

7. Differentiation within the population (ethnicities) and the different social layers

- favorable
- hesitant
- indifferent
- enemies

The politics in relation to each of those social layers.

a) The relationship between the combatants and the nation. Strengthening the relationship between the nation and the F.A.R.P. Respect for the habits and religion of each of those ethnic groups. Respect for the property and population
b) The people: source of recruitment, supply and information.
c) Support of the people – fundamental fact for the liberation struggle.
d) Tribalism and religions.
e) Relating the interests between our people and our combatants. (there is no contradiction of interest between the F.A.R.P. and our people)
f) Our weaknesses: a constant fight against our weaknesses

8. Our enemy

a) who is our enemy?
b) His goals (military, political and economic)
c) His strengths. His weaknesses. His allies (internal, African and international)
d) His tactics in war, psychology and politics
e) We and the Portuguese

9. Our struggle and Africa

The meaning of our struggle for "black" Africa. Our allies in the African plan. Our enemies in the African plan.

10. Our struggle and the struggle of the Portuguese colonies

11. Our struggle in the international context

Other national liberation struggles (Vietnam)
Imperialist countries and the O.T.A.N.
Socialist countries and the U.R.S.S.
Progressive forces in the capitalist countries

12. The oath of the F.A.R.P. combatant

Program of Study of the center for Political and Military Instruction (CIPM)
   One Version

1. Colonial domination in Guiné
   1. Its characteristics

2. Its consequences
   stress in particular:
   a) the misery and ignorance
   b) the injustices and abuses
   c) racism and economic discrimination

2. Colonial domination on Cape Verde
   1. Its characteristics
   2. Its consequences
   3. The PAIGC:
      1. Mobilization and organization
      2. Beginning of the armed struggle
      3. Development of the armed struggles, stress in particular:
         a) difficulties met with
         b) mistakes committed
      4. The present situation:
         a) with regard to politics and administration
         b) with regard to the armed struggle
         c) with regard to national reconstruction
   4. The Program of the Party (summary)

Some principles of the Party:

1. Criticism and self-criticism
2. Democratic centralism
3. Collective leadership
4. Revolutionary democracy
5. Training of the fighting men
1. What a fighting man of the Party is
2. For whom it is necessary to fight
3. Discipline and organization
4. Relations between the fighting men: comradeship and discipline

Source: Arquivo & Biblioteca Fundação Mário Soares. Lisbon
(translated from Portuguese)

Annex 13. CIPM curriculum. School for the education of the combatants. Program to prepare the F.A.R.P. soldier

POLITICS

First part – 8 hours

1) short notions of geography, history and economy of Guiné and Cape Verde. The P.A.I.G.C. and the history of our struggle.
   – the exploration of our people by the Portuguese colonizers. The oppression. How they create oppression and exploration. The exploration and oppression of our people is not done in the interest of the Portuguese people. Differentiation between the Portuguese people and the Portuguese colonialism.

2) The conviction of the colonialism and the crimes that the Portuguese colonizers committed to the whole world. The right of our people for Liberty and Progress. What is progress.

3) The necessity to struggle for the liberation of our countries, conditions for constructing progress. The place of the youth in this struggle.

4) THE UNITY of the nation as a condition to achieve Independence, to defend the achieved Independence and to create progress. The importance of protecting the unity of the nation. Conviction of Racism and Tribalism. Unity of the people of Guiné, unity of the people of the Cape Verde and the unity of the both countries.

5) The necessity to prepare the people for our struggle. The necessity to mobilize. What is mobilization. The necessity of organization and direction.

6) the P.A.I.G.C., the party of the people of Guiné and Cape Verde. Brief history of the party and the struggle. In the party work the best of our sons. Why is it that the Party is the HOPE of our nation? The duty to protect our party. The enemies of the party, are enemies of the nation. The duty to respect the Hymn, the Flag, the Emblem and the leaders of the party.

7) Today, our party has millions of members. The love of the people for it's party is our fundamental strength. The party is the legitimate representative of the nation. The course of our party is the course of our nation.

8) The direction of the party. The central committee. The congress as the assembly of the legitimate representatives of the nation. The members of the central committee as the most dedicated sons of our nation. Who is the president of the central committee of the party. Who is the general secretary of the party.

9) What is the right behavior of a militant with his comrades. What means criticism and self-criticism. Differentiation between positive criticism and negative criticism. Differentiation between fraternal competition and competition.

10) What is a responsible of the party. Qualities that a responsible should require.

Second part – 10 hours

11) The program of the Party-program

a) The happiness of our people as goal of our party. The Liberty as first condition for the happiness of our people. The Independence.

b) The necessity to defend constantly the Independence after the achievement. The prohibition of any military bases.

c) The necessity to prevent that the power could be taken over by individuals that act in their own interest, exploring the nation. Internal enemies. Justice and progress for everyone. The internal enemies in the time of our struggle. Traitors and Opportunists. The need of military surveillance against the internal enemies. The right of the people to punish the internal enemies.

d) The colonial administration is against the interests of our people. The necessity to erase the political organization and administration of the colonizers. The necessity of an organization in service of our nation.

e) Liberty and Justice for everyone. The need that the people are effectively the ones who lead through our best sons of our nation (the most honest, the most capable and most friends with the people). The need that the law is equal for everybody. The emancipation of the woman, requirement of justice and progress.

f) Respect of the right to live, for physical integrity and the freedom of the people (Human rights). Freedom of domicile, of religion and work. Necessity of freedom of marriage.

g) How to treat foreigners that respect the nation and the laws.

h) The education of the people as a condition for progress. The need for alphabetization of the mass. The need to send all children that reach the scholar age to school. The need to educate the cadres. Obligatory and free primary education. The need to create primary schools, secondary schools, technical schools and universities. Development of physical education and sports. What the party does already: alphabetization, creation of schools and scholarships for the future cadres.

i) How important it is that everyone works with enthusiasm for the progress of our countries. Condemnation of vagrants. Parasites as enemies of the nation and of the progress. The respect that the workers deserve. The love for working. Heros of work.

j) To destroy all the traces of the colonial and imperial exploration, so that the earnings of work will be for the people. The idea of economic independence and neo-colonialism.

k) The idea of planning. Advantages of planning.

l) Goods that should be states property, and why. The advantages of cooperation and collective property. The end of private property that doesn't serve the interest of economic development of our countries. The personal property.

m) The need for development of agriculture. Modernization of agriculture. The disadvantages of mono-culture of peanut in Guiné and the mono-culture of corn in Cape Verde.

n) The need of industrial and handicraft Development.

o) What the party did for the domain of agricultural and trade production.

p) Organization of social assistance for those who involuntary are in need, in case of unemployment, invalidity or illness.

q) The need of an effective national defense. Organization of a national Defense starting from the armed forces of the liberty struggle. The necessity to support the National Defense of our people. The need of discipline in the armed forces. Loyalty and submission of the armed forces to the political leaders.

r) African Union. Reasons. Conditions.

s) The need of fraternal collaborations with other nations. Explanation of the principles that should be the base for such collaborations.: respect and national sovereignty, respect of territorial integrity, non-aggression, not intervening in internal issues, equality and reciprocal advantages, peaceful coexistence.

Third part – Our party and the struggle in the world – 2 hours

14) Our party in the context of the world. The nations and the governments that help our struggle. The help of Africa. Our neighbor countries. The socialistic countries help the nations that struggle for national liberty. The help of the socialistic countries for our party. Anti-colonial organizations in the world. The existence of those in countries where the governments help the Portuguese colonizers.

15) The governments allied with Portugal. Portugal can't fight the colonial fight without them. The O.T.A.N.

Fourth part – The oath of the combatant, explication
Explication of the oath of the combatant of the F.A.R.P.
Source: Arquivo & Biblioteca Fundação Mário Soares. Lisbon
(translated from Portuguese)

Annex 14. Statutes of the Party Pioneers

1 The goal of the Organization of the Pioneers of our Party (PP) is to contribute
to a good education for our children. Acting on the political principles of the
Party our Organization of the Pioneers is aiming to reinforce the love of our
children to its people. Our children's dedication to the struggle, their respect
for the family and school, their fondness for justice, work, progress and liberty.

The Pioneers of the Party try to create in all their companions the desire to
deserve wearing the yellow scarf of the Pioneers and that they long to attain
being the best sons of our nation being inspired by the example of the heroes
of our struggle of national liberation.

Our organization of the Pioneers leads all its activities in the aim to make
all their members a worthy militant of our grand Party, just as an honest
and conscious citizen. Therefore, it is very important for the preparation of
our youth for their grand responsibilities of tomorrow in the construction
of our country. Also in the uncompromising defense of the conquest in the
Revolution of the people of Guinea and Cape Verde.

2 The Organization of the Pioneers of our Party (PP) constitutes the organization
of Vanguard, from which only – in our present situation of our lives - the students
of the party schools can be part of. They have to fulfill the following conditions:
   a) They are at least 10 years old, but never older than 15.
   b) They completed the first year of primary education.
   c) They are good students, disciplined and dedicated to their companions,
   their school their parents and our nation.
   d) They manifested love and interest for our Party and our struggle.

3 The slogan of our Pioneers of the Party is: "Education – Work – Struggle". The
salutation is: "By the PAIGC, strength, light, and guidance for our nation!".
The Pioneers of the Party also have their own symbol and flag.

4 In every Party school is going to be a group of Pioneers, which activities will
be orientated by the teacher of the school.

5 The teacher of the school who is determined to monitor, will supervise the
activities of the group. He will promote its intensification and watches over
the fulfillment of the orders of the Pioneers and the decisions of the Central
Direction of the organization.

6 The Group of Pioneers has a weekly meeting in order to discuss all the questions that deal with their activities.

7 This meeting elects a committee which will execute all decisions.

8 The committees of each sector gathers in the first holidays of the semester (December) in order to elect a committee of the sector.

9 Its tasks is to coordinate the activities of the Pioneers of all sectors by the direct orientation of the political commissary of the party.

10 The admission of a new Pioneer is always done by a solemn session on the sector level. A delegate of the Direction of the Party will be present.

   The candidate is proposed by the group of his school and the candidacy is presented by the instructor.

   After the reading of the "Instructions of the Pioneers" the candidate has to owe the following "Promise of the Pioneer":

   "I promise to study every day with more attention, work every time with more dedication, fight always with courage in order to always be worthy of the Title of being a Pioneer of our Party at the forefront of the youth of our homeland. To contribute to the realization of the program of our Party, to the service of the national liberation and the construction of peace, progress and happiness of our people in Guinea and Cape Verde"

11 The following are the "Instructions of the Pioneer":

   – The Pioneer of the Party loves the homeland, just like the organization for the struggle of constructing our homeland
   – The Pioneer of the Party prepares himself to become a good militant and a good citizen of Guinea and Cape Verde
   – The Pioneer of the Party loves his parents
   – The Pioneer of the Party is a good friend to his comrades and seeks the friendship of all the children of the school, trying to influence them with his good example of a Pioneer.
   – The Pioneer of the Party loves work and respects every worker
   – The Pioneer of the Party loves and defends justice, progress and liberty.
   – The Pioneer of the Party helps everyone who needs his help unwittingly and especially the victims and the families of the victims of our struggle for national liberation.
   – The Pioneer of the Party considers himself responsible for his school.
   – The Pioneer of the Party studies hard, is disciplined, respectful, tidy and seeks to be everyday better in all his activities.
   – The Pioneer of the Party is clean, watches over his health and loves physical exercise and sports

- The Pioneer of the Party does not lie, does not smoke, nor drinks alcohol. He fulfills his promises and executes all his tasks on time
- The Pioneer of the Party is happy, because he has confidence in the strength of our nation and in the future of our country. He likes to play, laugh and sing, to have fun in a healthy way.
- The Pioneer of the Party honors in every situation his yellow Pioneer scarf.

12 Activities

The group of Pioneers discusses and takes decisions in weekly meetings. All the questions that deal with our struggle of liberty, the life of the group, of the school and its region. The assembly can designate brigades of Pioneers to help the work of the committee.

The group of Pioneers promotes meetings with parents, with the leaders of the party, with the responsible politicians of the region, with the workers, the militants, the fighters, with our foreign friends that visit our country and with everybody who shows interest for the good work of our Group.

The Group of Pioneers has to organize sport competitions, drawing, hand-craft, musical and other contests, for the members of the group, the students of the school and other groups. In order to realize common activities for two or more groups they can create mixed committees of Pioneers which will work on the orientation of the supervisors.

Every two months the assembly chooses a group to "hold the flag" which must be the best of all the Pioneers.

The Group of Pioneers will keep a book in order, which is called "Our life and our struggle" and where they will put all their activities. The Group of Pioneers also owns their "book of honor" where they will register all approvals they received and in which visitors can leave their impressions that they had of the group.

13 Everybody who, for whatever reproachable action, was judged by the assembly in agreement with the supervisor, unworthy to wear the yellow scarf of the Pioneers of the Party must quit to be a Pioneers of the Party.

14 The Pioneer of the Party can be recompensed for special merits with the following awards:

a) approval in the assembly of the group
b) approval and registration in the "Book of Honor" of the group
c) a photography in front of the flag of the party
d) a quote in the "*Blufo*"

Source: Arquivo & Biblioteca Fundação Mário Soares. Lisbon
(translated from Portugese)

Annex 15. PAIGC's official information about the publication of the school manual for the first class

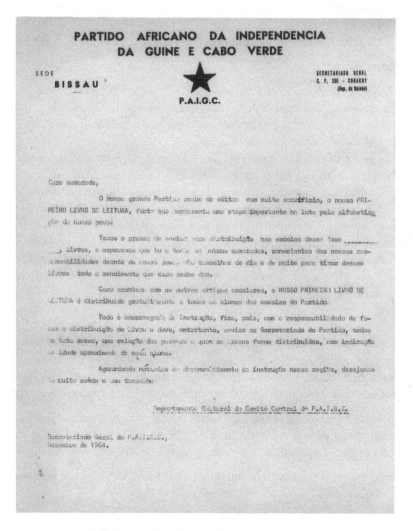

Source: Arquivo & Biblioteca Fundação Mário Soares. Lisbon

Annex 16. PAIGC's Program "*Semaine d'Information. Spectacle Artistique*" Palais du Peuple in Conakry, 17-22 July 1972

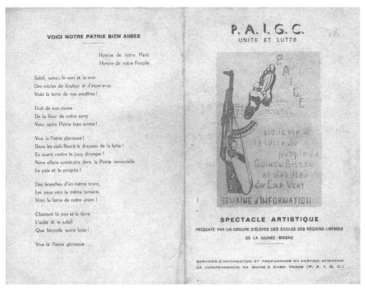

Source: Original brochure kindly offered by Arlette Cabral. Bissau 2014

Annex 17. *Escola Piloto* School exam for the politics

Positivo

ESCOLA-PILOTO DO P.A.I.G.C.

PONTO DE EXAME DE POLÍTICA

Nome : *Quessana Baian*

Classe : 4ª   Data : 14-5-68

– I –

1°) Que acontecimentos importantes se verificaram na vida do nosso povo nas seguintes datas :

– 19 de Setembro de 1956 – *Foi fundado o nosso partido*

– 3 de Agosto de 1959 – *Começou a luta armada*

2°) Risca as frases que não estiverem bem :

– ~~O nosso Partido foi fundado em Dakar~~

– ~~O nosso Partido foi fundado na Praia~~

– O nosso Partido foi fundado em Bissau.

– II –

1°) Responde SIM ou NÃO às seguintes perguntas :

– Um menino de 11 anos pode ser militante do Partido ? *Não*

– Um pioneiro pode ser ao mesmo tempo militante do Partido ? *Não*

– Um menino de 7 anos pode ser pioneiro do Partido ? *Não*

– Um velho de 80 anos pode ser militante do Partido ? *Sim*

2°) – Risca o que estiver mal :

– ~~A divisa do Partido é "Estudo, Trabalho e Luta".~~

– A divisa do Partido é "Unidade e Luta"

– A divisa do Partido é "Abaixo o colonialismo português!"

3°) – Preenche com números os espaços deixados nas seguintes frases :

"Na organização do Partido, a Guiné e Cabo Verde dividem-se em Regiões. Em Cabo Verde há *dois* Regiões; na Guiné há *sete* Regiões. As Regiões de Guiné estão reunidas em *dois* Inter-Regiões."

..../...

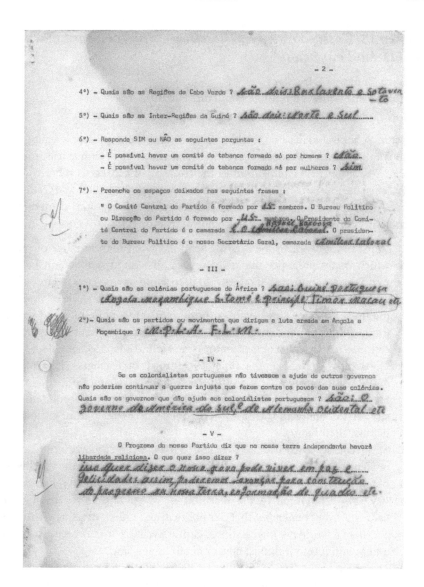

- 2 -

4º) - Quais são as Regiões de Cabo Verde ? *São dois: Barlavento e Sotavento*

5º) - Quais são as Inter-Regiões da Guiné ? *São dois: Norte e Sul*

6º) - Responde SIM ou NÃO as seguintes perguntas :

- É possível haver um comité de tabanca formado só por homens ? *Não*
- É possível haver um comité de tabanca formado só por mulheres ? *Sim*

7º) - Preenche os espaços deixados nas seguintes frases :

" O Comité Central do Partido é formado por *15* membros. O Bureau Político ou Direcção do Partido é formado por *15* membros. O Presidente do Comité Central do Partido é o camarada *Amilcar Cabral*. O presidente do Bureau Político é o nosso Secretário Geral, camarada *Amilcar Cabral*

- III -

1º) - Quais são as colónias portuguesas de África ? *São: Guiné Portuguesa, Angola, moçambique, S.tomé e príncipe, Timor, macau etc.*

2º) - Quais são os partidos ou movimentos que dirigem a luta armada em Angola e Moçambique ? *M.P.L.A. F.L.i.M.*

- IV -

Se os colonialistas portugueses não tivessem a ajuda de outros governos não poderiam continuar a guerra injusta que fazem contra os povos das suas colónias. Quais são os governos que dão ajuda aos colonialistas portugueses ? *São: O governo da América do Sul e da Alemanha ocidental etc*

- V -

O Programa do nosso Partido diz que na nossa terra independente havará liberdade religiosa. O que quer isso dizer ? *isso quer dizer o nosso povo pode viver em paz e felicidade assim, poderemos avançar para construção do progresso na nossa terra, enformação de quadros etc*

Source: Arquivo Amílcar Cabral- Fundação Mário Soares

Annex 18. *Cassacá Congress Directive – "Improve our knowledge and Defend our health"*

Cassacá Congress Directives[327]
" Improve our Knowledge and Defend our Health

To carry on the victorious development of our struggle, we must:

A. Set up schools and develop teaching in all liberated areas. Choose youngsters)boys and girls) between the ages of fourteen and twenty, with at least fourth-year education who can be used in the training of cadres. Combat without violence harmful practices , the, negative aspects of the beliefs and traditions of our people. Make responsible workers of the Party and all dedicated militants constantly improve their cultural training.

1. Improve the work in the existing schools, avoid high number of pupils which might prejudice the advantage of all. Found schools but bear in mind the real potential at our disposal, to avoid having later to close some schools through lack of resources. Frequently inspect work of teacher's methods they are using. Avoid corporal punishment of pupils and strictly follow programmes drawn up the Party for elementary and primary education. Set up special courses for the training and advancement of teachers.

2. Constantly strengthen the political training of teachers, their unlimited devotion to the Party and the people. Dismiss and punish all those teachers who fail in their duties. ºpersuade parents of the absolute necessity for the pupils in such a way that they can also be useful at home in helping their family.

3. Set up courses to teach adults to read and write, weather they are combatants or elements of the population. On all sides ensure respect for the watchword of our party – 'all those who know should teach those who do not know'.

4. pay closest attention to the recruitment of youngsters for training as cadres. Always remember that our political and military victories will lead nowhere if we do not have national cadres available for the reconstruction and scientific and technical development of our land.

   In choice of candidates for training cadres, give preference to the youngest, to the best militants of the Party, to individuals (boys and girls) who have given evidence of intelligence and willingness to learn.

---

327 The seventh of a total the eight directives giving theoretical and practical guidance for Party workers. The directives were written by Amílcar Cabral in 1965 after the Cassacá Congress held in 1964.

5. Combat among the youth , notably among the more mature (above the age of twenty), the obsession with
   leaving the country to go and study, the blind ambition to be a *doctor*, the inferiority complex and the mistaken notion that those who study and take courses will have privileges tomorrow in our land. Do not accept as a candidate for a scholarship any responsible worker of the Party with leadership duties, whatever his level of education. But combat above all among responsible workers who have devoted themselves to the struggle, ill will against those who study or want to study, the complex that makes them think that all students are dangerous and future saboteurs of the Party. (Winning the battle of training cadres, to ensure the cadres needed for the development of our land is one of the most important aspects of the action and programme of our Party.)

6. Protect and develop manifestations of our people's culture, respect and ensure respect for the usages, customs and traditions of our land, so long as they are not against human dignity, against the respect we must long for every man, woman or child. Support manifestations of art 8music, dance, painting and sculpture), hold competitions among artist, form groups for dancing, singing and theatre, make collections of works of art, collect text of legends and tales by the people. Combat all particularisms (separatist feeling) prejudicial to the unity of the people, all demonstrations of tribalism, of racial or religious discrimination. Respect and ensure respect for each one's religion and the right not to have a religion.

7. pay special attention to the life of the children, develop their personality and protect them against abuses, even on the part of parents and relatives. Defend the rights of woman, respect and ensure respect for women (in childhood, as young girls and adult women), but persuade women in our land that their liberation must be their own achievement through their work, dedication to the Party, self-respect, personality and firmness in the face of anything that might offend their dignity.

8. teach ourselves and teach others and the population in general to combat fear and ignorance, to stamp out little by little submissiveness before nature and natural forces which our system has not yet mastered. Struggle without unnecessary violence all the negative aspects, harmful man, which still form part of our beliefs and traditions. Little by little persuade militants of the Party particularly that we shall end up overcoming the fear of nature, knowing that man is the most powerful force in nature.

9. demand from responsible workers of the Party, that they devote themselves seriously to study, that they take interest in aspects and questions

of life and of the struggle in their essential basic character, and not merely superficially. Make every responsible worker constantly improve his knowledge, his culture, his political training. Convince everyone that no one can know without learning and the most ignorant person is the one who purports to know without having learned. Learn from life, learn with our people, learn in books and from the experience of other. Constantly learn. (responsible workers must put a definitive stop to the spirit of child-ishness, irresponsibility, carefreeness, friendship based on 'easy come', in order to face up to life with seriousness, full awareness of responsibilities, with concern for proper achievement, with comradeship based on work and duty done – as genuine responsible workers for our party and our people. None of this rule out joy at living, love of the life and amusements, confidence foe the future, which must enliven our action, our struggle and the work of each of us.)

10. little by little set up libraries ion the liberated areas, lend others the books we possess, help others to learns to read a book, the newspaper and to understand what is read. Give the widest possible distribution to the Party newspaper, hold sessions for collective reading (in a group) and lead those who are reading into discussion and into expressing views on what that have read.

11. always remember that a good militant (like a good citizen) is the one who does his duty properly. He is the one who, in addition to doing his duty, succeeds in improving himself each day so as to be able to do more and better."

Source: Amílcar Cabral, Revolution in Guinea: Selected Texts by Amílcar Cabral. (New York: Monthly Press Review, 1969, 242-244).

List of Photos

List of Figures

List of Tables

List of Annexes

Bibliography

Consulted Archives
In Portugal

Fundação Mário Soares Archive (AMS) - Amílcar Cabral Documents

PAIGC. "A nossa luta pela educação das massas e pela formação de quadros." Setembro 1965.

PAIGC. "Assembleia Nacional Popular (Guiné-Bissau). Lista dos Conselhos Regionais dos Deputados (representação popular)." Julho de 1973.

PAIGC. "Apontamentos das Aulas de Política. Centro de Aperfeiçoamento de Professores." Conackry, Julho/Setembro 1966.

PAIGC. "Blufo. Orgão dos Pioneiros do Partido." 1966-1973.

PAIGC. "Brochura." Calendário Escolar. Janeiro 1, 1971.

PAIGC. "Centro de Aperfeiçoamento de Professores." Julho/Setembro 1966. 6.

PAIGC. "Classificação e resultados finais dos alunos Instituto Amizade." 5 de Julho de 1969. 2.

PAIGC. "Elevar a Consciência Política e a Militancia dos Estudantes do Partido." Novembro 19-24, 1969. 10.

PAIGC. "Escola para a formação de combatentes." n.d. 16.

PAIGC. "Escola para a Formação de combatentes." n.d.

PAIGC. "Estatutos dos Pioneiros do Partido." n.d. 3.

PAIGC. "História de África. Lições feitas no Centro de aperfeiçoamento de professores em 1966." 60.

PAIGC. "La Republique de Guinee-Bissau en Chiffres." Comissariat d'Etat à l'Economie et aux Finances, Février 1974. 31.

PAIGC. "Lições de História da Guiné e Cabo Verde. IV Centro de Centro de aperfeiçoamento de professores." 1968, 30.

PAIGC. "Lista de estudantes do PAIGC no exterior." n.d.

PAIGC. "Notas de Amílcar Cabral para a conversa na Escola [Piloto] com os responsáveis." n.d.

PAIGC. "O analfabetismo na nossa terra. Suas causas e consequências." 1973. 7.

PAIGC. "O nosso Partido e a luta devem ser dirigidos pelos melhores filhos do nosso povo." Novembro 19-24, 1969. 14.

PAIGC. "Organização dos Estudantes do PAIGC em Moscovo. Criação da Secção do Partido. Pedido de aparelhos. Livros. Documentação de informação." Setembro de 1962, 8.

PAIGC. "Para a reorganização e melhoria do trabalho Brigadas de Acção Política." Sónia Vaz Borges, Fevereiro 1971. 7.

PAIGC. "Programa de estágio na Universidade Operária africana." n.d.

PAIGC. "O programa do PAIGC." 1973.

PAIGC. "Quadros formados pelo PAIGC desde o inicio da luta." n.d. 6.

PAIGC. "Relatório sobre a missão de alfabetização no interior." Agosto de 1964. 3.

PAIGC. "Reunião do Conselho Superior da Luta. Sobre alguns problemas práticos da nossa vida e da nossa luta. Intervenção do camarada Amílcar Cabral." Agosto 1971. 24.

PAIGC. "Reunião com o corpo do Centro [de Aperfeiçoamento de Professores]." Agosto de 1968, 6.

PAIGC. "Reunião com os Professores da Escola Piloto." Feveiro de 1970, 8.

PAIGC. "Sur la situation de Notre Lutte de Liberation Nationale. Rapport du Camarade Amilcar Cabral Secretaire Général du PAIGC." Décembre 1966. 30.

PAIGC. "The Party Program of the PAIGC." n.d.

CIDAC Archive – Centro de Intervenção para o Desenvolvimento Amílcar Cabral

PAIGC. "Reconstrução Nacional. Dados Estatísticos." n.d.

PAIGC. "Educação tarefa de toda a sociedade. Comissariado de Estado da educação Nacional.", 1978, 34.

Archive Instituto dos Arquivos Nacionais/ Torre do Tombo (IAN/TT) –

The collection of fourteen files produced about Amílcar Cabral political, diplomatic and military work and the ongoing operations of the liberation struggle. The collection was produced by the Portuguese Police PIDE/DGS during the years 1956-1974.

In Cape Verde

Archive Fundação Amílcar Cabral

Arruda, Marcos. "Uma educação criadora para as sociedades africanas independentes." Economia e Socialismo _ Revista Mensal de Economia Política, September 1978: 18–29.

PAIGC. "I Encontro de Ministros da Educação e educadores de Angola; Cabo Verde, Guiné-Bissau, Moçambique e S.Tomé: À procura de uma nova educação." O Militante, March/April 1978: 48–51.

PAIGC. O nosso livro 2. classe. Uppsala: Toffers/Wretmans Boktryckeri AB, 1970.

PAIGC. O nosso livro 3° classe. Uppsala: Toffers /Wretmans Boktryckeri AB, 1970.

PAIGC. O nosso livro 4° classe. Uppsala: Wretmans Boktreckeri AB, 1974.

PAIGC. O nosso primeiro livro de leitura. Conakry: Edição do Departamento Secretariado, informação, Cultura e Formação de Quadros do Comité Central do PAIGC, 1966.

PAIGC. "Reunião com os professores da Escola Piloto." 13-2-1970.

Ramos, Domingos. "Quadros formados pelo Partido até 1971." 31-12-1971.

In Sweden

Archive Nordiska Afrikainstitutet (NAI-Uppsala) – PAIGC Documents

PAIGC. "Formação Militante. programa da 4° classe." n.d.

PAIGC. "Instituto Amizade - Estatutos." Translated by Sónia Vaz Borges. Maio 1969. 4.

PAIGC. "Programa da 1° classe. Coordenadora: Maria Emília da Graça Vieira da Silva Ferreira." n.d.

PAIGC. "Programa da 2° Classe: coordenadora Fátima Barbosa Moura." n.d.

PAIGC. "Programa da 3° classe: Coordenadora da Classe María Emília das Neves Évora." n.d.

PAIGC. "Programa do Ensino para as escolas das regiões libertadas.", Departamento de Reconstrução Nacional / Serviço de Ensino, n.d. 17.

PAIGC. "Regulamento das escolas do Partido." Setembro 19, 1966. 3.

PAIGC. "Regulamento Interno dos Internatos das Regiões Libertadas.", 1971: Publicação do Serviço de Reconstrução Nacional/Ensino, n.d. 7.

PAIGC. "The Party Programm of the PAIGC." n.d.

UNSA of Sweden. "The Educational Systems of the Liberation Movements and the Portuguese in Angola, Mozambique and Guinea-Bissau." Nineteenth General Conference, n.d.

In Berlin -

Archive Arsenal – Institut für Film und Videokunst/ INCA -Instituto Nacional de Cinema e Audiovisual (Berlin/Bissau)

INCAGB_004: Description: A group of students from Guinea Bissau volunteering in Cuba. Among the volunteers are; Josefina Crato, José Bolama Cobumba, Sana Na N'hada and Flora Gomes. Who studied cinema at the Cuban institute of cinematographic art and industry (icaic), 1967.

INCAGC_009: Description: O Regresso de Cabral (The Return of Cabral) by José Bolama Cobumba, Josefina Crato, Flora Gomes and Sana Na N'hada, 1976.

INCAGB_025: Description: Amílcar Cabral youth (JAAC) meeting/homage to guerrilla martyr Tetina Silá. Women's meeting and speech. Commemoration walk to the rio Farim. 1976/77.

INCAGB?029: Description: unilateral declaration of independence. Footage by Sana Na N'hada. Boé forest, 24 September 1994./ the second PAIGC congresso. Boé forest, July 1973, 1973.

INCAGB_032: Description: The week of information, hosted by Amílcar Cabral in Conakry in September 1972 and held at the Palais du Peuple (people's palace). Features an exhibition about the liberation war in guinea. Among the special guests are Ahmed Sékou Touré, Hadja André Touré, Luís Cabral, Kwame Ture (Stokley Carmichael) and Miriam Makeba. PAIGC headquarters and the Pilot school. 1972.

INCAGB_102: Description: March 8, 1970. Cabral's speech on women: presented at the Pilot School of PAIGC in Conakry, on international women's day, the speech celebrates a cause that only in 1975 was recognized by the UN and, thus, international acclaimed. 1970.

Consulted personal Archives

Personal documents from Commander Agnelo Dantas (Cape Verde).

Personal documents from Amélia and Teresa Araújo (Cape Verde).

Personal documents from Arlette Cabral (Guiea Bissau).

Personal documents from Maria da Luz Boal and Manuel Boal (Cape Verde).

Personal documents from Birgitta Dahl (Sweden).

Personal documents from Lars Rudebeck (Sweden).

Personal documents from Löfgren Folke (Sweden).

Filmography

"Sans Soleil" Directed by Chris Marker, Argos Films, 100', 1983.

"Labanta Negro" Directed by Piero Nelli, 39', Italy 1966.

"No Pintcha" Directed by Tobias Engel, René Lefort and Gilbert Ingel. Performed by René Lefort; Gilbert Ingel, 65', France, 1970.

" En Nations Födelse" (Birth of Nation) Directed by Lennart Malmer and Ingela Romare, Sveriges Telivision (SVT), 48', Sweden, 1973.

"Navigating the Pilot School." Directed by Filipa César and Sónia Vaz Borges, 12', Berlin, 2016.

"Spell Reel" Directed by Filipa César, Spectre Productions, 96', Berlin, 2017.

Portuguese colonial legislation

Acto Colonial: Dec. no. 18.570, of 8 July 1930.

Código do Trabalho dos Indígenas nas colónias Portuguesas de África: Dec. no. 16 199, from 6 December of 1928.

Estatuto missionário: Dec. Lei n.º 31 207, of 5 April of 1941.

Estatuto dos Indígenas Portugueses das Províncias da Guiné, Angola e Moçambique, Dec.Lei n. 39 666, from 20 May of 1954.

General bibliography (books, magazines, articles and reports)

Achebe, Chinua. *The education of A British-protected child*. New York: Alfred A. Knopf, 2009.

Adi, Hakim, and Marika Sherwood. *Pan-Africanism History: Political figures from Africa and the Diaspora since 1787*. London: Routledge, 2003.

Agrippah, Mugomba T., and Nyaggah Mougo. *Independence without freedom. The political economy of colonial education in Southern Africa*. Oxford: Clio Press, 1981.

Ali A. Abdi and Ailie Cleghorn, *Issue in African history* (New York: Palgrave Macmillan, 2005), 12.

Anderson, Benedict. *Imagined Communities. Reflections on the origin and spread of nationalism*. New York: Verso, 2006.

Andrade, Mário de. *Amílcar Cabral: Essai de Biographie Politique*. Paris: François Maspero, 1980.

Andrade, Mário de. *A geração Cabral*. Editado por P.A.I.G.C. Conakry: Instituto Amizade, 1973.

Andrade, Mário de. *Origens do Nacionalismo Africano. Continuidade e ruptura nos movimentos unitários emergentes da luta contra a dominação colonial portuguesa: 1911-1961*. Lisboa: Publicações Dom Quixote, 1998.

Appiah, Kwame Anthony. *In my father's House: Africa in the Philosophy of Culture*. New York: Oxford university Press, 1992.

Arruda, Marcos. "Uma educação criadora para as sociedades africanas independentes." *Economia e Socialismo _ Revista Mensal de Economia Política*, September 1978: 18–29.

Asante, Molefi Keti. *The Afrocentric idea*. Philadelphia: Temple University Press, 1998.

Assie-Lumumba, N'Dri T. "Cultural foundations of the idea and practice of the teaching profession in Africa: Indigenous roots, colonial intrusion, and post-colonial reality." *Educational Philosophy and Theory*, 2012: 21–36.

Augel, Moema Parente. *O desafio do escombro: nação, identidade e pós-colonialismo na literatura da Guiné Bissau*. Rio de Janeiro: Garamond Universitária, 2007.

Bartkowski, Maciej J. *Recovering nonviolent history. Civil resistance in liberation struggles*. London: Lynne Reinner Publishers, 2013.

Battle, Vincent M., and Charles H. Lyons. *Essays in the history of African education*. New York: Teachers College University, 1970.

Bélanger, Paul. "Une pratique de Contre-ècole: L' expérience éducative du mouvement de libération nationale dans les zones libérées de lá Guinée-Bissau." *Sociologie et Sociétés*, 1980: 155–168.

Bell, Morag. *Geography and Imperialism, 1820-1940*. New York: Manchester University Press, 1995.

Biko, Steve. *I write what I like*. Johannesburg: Heinemann, 1987.

Borges, Sónia Vaz. *Amílcar Cabral: estratégias políticas e culturais para a independência da Guiné e Cabo Verde*. Lisbon: Universidade de Letras de Lisboa, 2008.

Bornat, Joanna. "Remembering in later life: Generating individual and social change." In *The Oxford handbook of oral history*, by Donald A. Ritchie, 202–218. Oxford: Oxford University Press, 2011.

Brodiez, Axelle. "Militants, bénevoles, affliés, affranchise: de l'applicabilite historique des travaux sociologiques." (2004), URL. https://halshs.archives-ouvertes.fr/halshs-00174309/document (accessed August 3, 2017).

Cá, Lourenço Ocuni. *Perspectiva histórica da Organização do sistema educacional da Guiné Bissau*. São Paulo: UNICAMP, 2005.

Cabral, Amílcar. *Unity and Struggle. Speeches and Writings.* New York: Monthly Review Press, 1979.

Cabral, Amílcar. *Análise de alguns tipos de Resistência.* Bolama: Imprensa Nacional, 1979.

Cabral, Amílcar. "A propósito da educação." *Boletim de Propaganda e Informação,* June 1951: 24–25.

Cabral, Amílcar. *Revolution in Guinea: Selected Texts by Amílcar Cabral.* New York: Monthly Press Review, 1979.

Cabral, Amílcar. *Unidade e Luta. A Prática Revolucionária.* Lisboa: Seara Nova, 1977.

Cabral Amílcar, *Unidade e Luta. A Arma da Teoria.* Lisboa: Seara Nova: , 1978.

Cabral, Luís. *Crónica da Libertação.* Lisboa: O Jornal, 1984.

Callewaert, Inger. *The birth of religions among the Balanta of Guinea-Bissau.* Lund: Department of History and Religions. University of Lund, 2000.

Carreira, António. "A educação dos indígenas africanos pela administração local." *Boletim Cultural da Guiné Portuguesa,* Janeiro 1953: 89–105.

Carreira, António. "Aspectos Históricos da evolução do Islamismo na Guiné Portuguesa. Achagas para o seu estudo." *Boletim Cultural da Guiné Portuguesa,* Outubro 1966, 84 ed.: 405–457.

Carvalho, Maria Adriana Sousa. *O Liceu em Cabo Verde, um imperativo de cidadania (1917-1975).* Praia: Edições Uni-CV, 2011.

Césaire, Aimê. *Discourse on Colonialism.* London: Monthly Review Press, 1972.

Chung, Fay. *Re-living the Second Chimurenga Memories from the Liberation Struggle in Zimbabwe.* Stockholm: Nordiska Afrikainstitutet, 2006.

Cleghorn, Ailie. "Language issues in African school setting: problems and prospects in Attaining Education for All." In *Issues in African Education. Sociological perspectives,* by Ailie Cleghorn and Ali A. Abdi, 101–122. New York: Palgrave Macmillan, 2005.

Cleaver, Eldridge. "Education and revolution." *The Black Scholar,* Vol. 1 Issue no. 1, the culture of revolution (1969): 44–52.

Conceição, Fernando. *Negritude Favelada (teoria e militância). A questão do Negro e o poder na "democracia racial brasileira".* Salvador: Edição do Autor, 1988.

Daled, Pierre. "Une définition des termes: la 'laïcisation' du militant au 19e et au début du 20e siècle" in Militantisme et militants, coordinated by José Gotovitch et Anne Morelli, (Bruxelles: EVO, 2000) 8–9.

Datta, Asit, and Gregor Lang-Wojtasik. *Bildung zur Eigenständigkeit. Vergessene reformpädagogische Ansätze aus vier Kontinenten.* Frankfurt am Main: IKO-Verlag für Interkulturelle Kommunikation, 2002.

Davidson, Basil. "Portuguese' Africa. The struggle for independence." in *The UNESCO Courier*. November 1973, 4-8.

Davidson, Basil. "On Revolutionary Nationalism: The Legacy of Cabral." *Latin American Perspectives 11*, 1984: 15–42.

Davidson, Basil. *No Fist is Big Enough to Hide the Sky: The liberation of Guinea and Cape Verde: Aspects of an African Revolution*. London: Zed, 1981.

Dei, George J. Sefa. *Teaching Africa: Towards a Transgressive Pedagogy*. New York: Springer, 2010.

Depelchin, Jacques. *Silences in African History. Between the syndromes of discovery and abolition*. Dar es Salaam: Mkuki Na Nyota Publishers, 2005.

Dhada, Mustafah. *Warriors at Work: How Guinea was really set free*. Niwot: University Press of Colorado, 1993.

Dahl, Birgitta; Andreasson, Knut. *Guinea-Bissau: rapport om ett land och en befrielserörelse*. Stockholm:Prisma, 1971.

Dewwes, Anthony; Arnove, Robert F. "Education in revolutionary Nicaragua, 1979-1990." *Comparative Education Review*, vol. 35, Issue no. 1, Special issue on education and socialist Revolution (1991): 92–109.

Diallo, Ibrahima. *Em torno da problemática da língua de ensino*. Bissau: Agencia Sueca para o Desenvolvimento Internacional (ASDI), 1996.

Diallo, Ibrahima. *L' incidence des facteurs sociolinguistiques sur l' usage et l' apprentissage des langues en Guiné-Bissau- Une étude des classes expérimentales CEEF avec créole comme langue d'enseignement dans la région de Catio*. Bissau: Agencia Sueca para o desenvolvimento Internacional (ASDI), 1995.

Enwezor, Okwui. "The short century: Independence and liberation movements in Africa 1945-1994: An introduction." In *The short century: Independence and liberation movements in Africa 1945-1994*, by Okwui Enwezor, 10–17. New York: Prestel, 2002.

Esedebe, Olisanwuche P. *Pan-Africanism: The idea and Movement, 1976-1963*. Washington D.C: Howard University Press, 1994.

Fanon, Frantz. *Os condenados da Terra*. Lisboa: Editora Ulisseia, 1961.

Faria, António. *Linha Estreita da Liberdade. A Casa dos Estudantes do Império*. Lisboa: Edições Colibri, 1997.

Förster, Steig, Ronald Robinson, and Mommsen J. Wolfgang. *Bismark, Europe, and Africa: The Berlin Africa Conference 1884-1885 and the onset partition*. New York: Oxford University Press, 1988.

Freire, Paulo. *Cartas à Guiné-Bissau. Registo de uma experiência em processo*. Lisboa: Moraes Editores, 1978.

Freire, Paulo. *Educação como prática da liberdade*. Rio de janeiro: Paz e Terra, 1967.

Freire, Paulo. *Pedagogy of the oppressed*. New York: The Seabury Press, 1970.

Freire, Paulo. *Amílcar Cabral. O Pedagogo da Revolução*. http://forumeja.org.br/files/amilcar.pdf (accessed November 18, 2016).

Freire, Paulo, and Sérgio Guimarães. *A África ensinando a gente. Angola, Guiné-Bissau, São Tomé e Príncipe*. São Paulo: Paz e Terra, 2003.

Geary, Maurice, "Education for revolution: a study of revolutionary strategies, and leadership from three ideological perspectives." PhD diss., Wayne State University of Detroit, University of Detroit, 1976.

Geiss, Imanuel. *The Pan-African Movement: A history of Pan-Africanism in America, Europe, and Africa*. New York: Africana, 1974.

George, Edward. *The Cuban intervention in Angola, 1965-1991. From Che Guevara to Cuito Cuanavale*. New York: Frank Cass, 2012.

Giroux, Henry. *Teachers as intellectuals: Toward a critical pedagogy of learning*. London: Bergin & Garvey, 1988.

Grovogui, Siba n'Zatioula. *Sovereigns, Quasi Sovereigns, and Africans: Race and Self-Determination in International Law*. Minneapolis: University of Minnesota, 1996.

Hamilton, Paula. "The Proust effect: oral history and the senses." In *The Oxford handbook of oral history*, by Donald A. Ritchie, 219–232. Oxford: University Press, 2011.

Harper, R. Charles, and J. William Nottingham. *Escape from Portugal - the church in action. The secret flight of 60 African students*. St. Louis-Missouri: Lucas Park Books, 2015.

Hatzky, Christine. *Kubaner in Angola. Süd-Süd Kooperation und Bildungstransfer 1976-1991*. München: Oldenbourg, 2012.

Hollander, Paul, *The many faces of Socialism. Comparative sociology and politics*. London: Transaction Books, 1983.

hooks, bell. *Teaching to transgress. Education as a practice of freedom* (New York. Routledge Taylor & Francis Group, 1994).

hooks, bell. *Teaching Community. A pedagogy of hope*. New York: Routledge, 2003.

Ion, Jacques. "Militant, militantisme" in *Dictionnaire de sociologie Le Robert*, (Paris: Seuil, 1999), 341.

Ion, Jacques. *Teaching to transgress. Education as a practice of freedom*. New York: Routledge Taylor & Francis Group, 1994.

Kelly, Gail P., and Philip G. Altbach. *Education and colonialism*. New York: Longman Inc., 1978.

King, Kenneth James. *Pan-Africanism and Education: a Study of race Philanthropy and Education in the Southern States of América and East Africa*. Oxford: Clarendon Press, 1971.

Laban, Michel. *Mário Pinto de Andrade. Uma entrevista dada a Michel Laban*. Lisboa: Edições João Sá da Costa, 1997.

Lara, Lúcio. *Documentos e comentários para a historia do MPLA*. Porto: Edições Afrontamento, 1995.

Lema, Elieshi, Marjorie Mbilinyi, and Rakesh Rajani. *Nyerere on Education*. Dar es Salaam: The Mwalimu Nyerere Foundation, 2004.

Lopo Vaz de Sampayo Mello, *Política Indígena*. Porto: Magalhães e Moniz Lda., 1910.

Machel, Samora. *Produzir é um acto de militância*. Maputo: Departamento do Trabalho Idelógico, 1979.

Machel, Samora. *Fazer da Escola uma base para o povo tomar o poder*. Liboa: Publicações Nova Aurora, 1974.

Madeira, Ana Isabel. *Popular education and republican ideals: The Portuguese lay missions in colonial Africa*. Vol. 47, in *Paedagogica Historica*, 123–138. Routledge Taylor&Francis Group, 2011.

Madeira, Ana Isabel. *Portuguese, French and British discourses on colonial education: church-state relations, school expansion and missionary competition in Africa, 1890-1930*. Vol. 41, in *Paedagogica Historica*, 31–60. Routledge Taylor &Francis Group, 2005.

Marah, John Karefah. "Educational adaptation and pan-Africanism: developmental trends in Africa." *Journal of Black Studies*, June 1987: 460–481.

Karl Marx, *A contribution to the critique of political economy*. Calcutta: Abinash Chandra Saha, 1904, 11–12.

McCorquodale, Robert. *Self-determination in International law*. Dartmouth: Aldershot Publishing Company, 2000.

Memmi, Albert. *The colonizer and the colonized*. UK: Earthscan Publications Ltd, 2003.

Mendy, Peter Karibe. *Colonialismo português em África: A tradição da resistência na Guiné-Bissau (1879-1959)*. Bissau: INEP, 1994.

Montero, Martiza, and Christopher C. Sonn. *Psychology of Liberation. Theory and applications*. Venezuela: Springer, 2009.

Mota, Avelino Teixeira. *Guiné Portuguesa*. Lisboa: Agencia Geral do Ultramar, 1954.

Moutinho, Mário. *O indígena no pensamento colonial português*. Lisboa: Edições Universitárias Lusófonas, 2000.

Mudimbe, V.Y. *The invention of Africa*. London: Indiana University Press, 1988.

Murray, Albert V. *The school in the bush: a critical study of the theory and practice of native education in Africa*. London: Cass, 1967.

N'Krumah, Kwame. *Africa must unite*. London: Panaf Books, 1998.

N'Krumah, Kwame. *Neocolonialismo. Último estágio do imperialismo*. Rio de Janeiro: Civilização Brasileira, 1967.

Pereira, Luísa Teotónio; Moita, Luís. *Guiné- Bissau. 3 anos de independência*. Lisboa: CIDAC, 1976.

"I Encontro de Ministros da Educação e educadores de Angola; Cabo Verde, Guiné-Bissau, Moçambique e S. Tomé: Àprocura de uma nova educação." In *O Militante*. March/April 1978: 48–51.

Oliveira, Olavo Borges de, Philip J. Havik, and Ulrich Schiefer. *Armazenamento Tradicional na Guiné Bissau*. Münster: Institut für Soziologie. Universität Münster, 1993.

Opalski, Krzysztof."Report of a vist to the liberated areas of Guinea-Bissau." Helsinki: International Union of Students (IUS) and National Union of Finish Students (SYL), 1971.

Padmore, George. *History of the Pan-African Congress*. London: Hammersmith, 1947.

Paulo, João Carlos. *Da "educação colonial portuguesa" ao ensino no ultramar*. Vol. 5, in *História da expansão portuguesa;5:Último império e recentramento: (1930 - 1998)*, by Francisco Bethebcourt and Maria F. Alegria, 304–333. Lisboa: Temas e Debates, 2000.

Paulo, João Carlos. "Vantagens da instrução e do trabalho. «Escola de massas» e imagens de uma «educação colonial portuguesa»." *Educação, Sociedade e Culturas*, 1996: 99–128.

Paulo, João Carlos. "Èducation Coloniale et «École Portugaise»." In *The colonial experience in education*, by António ́ Nóvoa, Marc Depaepe and Erwin V. Johanningemeier, Paedagogica Historica- International journal of History of Education: Paris, 1995: 115-138.

Pereira, Aristides. *Relatório do c.s.l. ao III Congresso do PAIGC*. Mindelo: PAIGC, 1978.

perspectives, by Ali A. Abdi, Korbla P. Puplampu and George J. Sefa Dei, 1–12. Oxford: Lexington Books, 2006.

Quaye, Christophern O. *Liberation Struggle in International Law*. Philadelphia: University Press, 1991.

Rabaka, Reiland. *Concepts of Cabralism. Amílcar Cabral and Africana Theory*. London: Lexington Books, 2014.

Ranger, Terence. "African attempts to control education in east and central Africa, 1900-1939." *Past & Present*, 1965: 57–85.

Read, Christopher. *Lenin. A revolutionary life.* New York: Routledge, 2005.

Rickford, Russel. *We are African people: We are African people. Independent Education, Black power and Radical imagination.* New York: Oxford University Press, 2016.

Ritchie, Donald A. "Introduction: the evolution of oral history." In *The Oxford handbook of oral history*, by Donald A. Ritchie, 3–23. Oxford: University Press, 2011.

Rodney, Walter. *How Europe underdeveloped Africa.* Dakar: Pambazuka, 2012.

Rudebeck, Lars. *Guinea-Bissau. A study of political mobilization.* Uppsala: The Scandinavian Institute of African Studies, 1974.

Sammoff, Joel, Socialist education? *Comparative Education Review*, Vol 35, No. 1, Special Issue on Education and socialist (R)evolution (1991).

Sellström, Tor. *Sweden and national liberation in Southern Africa: solidarity and assistance 1970-1994.* Uppsala: Nordiska Afrikainstitutet, 2002.

Sevilla-Borga, Horacio. "Report of the Special Mission established by the Special Committee at its 840th meeting on 14 March 1972." United Nations-General Assembly, July 3, 1972.

Shiza, Edward. *Linguistic independence and African education and development.* Vol. 21, in *The dialectics of African education and western discourses. Counter-hegemonic Perspectives*, by Handel Kashope Wright and Ali A. Abdi, 148–162. Oxford: Peter Lang, 2012.

Smith, Linda Tuhiwai. *Decolonizing Methodologies. Research and indigenous people.* New York: Zed Books Ltd, 1999.

Solidária, CIDAC: Terra. *Guiné Bissau. Tempo de Mudança.* Vol. 24. Lisboa: CIDAC, 1990.

Sousa, Julião Soares. *Amílcar Cabral (1924-1973) - Vida e Morte de um Revolucionário Africano.* Lisboa: Vega, 2011.

Thiong'o, Ngũgĩ wa. *Dreams in a time of war: a childhood memoir.* London: Harvill Secker, 2010.

Thomson, Alistair, and Robert Perks. *The oral history reader.* New York: Routledge, 2006.

Tomás, António. *O Fazedor de Utopias. Uma Biografia de Amílcar Cabral.* Lisboa: Tinta da China, 2007.

Touré, Ahmed Sékou. *África: ensino e revolução.* Lisboa: Via Editora, 1977.

UNESCO.Final report. *Conference of African states on development of education in Africa.* UNESCO: Addis Ababa: United Nations Educational, Scientific and Cultural Organization, 1961.

Urdgang, Stephanie. *Fighting Two Colonialism: Women in Guinea-Bissau.* London: Monthly Review Press, 1979.

Walters, Ronald W. *Pan-Africanism in the African diaspora.* Detroit: Wayne State University Press, 1993.

Wolfgang Leonard, *Child of the Revolution.* London: Collins, 1957.

Whyte, Martin King, *Small groups and political ritual in China,* London: University of California Press, 1974.

Additional Bibliography

Adi, Hakim, and Marika Sherwood. *Pan-Africanism History: Political figures from Africa and the Diaspora since 1787.* London: Routledge, 2003.

Besançon, Alain. *Las origenes intelectuales del leninismo.* Madrid: Ediciones RIALP, 1980.

Cabral, Amílcar. "Em defesa da terra. a erosão e os seus efeitos." *Boletim de Propaganda e Informação,* November 1949: 2–4.

Cabral, Amílcar. *Sou um simples Africano.* Lisboa: Fundação Mario Soares, 2001.

Chabal, Patrick. *Amílcar Cabral. Revolutionary leadership and people's war.* New York: Cambridge University Press, 1983.

Cissoko, Mário A.R. *Povo e Escola nos reinos felupes e noutras regiões da margem direita do Rio Cacheu.* Bissau: Agencia Sueca para o Desenvolvimento Internacional (ASDI), 1994.

Cissoko, Mário. *Três currículos, três problemas para a Guiné-Bissau. Introdução ao caso de uma região islâmica.* Pedagogic Study, Bissau: Agência Sueca para o Desenvolvimento Internacional (ASDI), 1996.

Collins, Robert O. *Problems in the history of colonial Africa, 1860-1960.* Englewood Cliffs: Prentice-Hall, 1970.

Davis, Angela Y. *The meaning of freedom and other difficult dialogues.* San Francisco: City Lights Books, 2012.

Dorman, Sara Rich. "Post-liberation politics in Africa: Examining the political legacy of struggle." Third World Quarterly, vol. 27, Issue no. 6 (2006): 1085–1101.

Drescher, Seymour. "The ending of the slave trade and the evolution of European scientific racism." In *The Atlantic salve effects on economies, societies, and peoples in Africa, the Americas, and Europe,* by Joseph E. Inikori and Stanley L. Engerman, 361–396. Duke University Press: North Carolina, 1992.

Edem, Kodjo, and David Chanaiwa. *Pan-Africanism and Liberation.* Vol. 8. Africa since 1935, in *gGeneral History of Africa,* by Ali A. Mazrui.

Oxford: Heinemann Berkeley: University of California Press, and Paris, 1993.

Enns, Diane. *Speaking of Freedom. Philosophy, politics and the struggle for liberation.* California: Stanford University Press, 2007.

Enwezor, Okwui. "The short century: Independence and liberation movements in Africa 1945-1994: An introduction." In *The short century: Independence and liberation movements in Africa 1945-1994*, by Okwui Enwezor, 10–17. New York: Prestel, 2002.

Fanon, Frantz. *Pele negra Mascaras Brancas.* Porto: Paisagem, 1975.

Ferreira, Eduardo Sousa. *O fim de uma era: o colonialismo português em África.* Lisboa: Sá da Costa, 1977.

Field, Sean. "Disappointed Remains: Trauma, testimony, and reconciliation in Post-Apartheid in South Africa." In *The Oxford handbook of oral history*, by Donald A. Ritchie, 142–159. Oxford: Oxford University Press, 2011.

Godinho, Patrícia. *Os fundamentos de uma nova sociedade: O PAIGC e a luta armada na Guiné-Bissau (1963-1973); Organização do Estado e as relações internacionais.* Torino: L' Harmattan Italia, 2010.

Gonçalves, José Julio. "O Islamismo na Guiné Portuguesa." *Boletim Cultural na Guiné Portuguesa*, Outubro 1952: 397–470.

Green, Anna. "Can memory be collective." In *The Oxford handbook of oral history*, by Donald A. Ritchie, 96–111. Oxford: Oxford University Press, 2011.

Gutmann, Amy. *Democratic Education.* New Jersey: Princeton University Press, 1999.

Hutching, Megan. "After action: oral history and war." In *The Oxford handbook of oral history*, by Donald A. Ritchie, 233–243. Oxford: University Press, 2011.

Johnson, Cedric J. *Black Marxism. The making of the radical tradition.* North Carolina: University North Carolina, 2000.

Lopes, José Vicente. *Cabo Verde. Os bastidores da Independência.* Cidade da Praia: Spleen edições, 2002.

Lorenz, Federico Guillermo. "How does one win and lost war? Oral history and political memories." In *The Oxford handbook of oral history*, by Donald A. Ritchie, 124–141. Oxford: University Press, 2011.

Madeira, João, Luís Farinha, and Irene Flunser Pimentel. *Vítimas de Salazar: Estado Novo e violência política.* Lisboa: ESfera dos Livros, 2010.

Marroni, Luisa. "Portugal não é um país pequeno". A lição do colonialismo na Exposição Colonial do Porto 1934." *Revista da FLUP*, 2013: 39–38.

Mercieca, Duncan. "Becoming-Teachers: desiring students." *Educational Philosophy and Theory*, 2012: 43–56.

Meyer, Alfred G. *Leninism*. Massachusetts: Harvard University press, 1957.

Monteiro, Augusto José. "A (re)valorização de outras fontes históricas: a problemática dos manuais escolares." in *Outros comabtes pela história*, by Maria Manuela Tavares Ribeiro, 343–377. Coimbra: Imprensa da Universidade de Coimbra, 2010.

Newton, Huey. *To die for the people*. New York: City lights Publishers, 2009.

Nóvoa, António, Marc Depaepe, and Erwin V. Johanningmeier. *The colonial experience in education. Historical issues and perspectives*. Belgium: Paedagogica Historica. International Journal of History of Education, 1995.

Puplampu, Korbla P., Ali A. Abdi, and George J. Sefa Dei. "African Education and Globalization: An Introduction." In *African Education and Globalization. Critical*

Ritchie, Donald A. *Doing Oral History. A practical guide*. New York: Oxford University Press, 2003.

Robinson, Cedric J. *Black Marxism. The Making of the Black Radical Tradition*. London: Zed Press, 1983.

Shiza, Edward. "Reclaiming our memories: the education dilemma in post-colonial school curricula." In *Issues in African Education. Sociological perspectives*, by Ali A. Abdi and Ailie Cleghorn, 65–81. New York: Palgrave Macmillan, 2005.

Stauffer, Martin. *Pädagogik zwischen Idealisirung und Ignoranz. Eine Kritik der Theorie, Praxis und Rezeption Paulo Freires*. Bern: Peter Lang, 2007.

Tedla, Elleni. *Sankofa: African thought and education*. New York: Peter Lang, 1995.

Thomson, Vincent Bakpetu. *Conflict in Horn Africa. The Kenya-Somalia border problem 1941.-2014*. UK: University Press of America, 2015.

Thomson, Alistair. "Memory and Remembering in Oral History." In *The Oxford handbook of oral history*, by Donald A. Ritchie, 77–95. Oxford: Oxford University Press, 2011.

Torgal, Luís Reis. "Nós e os outros: Portugal e a Guiné-Bissau no ensino da memória histórica." in *Para uma história da educação colonial*, by António Nóvoa, Marc Depaepe, Erwin V. Johanninmeier and Diana Soto Arango, 363–378. Lisboa: Sociedade Portuguesa da Educação, 1996.

Vambe, Maurice Taonezvi. "Contributions of African literature to the African Renaissance." *International Journal of African Renaissance Studies -Multi-, Inter- and Transdisciplinarity 5 (2)*, n.d.: 255–269.

Wright, Handel Kashope, and Ali A. Abdi. *The dialectics of African education and western discourses. Counter-hegemonic perspectives.* Oxford: Peter Lang, 2012.

Wright, Michelle. *Becoming black. Creating Identity in the African Diaspora.* Duke University Press, 2004.

Index

Interviews Index

Studia Educationis Historica

Bildungsgeschichtliche Studien / Studies in the History of Education /
Estudios de Historia de la Educación

Herausgegeben von/ edited by
Marcelo Caruso, Eckhardt Fuchs, Gert Geißler, Sabine Reh, Eugenia Roldán Vera, Noah W. Sobe

Vol. 1 Anna Larsson / Björn Norlin (eds.): Beyond the Classroom. Studies on Pupils and Informal Schooling Processes in Modern Europe. 2014.

Vol. 2 Marcelo Caruso (ed.): Classroom Struggle. Organizing Elementary School Teaching in the 19th Century. 2015.

Vol. 3 Cristina Alarcón / Martin Lawn (eds.): Assessment Cultures. Historical Perspectives. 2017.

Vol. 4 Sónia Vaz Borges: Militant Education, Liberation Struggle, Consciousness. The PAIGC education in Guinea Bissau 1963-1978. 2019.

www.peterlang.com